THE HOLOCAUST AND THE ARMENIAN CASE IN COMPARATIVE PERSPECTIVE

Yücel Güçlü

Studies in Judaism

University Press of America,® Inc.
Lanham · Boulder · New York · Toronto · Plymouth, UK

Library of Congress Control Number: 2011941106
ISBN: 978-0-7618-5782-2 (paperback : alk. paper)
eISBN: 978-0-7618-5783-9

™
⊖ The paper used in this publication meets the minimum
requirements of American National Standard for Information
Sciences—Permanence of Paper for Printed Library Materials,
ANSI Z39.48-1992

Contents

Preface

Up to the present, most of the information available to European and American students of Ottoman and Turkish history in the period from the late 19ᵗʰ century, through the First World War, and to the establishment of the Republic of Turkey in 1923 has been viewed primarily through a European and an Armenian prism. In that context, the Ottoman Empire is portrayed largely as an enemy state in the war and the primary cause of the suffering of many innocent men, women and children in that war and its immediate aftermath.

This reading of history is selective and incomplete. What has always been missing is an understanding of the full context for the events of that period. This context was not always available, due to lack of access to primary research materials, especially those located in Ottoman and Armenian archives. While Armenian archives remain off-limits to most scholars, Ottoman archives have become available, and provide a rich vein for inquiry.

One finds in them documents, letters, reports, and other evidence suggesting that Ottoman actions prior to, during, and immediately after the First World War do not justify the term "genocide," nor do those actions bear any semblance to the actions of Nazi Germany prior to and during the Second World War against European Jewry.

The judgment of this work is that the history of the period is intricate and does not lend itself to simple judgments and labels. Reputable scholars of varying perspectives have failed to reach a consensus on basic facts, assumptions and key implications of events of that period.

Whereas scholars of the Holocaust have delved deeply into Nazi aspirations, ideology, actions, directives and contemporary accounts, the scholars of the Ottoman-Armenian conflict have tended to focus almost exclusively on the suffering of the Armenians. This has led to a near-total lack of awareness of Ottoman perspectives and experiences.

Very few studies have been undertaken from the view of policy makers in İstanbul. Many authors rarely discuss Ottoman decision-making and operational control. And importantly, most scholars misrepresented the goals of the Ottoman policy of moving Armenian populations from eastern Anatolia.

This survey seeks to close the gap of study and awareness of Ottoman actions, and the context for those actions. It places in perspective the events of 1915-1918, and seeks in particular to distinguish those events from the Nazi Holocaust. This is because the Nazi Holocaust was not only much different in multiple ways, but it is often used as a comparison to the Armenian tragedy, and even a precursor to it. The historical evidence does not support this claim in any meaningful way.

This study, organized into five basic chapters, is intended to rectify this lacuna in the Western perception of Turkish history.

Acknowledgments

This work has been sustained by a deep desire to make clear that whatever debates exist over history, the events themselves must be understood, interpreted and remembered first on their own, and only after, in comparison to other events. Comparative history is never done well when the historian is operating with only an awareness of one historical narrative or era and merely a passing understanding of another. Therefore, I am most grateful to many historians whose work on the Holocaust has greatly informed this study, and who are quoted throughout. I am of course indebted as well to the librarians and researchers who do the hard work of maintaining and cataloguing vital archives.

In particular, I am grateful to Noam Neusner for his trenchant criticism and incisive suggestions on this study. He helped me generously with information and advice in my work, and I feel a special obligation to him for his interest and unstinting support. I am indebted as well to Jeff Weintraub, Jay Footlik and Ralph Posner for reading early drafts and sharing their invaluable recommendations. I should also like to thank Şükrü Hanioğlu, Garrett Professor in Foreign Affairs and head of Near Eastern Studies Department at the Princeton University, for helpful comments.

The author also wishes to thank the directors and staffs of the Prime Minister's Office Ottoman Archives in İstanbul, Turkish General Staff Directorate of Military History and Strategic Studies Archives in Ankara, United States National Archives at College Park, Maryland, United States Holocaust Memorial Museum Archives in Washington D.C., British National Archives at Kew, London, National Library in Ankara, Turkish Historical Society in Ankara, Library of Congress in Washington, D.C. and the Houghton Library at Harvard

University.

Needless to say, any errors or shortcomings in this work are solely my own responsibility.

Introduction

The basic events in Asia Minor during the First World War, though subject to significant debate and discussion nearly a century later, are not disputed. Beginning in early November 1914, the Ottoman Empire, under attack by Russians from the north and the British and French from the south and west, was crumbling. In eastern Anatolia, an uprising of Armenians in support of the Russians and other Entente forces caused significant losses to the Ottoman army and population. In response, the Ottoman government forcibly removed hundreds of thousands of Armenians from their homes and transported them east and south. The forced marches and associated violence led to many deaths. While the total number of Armenian deaths is in dispute, there is no doubt that the number rose to the hundreds of thousands.

Approximately 4 million people of all religions died in the Ottoman Empire during the First World War and during the Turkish War of Independence that followed until 1922, and many of these did die from massacres and counter massacres. These deaths were not limited to Armenians, though they certainly lost a higher percentage of their people than did any other group. During this period, deaths could be ascribed to many causes, but especially massacres and counter massacres, foreign invasion, internal attacks by bandits, famine and disease.

While these broad outlines are not in dispute, the details of these events – how many perished, which parties were responsible, the cause and level of suffering – is subject to significant debate among historians. These debates have become particularly emotional, are the source of major scholarly disputes and enter into modern day foreign policy discussions. Most critically, Armenian communities around the world have sought to categorize the events of 1915 as a genocide – a particular term that some historians inaccurately applied and most Turks find risible.

The term "genocide" was coined in the 20th century, and has a special meaning. It is defined not only by the characteristic of mass death, but by the characteristic of mass death caused intentionally by the policies and actions of a state, with the expressed purpose of wiping out a national, ethnographic, religious or other group. There are only a small handful of mass deaths in all of history that have been deemed, by consensus, a genocide. The tragedy of the Armenians is not one of those events.

For that reason, those who view the Armenian tragedy as a genocide have long sought to connect it explicitly to the single event that is most clearly associated with the word genocide – the Holocaust. Armenians and ethnic Armenians living elsewhere have routinely tried to argue that the Armenian tragedy inspired Nazi Germany's efforts to exterminate all of European Jewry. Such an argument of causation is significant, and carries significant implications, both for the way the Armenian tragedy is understood, and the way the Holocaust is understood.

Many ethnic groups in history have suffered massacres, forcible mass exiles, and the like. The Holocaust is unique, and stands alone as the archetype of a rare class of historical events. Therefore, the effort to equate the suffering of Armenians with that of Jews is not accidental. Should the Armenians establish that they were victim of a national program of extinction, as the Jews of Europe were, they would equate their national and personal suffering with that of the Jews, and derive from that legacy of suffering a unique position in history and on the world stage today. For example, the successor state of the Ottoman Empire, the Republic of Turkey, could be held to account by the Armenians.

This study explores the effort to make this comparison in three distinct ways:

One, through the prism of the events themselves: What do we know about the events and how they came about? Were there qualities to each event so similar as to make the comparison apt? Or did the events feature significant differences, rendering them incomparable in meaningful ways?

Two, through the historical evidence connecting the two events: This is not merely a debate about historiography, where historians connect historical events by analogy and comparison, looking for similarities and differences. In this case, Armenians frequently say that the Holocaust was inspired, to a significant extent, by the Armenian tragedy. They make this comparison by citing evidence. This study asks whether the evidence is accepted as plausible and authentic, and explores the implications of evidence countering this claim.

Three, through the battle waged for more than a decade to feature the Armenian tragedy within the exhibition of the United States Holocaust Memorial

Museum in Washington D.C. This extended drama features elements of the debate, as it is conducted among genocide scholars, but also shows how a debate over history can have real-life, present-day implications on the way events are retold, emphasized, and shape modern opinions. Just as history textbooks are often the result of significant debate over the meaning and accuracy of historical evidence, the decision to mention – in any way – the Armenian tragedy in the Holocaust Museum was a revealing episode, and explains to a great extent why issues which typically only interest historians came to become a rallying cry for two different ethnic communities.

This monograph attempts to explore the argument and evidence of those who seek to make this connection. Rather than engage in a debate over the fundamental truths of the Armenian tragedy – those losses which cannot be denied – this book will seek to engage with the evidence of the Armenian tragedy and its connection to the Holocaust, and whether the two events can be compared on the same terms.

The study will explore how the comparison between the Armenian tragedy and the Holocaust is not merely made as a metaphor. There is a sustained and deliberate effort to link the tragedy of the Armenians to the Holocaust, in order to say that one led very clearly to the other, and that without one, the other would not have occurred. The Armenian case is cited as the direct precursor to the Jewish catastrophe and as a precedent for the horrors of mechanized murder, so common in the 20th century.

In general, this study will argue that while the deaths of many thousands of Armenians were a terrible tragedy which could have been avoided, these deaths were not an outcome of deliberate policy of the Ottoman government – as were the deaths of 6 million Jews during the Second World War. It will show that official policy towards the Armenians was quite different than the manner in which the Armenians were sometimes treated, to ill-effect. This survey also shows that the deaths followed a period of insurrection and rebellion by the Armenians, a distinct difference from the example of the Jews a few decades later. Moreover, the survey notes, the Nazi genocide was deliberate and planned, while the Armenian deaths that followed from forced migrations was not.

Some of the evidence presented here is new, and some is familiar. The critical contribution of this study is its consultation of original and reliable sources as much as possible. This is in contrast to the often indirect and sometimes mistaken sources consulted by Armenians and their supporters, who have been trying to situate the Armenian episode squarely within the history of the Holocaust. For example, they allege that Adolf Hitler said, on the eve of Germany's invasion of Poland, that the Armenian tragedy proves that the world is indifferent to mass death – though the evidence of Hitler actually saying this is subject to significant doubt, and most regard it as a fabrication.

That citation is critical, because the connection to Hitler is deliberate.

Whether Hitler knew about the events in Anatolia is debatable. But by alleging that as Hitler plotted the Holocaust, he was emboldened by the international community's failure to condemn and remember the Armenian tragedy, Armenians and their supporters in the scholarly community seek to take a historical analogy and make it a historical connection, even a cause. It is alleged that Hitler noted the world's indifference to Armenian suffering, and pointed to that indifference to reassure doubters in his ranks and as a license to proceed at will with the destruction of the Jews without the fear of permanent negative consequences. [1]

If that were true, the Jews of Europe were doomed by the silence of the world in the face of Armenian suffering. But, as the evidence will show, the Jews of Europe faced a distinctly different threat in Nazi Germany, and the doom they met was not dependent on the suffering of the Armenian people.

Ultimately, those who make this connection assert that had the world paid more attention to the events and lessons of 1915, the tragedy of the Holocaust might have been prevented or mitigated.[2]

This is a powerful charge, and elevates the suffering of the Armenians, which I will make clear were an unfortunate outcome of a brutal war and rebellion, to the level of the suffering of Europe's Jews, which remains unparalleled in human history in significant respects. These comparisons and evocations carry with them significant implications in current events. Four members of the Foreign Affairs Committee of the United States House of Representatives on 10 October 2007 cited Hitler's alleged statements on the Armenian tragedy as a justification for supporting a resolution deeming the Armenian tragedy a genocide, as if to claim that the Armenian tragedy was to take the point of view of Hitler.[3] Therefore the comparison, and linkage, between the Armenian tragedy and Holocaust no longer is a matter merely of concern to scholars and those interested in historiography. The matter now affects public policy debates, with wide-ranging geopolitical implications. It is therefore vital that this comparison and linkage be explored fully, with the best possible access to relevant historical evidence.

Yet among scholars of Armenian history, there are relatively few serious studies of this period of history rooted in original and archival documentation. Most scholars sympathetic to the cause of Armenian claims of genocide tend to focus much more on "genocide denial" and on forging linkages with the field of Holocaust studies. A common denominator to these works is an assumption that what has been asserted about this period, especially those assertions related to Armenian losses and Ottoman intent, are settled matters, and no further discussion or exploration is needed. Because of this assumption, the exploration of the events of the Armenian tragedy is left to non-specialists, primarily journalists, whose lack of facility with relevant languages and original materials leaves them working solely with secondary studies.

Totally absent in the works published by Armenian and Western specialists on Armenian history is anything resembling a book or monograph specifically related to the historiography of the genocide claim. A thorough examination of the existing literature fails to uncover a single book or monograph by an Armenian (or, indeed a Western expert) which attempts to systematically set forth the case for the Armenian claim of genocide. While many works simply assume the historical accuracy of such a claim, none makes the claim in a scholarly manner – assembling relevant evidence, responding to specific challenges to thesis, and so forth.

What remains, within the field of Armenian studies, may be oral histories at best. But for those eager to explore the core issues at the heart of the dispute over the way to understand the Armenian tragedy, there is on one side, certitude based on assumption, and on the other side, a sincere effort to explore original resources not previously consulted.

Emotional and biased posture of many Armenian scholars has led to a distorted history that ignores the time-tested principles of historical research.[4] Yet when the shared history of the Turks and Armenians is approached with the normal tools of history, a logical and consistent account results. "Let the historians decide" is a call for historical study like any other historical inquiry, one that looks at all the facts, examines all the theories, applies historical principles, and comes to logical conclusions.

Armenian historians refer to the "evidence" of British wartime propaganda, Christian missionary reports, statements by Armenian revolutionaries, and the like. They seldom refer to Ottoman documents, thousands of which have been published in recent years, except using them out of context. This monograph argues that these documents show the Ottoman government planned no genocide. The fact that these contradict the Armenian sources is all the more reason that they should be consulted. Good history can only be written when both sides of historical arguments are considered.

Most significant of all failures by Armenian sympathists is their regular oversight of Muslim dead at the hands of Armenians during this period. Given the nature of the Armenian insurrection, it is only fair to call the period a form of secessionist rebellion, or an intercommunal strife. Any insurrection or intercommunal strife will appear to be genocide if only the dead of one side are counted. Therefore it is essential that historians account for the deaths of nearly two-thirds of the Muslims of the province of Van, deaths caused by the Russians and Armenians. Histories that strive for accuracy must include all the facts, and the death of millions of Muslims is surely a fact that deserves attention. Justin McCarthy, professor of Middle Eastern history and demographer at the University of Louisville, one of the few Western scholars to have done systematic research in the Ottoman archives, comments: "To mention the sufferings of one group and avoid those of another gives a false picture of what was a human, not simply an ethnic, disaster." Moreover he finds that:

> In the east (of Anatolia), the areas of Muslim deaths and Armenian deaths were
> almost perfectly correlated...In numbers, the Muslims lost many more persons
> than did the Armenians; in percentage of total population, less. The great mor-
> tality of both Muslims and Armenians does not fit into any theory that posits
> one group of murderers, and another group murdered.[5]

Of the evidence for genocide, there are several primary pieces of alleged evidence. Guenter Lewy, who for many years taught political science at the University of Massachusetts-Amherst and has a distinguished record of publications on genocide cases, identifies the three pillars of the genocide argument: the actions of Ottoman courts martial of 1919-1920, which convicted Ottoman government officials of organizing massacres of Armenians; the role of the Ottoman Special Organization accused of carrying out the massacres, and Aram Andonian's Memoirs of Naim Bey[6] which contain alleged telegrams of Interior Minister Talat Paşa[7] conveying the orders for the extermination of the Armenians.[8]

Yet these pillars are not as solid as Armenian sympathists would have you believe. Much was made of postwar courts martial in İstanbul[9] that accused the leadership of the Committee of Union and Progress[10] of crimes against the Armenians.[11] By all accounts, the primary reason for convening military tribunals was pressure from the Allied powers, which insisted on retributions for the Armenian killings. The Ottoman government of the day also hoped that by placing blame on a few members of the Committee of Union and Progress, they might receive more lenient treatment at the Paris Peace Conference.

Given these pressures, the trials were hardly definitive as fact-finding panels. For example, the tribunals lacked the basic requirements of due process. The right of cross-examination was not acknowledged. The judge weighed the probative value of all evidence submitted during the preparatory phase and during the trial, and he questioned the accused. At the 1919-1920 trials, the presiding officer acted more like a prosecutor than an impartial judge. Defense counsel was barred access to pretrial investigatory files and from accompanying their clients to pretrial interrogations. According to trial transcripts, although charges of mistreatment of Armenians were leveled, a majority of the charges and convictions were mainly motivated by political retribution, related not to crimes against civilians, but to the management or mismanagement of the war. Four members of the principal military tribunal were later arrested by the government on charges of contravening judicial procedure. The ultimate value of the evidence is best appreciated by a single point: When the British government considered holding trials of alleged Ottoman war criminals in Malta, it declined to use any evidence developed by the courts martial of 1919-1920.[12]

The second pillar for the case for genocide relates to the role of the Ottoman

Special Organization, which is alleged to have played a direct role in implementing the Armenian relocations.[13] The evidence, however, does not support this assumption. The Special Organization, established in November 1913, was used for special military operations in the Caucasus, Egypt, and Mesopotamia. It was also employed in dealing with the cause of Arab separation in Syria. The Special Organization played no role in the Armenian population displacements. While the indictment of the 1919 court martial linked the Special Organization to the Armenian killings, neither the trial's proceedings nor its verdict support the claim. Rather, defendants described the Special Organization's role in covert operations behind Russian lines. Since these trials were organized by the political enemies of the accused, not everything alleged by the Prosecutor General is necessarily true.

The third pillar of the genocide claim is documents reproduced in the Memoirs of Naim Bey. Indeed, these documents paint a chilling picture of Ottoman intent.[14] Particularly suggestive are the telegrams of Interior Minister Talat Paşa. In them, he appears to give explicit orders to kill all Ottoman Armenians. One telegram dated 16 September 1915 notes that the Committee of Union and Progress had decided to destroy completely all Armenians living in the Ottoman Empire.

Yet these documents are, in fact, forgeries. Two Turkish authors, Şinasi Orel and Süreyya Yuca, who undertook a detailed examination of the authenticity of the documents in the Andonian book, proved this beyond any doubt.[15] Turkish scholars are not alone in their assessment of that the Andonian documents are fakes. Michael Gunter immediately questioned the validity of them. He says the manifest inconsistencies in Naim-Andonian documents indicate that they are likely forgeries.[16] Others also dismiss them as inventions.[17] Moreover, while telegrams from Andonian book were included in the files of the Malta detainees, the British government never made use of them, suggesting the British knew they were counterfeit.

THE PROBLEM OF EVIDENCE

This study is an attempt to demonstrate that the Armenian experience during the First World War is not the equivalent of the Holocaust and the Armenian allegation of genocide is invalid. This work addresses the misconceptions inherent in the consensus view of modern Middle Eastern history, which regards the Ottoman Turks solely as oppressors and their non-Muslim subjects solely as victims.

In particular, this study reveals significant new evidence that while the Armenians suffered terribly, there were many examples of Ottoman efforts to minimize that suffering – surely a major distinction with the experience of Jews at the hands of the Nazis. The book reviews the record of Fourth Ottoman Army commander Cemal Paşa's[18] assistance and protection of Armenians, and the Turkish position that not all Armenians residing within the empire represented a threat.

The methodological approach adopted is comparative/contrastive analysis. The Armenian tragedy during the late Ottoman period should not be examined in isolation, but in the context of other similar human dramas – especially since it is often compared to those dramas. The comparative method broadens our horizons. It opens up new and unexplored avenues and is useful in reminding one of the distinctive factors of historical events, and the uniqueness of the human experience, even in tragedy.

By employing an array of indigenous sources generated from within the Ottoman and Republican Turkish world and various reliable evidences from Western sources, this study endeavors to provide a new prism through which to view the Armenian conflict and its consequences. Particular emphasis is placed on historical nuance. Attention is paid to the detail.

General Records of the State Department, Record Group 59, in the United States National Archives were a helpful resource. To the best of the present author's knowledge, the bulk of documentation obtained from the repositories at the University of Maryland's College Park campus is published here for the first time. These include correspondence between the Department of State, its diplomatic and consular missions in the Ottoman Empire and Ottoman authorities. The records, consisting of unbound documents, are mostly instructions and dispatches, memoranda of conversations, telegrams, and airgrams from diplomatic and consular officials. The dispatches are often accompanied by enclosures. In addition to official exchanges between the Department of State and its field representatives, there are notes exchanged between the Department of State and foreign diplomatic and consular representatives in the United States, memoranda by officials of the Department, correspondence and memoranda exchanged with other agencies of the United States government, and correspondence with private firms and persons.[19]

The United States Holocaust Memorial Museum archives is one of the world's major repositories of Holocaust documentation, the central node of an international network of inventories and catalogs of Holocaust records in other institutions, and a national center for Holocaust research. The archives also contain the records of the President's Commission on the Holocaust and the United States Holocaust Memorial Council.

A few of the papers of the American Board of Commissioners for Foreign Missions (now the Wider Church Ministries) at the Houghton Library, Harvard University have been of assistance. Use has been made of memoirs and autobiographies of pertinent Turkish, Armenian and German statesmen and officials. Scattered literature in international periodicals and law journals and Turkish,

Armenian, British and American newspapers have been utilized. *The Orient*, a well-edited weekly record of the religious, educational, political, economic, and other interests of the Ottoman Empire and the Near East, published between 1910 and 1923 in English at the American Bible House in İstanbul, proved helpful. The Bible House represented both the American and the British Bible Societies, and it was also the center of the administration of the American Board of Commissioners for Foreign Missions in Asia Minor. Findings of a number of acknowledged specialists in the interrelated areas of history, political science, religion, and philosophy are also widely drawn on.

The full opening of the Ottoman archives in 1989 has provided historians with masses of material relevant to the study of the Armenian question, including its political, economic, religious and socio-cultural attributes. This resource has enabled many of the uncertainties of the past to be rendered more definitive. There are approximately 150 million ancient documents and 366,000 registers of inestimable value in the Ottoman archives. Even now, new collections are opened and made readily available to researchers. They constitute an unequaled trove of reliable information about how people lived from the fifteenth through the early twentieth centuries in a territory now taken up by thirty-nine nations. Scores of experts pore over troves of centuries-old documents, accessible to any scholar.

In particular, the records of the Ottoman Ministry of the Interior were critical. The ministry was the most important government department directing and supervising the relocation and resettlement of the Armenian population. The collection of the ministry documents covers the period from 1866 through 1922 and consists of 4,598 registers or notebooks. It is classified according to twenty-one-sub-collections, according to office of origin. Among the available documents in the Ottoman archives are several dozen bound handwritten registers containing the record of the deliberations and decisions of the Council of Ministers which set policies, received information, and discussed the problems that arose regarding the relocations and other wartime events in the empire. The minutes of its meetings, deliberations, resolutions, and decisions on important matters are bound in 224 volumes covering the years 1885 and 1922. These registers include each and every decree pertaining to the decision to relocate the Ottoman Armenians away from strategically sensitive war zones during the First World War.[20] Substantial documentation is also found in the Records Office of the Sublime Porte.[21] The importance of these materials to determining the true nature of the Armenian events of 1915 is apparent.[22]

Documents at the renovated Ottoman archival facilities at Sultan Ahmet area in İstanbul are categorized and filed by the government agency—Prime Minister's Office Directorate General of State Archives Department of Ottoman Records—that originally created them, forcing researchers to sort through decades-old record-keeping systems. Dozens of specialists a day make relentless demands for documents, often the same documents at the same time. Amid these mountains of files archivists function as guides to the information researchers need.

Bernard Lewis, Cleveland Dodge Professor Emeritus of Near Eastern Studies at Princeton University and one of the best living authorities on the Middle East, was one of the first among Western scholars to use the Ottoman archives. Lewis began to work in them as early as 1949 and after two years used these archives and their contents to produce the period's most detailed and accurate survey.[23] He says Ottoman archivists at İstanbul are ready to provide assistance and advice and gives them credit appropriately:

> The Ottoman archives are in the care of a competent and devoted staff who are always willing to place their time and knowledge at the disposal of the visiting scholar, with a personal helpfulness and courtesy that will surprise those with purely Western experience. [These records] are open to all who can read them.[24]

Taner Akçam of Clark University, one of most vocal Armenian genocide allegations proponents, said in 2006 that the working conditions in the Prime Minister's Office Ottoman Archives at İstanbul have improved enormously in the past few years. Akçam thanks the staff, and especially Deputy Director General of State Archives Associate Professor Mustafa Budak, for their generous help and openness during his last visit. He says this is a very hopeful development, and all scholars interested in the period should use this new opportunity to examine these materials.[25]

The archives of the Turkish General Staff Military History and Strategic Studies Directorate at Ankara provide a military perspective. They are vast and the First World War and the War of Independence collections alone number over five and a half million documents. Since the Ottoman government was controlled almost entirely during the First World War by the martial law administration, a part of the Ministry of War, this archive, more than the Prime Minister's Office Ottoman archives, has most of the documents concerning internal conditions in the empire at that time as well as those on operations of the Ottoman army and the Special Organization.[26] The files of the Vehip Paşa's Third Army (Erzurum), Cemal Paşa's Fourth Army (Damascus), and Ali İhsan Paşa's Sixth Army (Baghdad) are notably large. The cataloging and microfilming of these archives repository up to the end of 1922 is completed. Sifting through thousands of files and millions of documents now unclassified, researchers are anticipating further revelations about what happened in wartime. And they expect once-secret documents to shed a more intense light on the Armenian issue than in the past.[27]

Quite a number of doctoral dissertations and monograph studies have been published on the basis of army records in Turkey. These materials have also been used extensively by such Western historians as Stanford Shaw, Edward Erickson, Tim Travers, Michael Reynolds and Harvey Broadbent. There are several scholars working in the military archives at present, and the Turkish General Staff Military History and Strategic Studies Directorate itself publishes volumes from its collection, including both photographs and Latin transliteration of all documents. Each document is preceded by a brief introduction regarding its contents. A list of documents appears together with source information at the end of each volume. The wording of the translated documents is clear and concise, with the translators doing their best to convey their meaning in English. For the military historians of the Middle East in particular, these represent a treasure.

To achieve a full understanding of the Turkish-Armenian conflict, studies in the Ottoman archives alone would be insufficient. Also important is the need to do research in the archives of the Armenian revolutionary committees and guerrilla armies that were active in the Ottoman Empire during and after the First World War which are kept at the repositories of the Dashnak Party (Dashnaksutiun, the Armenian Revolutionary Federation) and the First Republic of Armenia in the Hairenik Association building in Watertown, Massachusetts. In contrast to open Ottoman archives, the above holdings and the archives of the Armenian patriarchate in Jerusalem and the Catholicosate (seat of the supreme religious leader of the Armenian people) in Etchmiadzin in Armenia, remain closed to non-Armenian researchers.

This is a serious problem. Consider the recent case of Associate Professor Göknur Akçadağ at Turkey's İnönü University in Malatya. In response to his letter of 20 June 2008, requesting the opportunity to use sources available in the Armenian archives in Watertown/Massachusetts the Turkish academic was informed that although the repositories (1890-1922), until very recently, were open for research to qualified scholars, access to them has been temporarily suspended, as they were in process of implementing necessary repairs in the facilities and upgrading of technology. The Turkish scholar was told that it was difficult, at this stage, to assess the time that would be required to complete the planned improvements. [28]

Dashnaksutiun archives are also not available to those Armenians who do not subscribe to the maximalist claims of the Armenian diaspora's political leaders. Historian Ara Sarafian, director of the Gomitas Institute in London, complained that:

> Some Armenian archives in the diaspora are not open to researchers for a variety of reasons. The most important ones are the Jerusalem Patriarchate archives. I have tried to access them twice and [been] turned away. The other archives are the Zoryan Institute archives, composed of the private papers of Armenian survivors, whose families deposited their records with the Zoryan Institute in the 1980s. As far as I know, these materials are still not cataloged

and accessible to scholars.[29]

Not only do these institutions close their archives to non-Armenian and even to some Armenian scholars, they do not even allow the public to access catalogs detailing their holdings.

From both historical and historiographical perspectives, in matters concerning Armenian actions, policies, and experiences, Armenian sources must be consulted. One would think, therefore, that it is incumbent on Armenians to open all the archives so that the scholarly community will have a far clearer picture of what precisely happened in the Ottoman Empire during the First World War. To the extent that some of the Armenian archives are already open and available, catalogs and descriptions should be published telling people where they are and how they could be used.

In case of Britain's National Archives (formerly Public Record Office) in Kew/London, not all papers relating to the First World War and its immediate aftermath are released yet. While much of the relevant British records are available for study, the materials left from the British occupation of İstanbul and other parts of Turkey following the First World War, including evidence regarding the returning Armenian refugees, and the dossiers of the British intelligence organizations, have been withheld from research by the British government under the authority of the Official Secrets Act as well as other pretexts, and have been only partially available in the archives of the Government of India in Delhi.

Ninety-three years after the end of the First World War files of the British Eastern Mediterranean Special Intelligence Bureau still remain closed. The opening of these records will enable historians and others to find more on the British campaign of espionage and sabotage, demoralizing propaganda, and attempts to provoke treason and desertion from Ottoman ranks during and immediately after 1914-1918. Such evidence could well reveal details about the misuse and deliberate misstating of the historical record by British officials of the time. The documents of the Secret Office of War Propaganda, a branch of the British Foreign Office (known only by the name of the building where it was located, Wellington House), which was in charge of developing propaganda used against the Central Powers during the First World War, under the direction of Lord James Bryce and Arnold Toynbee, likewise for the most part been concealed from researchers and must be made fully available for examination.

The Armenian question occupied a prominent place in 20th century Middle Eastern historiography and remains controversial at the beginning of the 21st. Most intense debates on what actually took place have been going on for more than nine decades and show no sign of resolution. The task for historians of the region is to discover as much source material as exists about the Armenian tragedy and determine, in as unified a manner as possible, a fact-based narrative. It is only after all these materials have been examined, published, studied, and discussed that a definitive history of the tragedies of the First World War can be written.

Therefore, even as this study puts forward new evidence, the author recognizes that it cannot hope to be definitive until all relevant archives are open to anyone who wishes to examine them. Only by this means will we be able to guarantee that the real history of the period of the First World War becomes fully known and understood.

NOTES

1. See for example, Kevork Bardakjian, *Hitler and the Armenian Genocide* (Cambridge, Massachusetts: The Zoryan Institute, Special Report No. 3, 1985); George Aghjayan, *Genocide Denial: The Armenian and Jewish Experiences Compared* (Worcester: Armenian National Committee of Central Massachusetts, 1998); Vahakn Dadrian, *The History of the Armenian Genocide: Ethnic Conflict from the Balkans to Anatolia to the Caucasus* (New York: Berghahn Books, 6th ed., 2003), pp.394-419; Robert Melson, *Revolution and Genocide: On the Origins of the Armenian Genocide and the Holocaust* (Chicago: University of Chicago Press, 1992); Yves Ternon, *La cause arménienne* (Paris: Editions du Seuil, 1983).

2. Max Laufer, "A Tale of Two Genocides," *Journal of Armenian Studies*, Vol. 2, No. 2 (Fall-Winter 1985-1986), pp. 75-86; Edward Gulbekian, "The Poles and Armenians in Hitler's Political Thinking," *The Armenian Review*, Vol. 41, No. 3-163 (Autumn 1988), pp. 1-14 and Christoph Dinkel, "German Officers and the Armenian Genocide," *The Armenian Review*, Vol. 44, No.1 (1991), pp.77-133.

3. See the remarks of Representatives Brad Sherman, Christopher Smith, Donald Payne and Edward Royce in Congressional Transcripts, Congressional Hearings, 10 October 2007. House Foreign Affairs Committee Holds Markup of House Resolution 106 on United States Foreign Policy and the Armenian Genocide.

4. For bibliographies on the Armenian literature in the field see, for instance, Richard Hovannisian, *The Armenian Holocaust: A Bibliography Relating to the Deportations, Massacres, and Dispersion of the Armenian People 1915-1923* (Cambridge, Massachusetts: Armenian Heritage Press, 1980) and Hamo Vassillian, ed., *The Armenians: A Colossal Bibliographic Guide to Books Published in the English Language* (Glendale, California: Armenian Reference Books, 1993).

5. Justin McCarthy, *Muslims and Minorities: The Population of Ottoman Anatolia at the End of the Empire* (New York and London: New York University Press, 1983), pp. 137-138. This work is clearly the best available on the subject and merits the close attention of any serious, disinterested reader. It has been referred to as a definitive book on the floor of the United States Senate. See Congressional Record, Vol. 136, 27 February 1990, p. 1694.

6. Bey and Paşa are Ottoman civilian/military titles that are generally treated as part of a name. Neither word is a surname.

7. Talat Paşa, the moving spirit of the Committee of Union and Progress throughout , was a steady, well-balanced, and able statesman. His was the will, the brain and

the hand. He had critical skill of a high order, great organizing ability and a remarkable grasp of public administration—qualities which he combined with a powerful and impelling personality. Yet very little serious scholarship has been devoted to Talat Paşa's career as a whole. The biographies that exist are superficial and undisciplined in their addressing of his career. Studies of his time as minister of the interior, or as grand vizier, are few and those that exist are dated. In particular, there is no comprehensive survey of his time as minister of the interior. This lack of extensive study of one of the most consistently important men in the Ottoman policy making elite is a fascinating omission in the inquiry of the Ottoman Empire's effort during the First World War.

8. Guenter Lewy, *The Armenian Massacres in Ottoman Turkey: A Disputed Genocide* (Salt Lake City: The University of Utah Press, 2005), pp. 63-89.

9. Except in quoted passages, Turkish place names will be used in the text: İstanbul for Constantinople, Ankara for Angora and İzmir for Smyrna.

10. The Committee of Union and Progress, usually known to Europeans as the "Young Turk Party," is the political body which except for a brief period practically held power in the Ottoman Empire between 1908 and 1918. The Young Turks were reformers imbued with modern thoughts and resolutely determined to make an earnest effort to save the country from disintegration. Their primary purpose was to renovate the empire in order to preserve it. They provided most of the ideas and cadres on which later the Turkish War of Independence and the republican movement were based upon. See in particular, Tarık Zafer Tunaya, *Türkiye'de Siyasi Partiler* (Political Parties in Turkey), Vol.3: *İttihat ve Terakki, Bir Çağın, Bir Kuşağın, Bir Partinin Tarihi* (Committee of Union and Progress, the History of an Age, a Generation, a Party), (İstanbul: İletişim Yayınları, 3rd ed., 2000); Sina Akşin, *Jön Türkler ve İttihat ve Terakki* (Young Turks and the Committee of Union and Progress), (Ankara: İmge Kitabevi, reprinted, 2006) and Muhittin Birgen, ed., Zeki Arıkan, *İttihat ve Terakki'de On Sene* (Ten Years in the Committee of Union and Progress), Vol.1: *İttihat ve Terakki Neydi?* (What Was the Committee of Union and Progress?) and Vol.2: *İttihat ve Terakki'nin Sonu* (End of the Committee of Union and Progress), (İstanbul: Kitap Yayınları, 2006).

11. See, for instance, Dadrian, *The History of the Armenian Genocide*; idem, "The Documentation of the World War I Armenian Massacres in the Proceedings of the Turkish Military Tribunal," *International Journal of Middle East Studies*, Vol. 23, No. 4 (November 1991), pp. 549-576; idem, "A Textual Analysis of the Key Indictment of the Turkish Military Tribunal Investigating the Armenian Genocide," *Journal of Political and Military Sociology*, Vol. 22, No. 1 (1994), pp. 133-172; idem, "The Turkish Military Tribunal's Prosecution of the Authors of the Armenian Genocide: Four Major Court Martial Series," *Holocaust and Genocide Studies*, Vol. 11, No.1 (Spring 1997), pp. 28-59.

12. A sound analysis of the Ottoman courts martial of 1919-1920 can be found in Feridun Ata, *İşgal İstanbul'unda Tehcir Yargılamaları* (Trials for Relocations in Occupied İstanbul), (Ankara: Türk Tarih Kurumu, 2005). Ata's exemplary book should be translated quickly into English as a potential goad in debating this important historiographical question.

13. See, for instance, Dadrian, *The History of the Armenian Genocide*; idem, "The Role of the Special Organization in the Armenian Genocide during the First World War," in Panikos Panayi, ed., *Minorities in Wartime: National and Racial Groupings in Europe, North America and Australia during the Two World Wars* (Oxford: Berg Publish-

ers, 1993), pp. 50-82. Throughout this study, "Armenian relocations" and "Armenian events of 1915" are used interchangeably. The term "deportation" is commonly applied to the Armenian experience, but it is erroneous. The Armenians were moved within the same country, not expelled to another country, as "deportation" implies. In wartime Ottoman Empire, most displaced people did not cross an internationally recognized border; they were and remained subjects of the sultan.

14. Aram Andonian, comp., *The Memoirs of Naim Bey: Turkish Official Documents Relating to the Deportations and Massacres of Armenians* (New Square, Pennsylvania: Armenian Historical Research Association, reprinted, 1965). Also Vahakn Dadrian, "The Naim-Andonian Documents on the World War I Destruction of Ottoman Armenians: The Anatomy of a Genocide," *International Journal of Middle East Studies*, Vol. 18, No. 3 (August 1986), pp. 311-360.

15. Şinasi Orel and Süreyya Yuca, *The Talat Pasha Telegrams: Historical Fact or Armenian Fiction?* (Nicosia: Rustem, 1986).

16. Michael Gunter, "Notes and Comments," *International Journal of Middle East Studies*, Vol. 19, No.4 (November 1987), pp. 523-524 and idem, "Notes and Comments," *International Journal of Middle East Studies*, Vol.40, No.4 (November 2008), pp. 728-729.

17. See, for instance, Guenter Lewy, "The First Genocide of the 20th Century?" *Commentary*, Vol. 120, No. 5 (December 2005), p. 50 and idem, *The Armenian Massacres in Ottoman Turkey*, pp. 63-73; Erik Jan Zürcher, *Turkey: A Modern History* (London and New York: I.B. Tauris, 3rd ed., 2004), pp. 115-116; Andrew Mango, "Turks and Kurds," *Middle Eastern Studies*, Vol. 30, No. 4 (October 1994), p. 985.

18. The Turkish names, titles, and places are frequently spelt in more than one way by different, or even the same, writers. The orthography used in this study is that of modern Turkish except when quoting from non-Turkish sources. Hence "Cemal Paşa" rather than "Jemal or Djemal Pasha" and "Maraş" for "Marash."

19. For a general description of these records see *Guide to the National Archives of the United States* (Washington, D.C.: National Archives and Records Service, 1974), particularly pp. 131-140.

20. Yusuf İhsan Genç et al., *Başbakanlık Osmanlı Arşivi Rehberi* (Guide to the Prime Minister's Office Ottoman Archives), (Ankara: Başbakanlık Basımevi, 1992), pp. 384 and 352.

21. In modern European history, the Sublime Porte is the familiar Ottoman equivalent of Downing Street, the Elysée Palace, the Ballplatz, the Wilhelmstrasse, and more recently, the Kremlin and the White House. Within the courts of the Sublime Porte were the various offices of the government, including the old council chamber, and from this the name had been taken as a synonym of Ottoman government. The Sublime Porte was in fact the entrance to the premises of the grand vizier, who conducted the business of government on behalf of the sultan. For particulars, see Bernard Lewis, *The Political Language of Islam* (Chicago and London: The University of Chicago Press, 1988), pp. 38-39 and 41; Nermi Haskan and Çelik Gülersoy, *Hükümet Kapısı Bab-ı Ali Kuruluşundan Cumhuriyete Kadar* (Government Gate The Sublime Porte: From Its Founding Up to the Republic), (İstanbul: Çelik Gülersoy Vakfı Yayını, 2000).

22. Yusuf Sarınay, "Türk Arşivleri ve Ermeni Meselesi" (Turkish Archives and the Armenian Question), *Belleten*, Vol. 70, No. 257 (April 2006), pp. 290-310. On Ottoman archival depositories see in particular Mustafa Küçük et al., *Başbakanlık Osmanlı Arşivi*

Kataloglatı Rehberi (Guide to the Prime Minister's Office Ottoman Archives Catalogs), (Ankara: Başbakanlık Basımevi, 1995). The first published catalog of Ottoman archival holdings authored by Murat Sertoğlu, director of the Prime Minister's Office Archives, appeared in 1955 and consisted of ninety pages of archival inventory and commentary. It is a general survey of the archives, with a description and classification of the papers and registers. A far more complete catalog followed in 1979, comprising 171 pages of catalog entries and other archival data. This authoritative work was translated into Italian in 1985. As the classifying and organizing of the archives continued, the catalog grew accordingly and reached 634 pages in the 1992 edition. These catalogs make clear the abundance of material available to scholars doing research on topics relating to Ottoman history. See Murat Sertoğlu, *Muhteva Bakımından Başvekalet Arşivi* (Contents of the Prime Minister's Office Archives), (Ankara: Türk Tarih Kurumu Basımevi, 1955); Attila Çetin, *Başbakanlık Arşivi Kılavuzu* (Guide to the Prime Minister's Office Archives), (İstanbul: Enderun Kitabevi, 1979); Genç, *Başbakanlık Osmanlı Arşivi Rehberi*, 1992; Donald Quataert, "Ottoman History Writing at a Crossroads," in Donald Quataert and Sabri Sayarı, eds., *Turkish Studies in the United States* (Bloomington, Indiana: Indiana University Ottoman and Modern Turkish Studies Publications, 2003), pp. 15-30 and idem, "Recent Writings in Late Ottoman History," *International Journal of Middle East Studies*, Vol. 35, No. 1 (February 2003), p. 138.

23. Bernard Lewis, "The Ottoman Archives as a Source for the History of the Arab Lands," *Journal of the Royal Asiatic Society*, Nos. 3-4 (October 1951), pp. 139-155. See also idem, *Notes and Documents from the Turkish Archives: A Contribution to the History of the Jews in the Ottoman Empire* (Oriental Notes and Studies, No. 3), (Jerusalem: The Israel Oriental Society, 1953), pp. 1-52 and "Studies in the Ottoman Archives, I," *Bulletin of the School of Oriental and African Studies*, Vol. 16 (1954), pp. 469-501.

24. Bernard Lewis, *From Babel to Dragomans: Interpreting the Middle East* (Oxford and New York: Oxford University Press, 2004), pp. 418-419.

25. Taner Akçam, "Deportation and Massacres in the Cipher Telegrams of the Interior Ministry in the Prime Ministerial Archive (Başbakanlık Arşivi)," *Genocide Studies and Prevention*, Vol. 1, No. 3 (December 2006), pp. 320-321 fn6.

26. Türkiye Cumhuriyeti Genelkurmay Askeri Tarih ve Stratejik Etüt Başkanlığı Arşivleri (Archives of the Turkish General Staff Directorate of Military History and Strategic Studies), Ankara (henceforth referred to as ATESE), Genelkurmay Başkanlığı Harp Tarihi Dairesi Tarihçesi (A Brief History of the War History Department of the Turkish General Staff) (henceforth referred to as HTDT), Folder: 1, File: 5, No. 1-14. On the importance of the Ottoman military archival sources see in particular Edward Erickson, "The Turkish Official Military Histories of the First World War: A Bibliographic Essay," *Middle Eastern Studies*, Vol. 38, No. 3 (July 2003), pp. 190-198.

27. Author interview, Colonel Ahmet Tetik, chief of the archives division of the Turkish General Staff Military History and Strategic Studies Directorate, 11 July 2008; ATESE, HTDT, Folder: 1, File: 7, No. 1-15; *Türkiye Cumhuriyeti Genelkurmay ATESE ve Denetleme Başkanlığı Yayın Kataloğu* (Publication Catalog of the Turkish General Staff Directorate of Military History and Strategic Studies and Directorate of Inspection), (Ankara: Genelkurmay Basımevi, 2005).

28. Letter from Tatul Sonentz-Papazian, Armenian Revolutionary Federation Archivist, to Göknur Akçadağ, Associate Professor at İnönü University in Malatya/Turkey, 30 June 2008.

29. Ara Sarafian, "Génocide arménien et la Turquie," *Nouvelles d'Arménie*, September 2008, p. 1.

Chapter One
The Events of 1915

The events in the Ottoman Empire in 1915 and those in Germany and Eastern Europe in 1939-1945 are contextually and morally distinct. Scholars who have studied the Armenian tragedy, and reached the conclusion that these events have significant differences with the Holocaust and do not merit being considered a genocide include: Bernard Lewis, the late Stanford Shaw, Guenter Lewy, Justin McCarthy, Norman Itzkowitz, Brian Williams, David Fromkin, Avigdor Levy, Michael Gunter, Pierre Oberling, the late Roderic Davison, Michael Radu, and Edward Erickson.[1] Outside of the United States even more scholars have endorsed a contra-genocide analysis of the history of the Ottoman Armenians, among them Gilles Veinstein of the College de France, Stefano Trinchese of the University of Chieti, Augusto Sinagra of the University of Romae-Sapienza, Norman Stone of Bilkent University, and Andrew Mango of the London University.

As Barbara Lerner—a commentator on Middle Eastern affairs based in Chicago—aptly points out, to judge whether the Holocaust analogy fits the historical facts one cannot just look at dead Jews in the Second World War, then at dead Armenians in the First World War, and extrapolate the rest. One has to look at live Armenians and Turks in 1915; at the desperate, multi-front situation of the Ottoman Empire and how people and leaders reacted to those conditions.[2] But in order to appreciate these conclusions, one must have a grounding in the actual events preceding the 1915 events, as well as the events themselves.

OTTOMAN-ARMENIAN CONFLICTS PRIOR TO SUMMER 1915

The history of Turkish-Armenian relations amounts to about a thousand years of shared experiences. The Turks began to coexist with the Armenians following the defeat of the Byzantine army by the Seljuk ruler Alparslan at the battle of Malazgirt in eastern Anatolia in 1071. The whole Asia Minor came under Ottoman sovereignty after Sultan Selim I's route of the Safavides at the battle of Çaldıran in 1514 and thereafter the Armenians in the region became the subjects of the government in İstanbul. Throughout their long history, Turks and Armenians lived together – often amicably. The Presbyterian historian Joseph Grabill says quite correctly: "The Turks leniently treated the Armenians, who became the favorite non-Moslem minority of the Ottoman government."[3]

Into the early nineteenth century the system of wide autonomy for the non-Muslim peoples largely satisfied the Armenians to the degree that they were known to the Turks as the *milleti sadıka* (loyal community). The rise of nationalism among the Armenian populace and decline of the multinational Ottoman Empire, however, began to change this circumstance as the nineteenth century reached its final decades. As a result, some Armenians started to look to Europe as their savior and protector.

The Ottoman-Russian War of 1877-1878 proved a major step in the development and internationalization of the Armenian question. Article 61 of the Treaty of Berlin of 13 July 1878 read:

> The Sublime Porte undertakes to carry out, without further delay, the amelioration and reforms demanded by local requirements in the provinces inhabited by the Armenians, and to guarantee their security against the Circassians and Kurds. It will periodically make known the steps taken to this effect to the Powers, who will superintend their application."[4] With this article, the signatory Powers had established an explicit right to interfere in the internal affairs of the Ottoman state, as it pertained to the question of the Armenian people. The role of international interference in Armenian matters therefore became a recurrent theme in Ottoman-Armenian relations. With this influence, as well as that of Russian terrorist groups such as the *Narodniki*, Armenian nationalism eventually manifested itself in the formation of the Marxist revolutionary Huntchaks in 1887 and the more nationalistic Dashnaks in 1890. Article 6 of the program of the Huntchak party stated: "The time for the general revolution (in Armenia) will be when a foreign power attacks Turkey externally. The party shall revolt internally."[5] The central plank of the Dashnaks read: "It is the aim of the Armenian Revolutionary Federation to bring about by rebellion the political and economic emancipation of Turkish Armenia." Revolutionary bands were "to arm the people," wage "an incessant fight against the (Turkish) Government," and "wreck and loot government institutions." They were "to use the weapon of the terror on corrupt government officers, spies, traitors, grafters, and all sorts of oppressors.[6]

In the summer of 1894 the Armenian armed bands incited the Armenian villagers of Sassun in the province of Bitlis in eastern Anatolia to revolt against the government. Troubles had been preceded by Armenian attacks on Muslim tribesmen. Troops were sent to establish order. Such authors as William Langer and Justin McCarthy put forth the argument that this and other incidents were part of a strategy on the part of Armenian revolutionaries, especially, the Huntchaks, to provoke the Ottoman government to take drastic measures that would draw the attention of Europe and bring about outside intervention.[7]

Armenian insurrectionary preparations were meticulously made in the region of Cilicia in southern Anatolia before the First World War. In 1895 Armenian revolutionaries had already started troubles in the rugged mountain town of Zeytun, about fifty kilometers northwest of Maraş. Violent clashes had also occurred between the Cilician Armenians and Turks in April-May 1909. The Armenians, influenced mainly by the Huntchaks, rose up in Adana, the principal city of Cilicia, presumably with the goal of attracting Western intervention at the nearby port of Mersin.[8]

Reliable contemporary accounts of this period are rare, yet one comes by way of J.A. Zahm, an American missionary who visited the area immediately after the First World War. He wrote in 1922 that while in Cilicia he made a special effort to ascertain the truth regarding the accusations of a massacre of Armenians that so stirred Europe and America to horror earlier in the century. His research called on the testimony and evidence of that region, with a focus on events dating back several decades.[9] In his view, the accusations of massacres against the Ottomans was highly flawed, and driven by broader, pan-nationalist demands by Armenians.

Cilicia was a district closely connected with Armenian history and independence. After the downfall of Sultan Abdülhamid II, the Armenians there enjoyed significant new freedoms, and gave vent to their aspirations not just for sovereignty but for vengeance. Their clubs and meeting places were loud with boastings of what was soon to follow. Postcards were printed showing a map of the future Armenian kingdom of Cilicia and circulated throughout the Ottoman post. Armenian nationalists marched in procession in the streets bearing flags purporting to be the flag of Lesser Armenia. The name of the future king was bandied about – a well-known Armenian landowner of the Cilician plain, held in peculiar disfavor by the Muslims. In addition, there was speculation that an Armenian army was gathering in the mountains by Hacin and Zeytun, preparing to march upon Adana and set up an Armenian kingdom again. Though some Armenians in Cilicia opposed violence, the nationalist movement had gotten beyond their control.[10]

Meanwhile, in eastern Anatolia, Armenian revolutionaries had also accelerated their efforts to spread propaganda about Ottoman actions against Armenians in certain parts of Asia Minor. These reports were often glaringly exaggerated and one-sided, with a special emphasis on the condemnation of the "bloodthirsty" Turk. [11]

An 1896 incident in İstanbul was, like that in Adana, provoked by the revolutionary activities of the Armenians. After having boldly announced their intention of applying the torch to the city and "reducing it," as their posted placards phrased it, "to a desert of ashes," a party of audacious young conspirators proceeded to blow up the Ottoman Bank, while their associates attacked innocent Turks in the Samatya quarter. During eighteen hours of terror, Armenian use of dynamite and bombs thrown from the windows upon the Ottoman soldiers rivaled anything recorded in the worst days of the Paris Commune of 1871. [12]

Considering the Ottoman reaction to these provocations, Zahm asks,

> What would the people of New York do if a foreign mob from the East Side with the red flag at their head were to attempt to blow up the Subtreasury Building and to make the same use of high explosives in their wanton destruction of life and property as did the Armenians in their ghastly work in Constantinople?

While the rhetorical question leads a modern reader to one conclusion, contemporary views of the incidents laid the blame for deaths in İstanbul, Adana and elsewhere squarely at the feet of the so-called "unspeakable Turk." [13]

That Zahm reported these events even-handedly is notable, since he had long sympathized with the cause of the Armenians. He began to recognize that behind much of the anti-Turk propaganda lay the truth; that Kurdish attacks on Armenians were ascribed to Turks; that Russian intrigue and aggression was often behind false reports; that Armenians were often set upon by Huntchaks and revolutionary Armenians of foreign extraction. Zahm recognized that Ottoman reprisals against Armenians served a larger purpose to tilt Western opinion against the Turks, ultimately driving the Great Powers to enter the fray. Always, the Armenian nationalists were free from responsibility while the ever-vilified Ottoman was pilloried before the world as "a monster of iniquity and a demon incarnate." [14]

Pierre Loti tells of a French consul in Asia Minor who barely escaped assassination at the hands of an Armenian agitator who, when questioned regarding his attempts on the life of the functionary, coolly replied: "I did this in order that the Turks might be accused of it and in the hope that the French would rise up against them after the murder of their consul." [15]

Halil Halid, who was born and bred in Asia Minor and who spent many years in Britain, asked at the time:

> Did the humanitarian British public opinion know these things? No; it does not care to know anything which might be favorable to the Turks. Have the political journals of this country—Britain—mentioned the facts I have stated?

Of course not, because—to speak plainly—they know that in the Armenian pie there were the fingers of some of their own politicians.[16]

And those that were well informed knew the reason of Britain's attitude toward the Ottoman Empire, for they knew that

> Since 1829, when the Greeks obtained their independence, England's Near East policy has been remorselessly aimed at the demolition of the Turkish Empire and the destruction of Ottoman sovereignty.[17]

Did France, the first nation of Europe to form an alliance with the Sublime Porte, know about the Armenian treachery? It did, but, at the time, it was easier to feign ignorance and to follow the policy of Britain. It did not even allow an academic, Pierre Loti—who knew the Turks better than any man in France—to make a statement in their favor, without censoring it, for fear he would comment on France's own policies regarding the alliance. Zahm asks:

> Does [the United States], whose people are supposed to be always on the side of justice and fair play, know the truth about the Turks and Armenians in Asia Minor?

He answers his own question:

> Not one in a hundred; not one in a thousand. The reason is simple. They have heard only one side of the Armenian question, and, in most cases, are quite unwilling even to hear anything to the advantage of the long-defamed Turks. With most of our people the case of the Turks has been prejudged and thrown out of court.

Zahm concludes that his sole desire was to make known the truth as he had found it, and he had found that it was not at all on the side of the Armenians.[18]

The incidents of 1894-1896 and those of 1909 were important in creating the psychological climate of 1915. The Ottoman government was convinced that the Armenians were planning a rebellion.[19]

Indeed, the Ottomans were correct. As the First World War began, the Armenian inhabitants of Zeytun refused to obey government orders and attacked Ottoman troops in August 1914. Ottoman army sent two divisions against this insurrection, and lost 500 men.[20]

Towards the end of February 1915, the Armenians at the eastern Anatolian cities of Van and Bitlis, who had heard that the Russians meant to occupy these areas, turned upon the Muslim population. Though Muslims comprised the vast majority, they were defenseless, since able men had been conscripted into military service. Armenians succeeded in massacring more than three-quarters of the people. In the district of Tavskerd, in the province of Erzurum, the local

Armenians and Armenian soldiers in the Russian army, annihilated a population of 40,000 souls. In the province of Trabzon, a similar attempt to exterminate the Muslim population was made. This was before Armenians suffered at the hands of the Muslims during forced removals. In an appeal addressed to the Allied powers by the Turkish government directly after the armistice, it was stated that the Armenians in the eastern provinces of Anatolia massacred a million Muslims before the relocation order was promulgated.[21]

In March 1915, the Armenians at Van quickly distributed large quantities of pre-positioned weapons and revolted in concert with a Russian offensive. These attacks and revolts against Ottoman forces began before the order of relocation (27 May 1915). What is now clear, the rebels at Van were in direct contact with fellow committeemen in the Armenian volunteer regiments fighting alongside the Russians. As the Armenians advanced and defeated Ottoman troops in Van, they burned the Muslim quarter and killed the Muslims who fell into their hands. With few exceptions, the only Muslims who survived were those who managed to flee, primarily those who fled with the Ottoman army. Everything Islamic in Van was destroyed.[22] Justin McCarthy notes:

> When the Ottomans evacuated Van, many of those who had been able to flee were set upon by Armenian bands on the roads. Approximately 400 from one group were killed between Erçiş and Adilcevaz. Armenians also killed 300 Jews who tried to escape toward Hakkari. Other refugees found their way blocked by Armenian bands and armed Armenian villagers, who attacked all Muslims passing by.[23]

These crimes of the Armenians were denounced in the Russian Duma of the time, but were not published in any British newspaper, though *The Times'* correspondent did let out, in an unguarded moment, that the Armenians at Van "took bloody vengeance on their enemies." On the continent of Europe it was generally recognized, even during the war, that the Armenian trouble had originated in a rebellion or attempted in the Ottoman provinces. Interestingly, while Armenians were portrayed in France and Italy as courageous defenders of their national identity, to the point that they extracted vigilante justice on Muslims, in Britain and the United States they were portrayed as mere lambs, having committed no offense.[24]

Perhaps the most compelling evidence to Armenian actions against Muslims comes from their Russian allies. While the Russian army occupied the greater part of eastern Anatolia, they were witnesses to Armenian-led atrocities and Russian officers deplored it. The Commander-in-Chief of the Russian Army, General Odichelidze, Lieutenant Colonel Tredokhleboff, Captain Youlkevitz, the Commissary Zelatoff, Lieutenants Lipsky and Stravosky, General Galitine, Lieutenant Colonel Grianznoff and about a hundred other Russian officers—all of whom were fighting against the Turks and had no reason to be sympathetic to them—were disgusted and outraged by Armenian savagery.[25]

ARMENIAN DISLOYALTY DURING THE FIRST WORLD WAR

Armenian terror against the Ottoman government had grown for six decades before the First World War. The Armenian patriarch Khorene Ashikian, who was accused by the Huntchak party of being on friendly terms with the Sublime Porte , was almost assassinated in 1894, and an attempt was made on the life of the Sultan Abdülhamid II while he was leaving the Friday prayer in 1905. Ottoman Armenians saw the First World War as an opportunity to carve out a separate state from the crumbling Ottoman Empire.[26]

After Russia formally declared war against the Ottoman Empire on 2 November 1914 and Britain and France followed suit two days later, a large number of young Armenians who had been drafted into the military deserted or evaded conscription and took up arms as rebels. They were active in various parts of the country. An official communication from the general staff of the Russian Caucasian army under the date of 10 November 1914 said:

> In several towns occupied by the Russians the Armenian students have shown themselves ready to join the invading army. Reports tell of armed conflicts arising from the refusal of Armenians to become Turkish conscripts and surrender their arms. It is now rumored that the important city of Van besieged by Armenian guerrilla bands in great force. In Zeitun the Armenians are said to exceed 20,000 in number, and they are reported to have defeated all the Turkish troops sent against them, causing the Turks heavy losses.[27]

Nerses Kouyoumjian, an Ottoman Armenian soldier, in an interview with the *Boston Sunday Globe* of 30 May 1915, made the following detailed confession on how he abandoned his unit at the first opportunity and joined the Russian army. Due to its relevancy, it is worthwhile to give the text of his statement in entirety:

> I should like to say a few words about why the Armenian people did not wish to enlist and fight with Turkish comrades. The Turkish people had always been regarded as enemies by the Armenians. Being 24 years of age, I had to join the army. My parents tried to protect me by keeping me in the house, and for two weeks I did not go out at all. By that time the Government was making a house-to-house search for missing young men and taking them by force. I was taken to the army and drilled. We took the boat from Constantinople and went to Drabizond, a port in the Black Sea. When we reached there we were joined with the other army who were waiting for us and advanced on to the Russian soil. Many of our men deserted and many were stranded willingly. From our company more than 75 men, all Christians, were going to the other side. I, also,

took advantage of a guard duty and flew to the other side. I was very glad, for I could fight for civilization in the Russian Army. For three days the Russians were inactive, merely protecting themselves. When reinforcements arrived we took the offensive, and destroyed a great Turkish Army and chased them to the other side of the River Jorukh. By forcing the enemy away, we took possession of a high land and were able to control the whole prairie below. We could plainly see the Turkish soldiers and kept cannonading them for a long time. In three days we reached Olttie Sarikamish. Another Russian Army advanced from the right under the protection of Russian battleships. They also succeeded in taking possession of Khoppa. The same day I received mail from Tiflis in answer to my letter and was invited to join an army with a group of volunteers, as they were going to Alashgerd on the Persian frontier to fight their way into Armenia. I was excused by our commanding captain because I could not talk Russian and could not understand them and joined the volunteers.[28]

At a time when the Ottoman army was fighting a war on several fronts, Armenian bands were attacking government offices, killing gendarmes and civilians, and burning villages. They also began to attack vulnerable Ottoman lines of communications by severing telegraph wires and conducting road sabotage to cut and block highways.[29]

The rebels were assisted by local Armenians, who provided sanctuary when the former were pursued by the gendarmes and at times ran to their rescue in conflicts, taking with them weapons that had been hidden in churches. Thousands of Armenians crossed the porous eastern border and joined Caucasian Armenians fighting in the Russian army or in the volunteer units formed alongside it for the specific purpose of "liberating" the "Armenian provinces" of the Ottoman Empire in the name of Christianity. Garegin Pasdermadjian, who represented Erzurum in the Ottoman Chamber of Deputies during 1908-1912, went over to the Russian side with almost all the Armenian soldiers in the Ottoman Third Army in eastern Anatolia at the outbreak of the war and returned at their head—burning villages and killing the Muslims who fell into his hands.[30]

At the end of 1914 *İkdam*, an influential İstanbul journal, warned Armenians that they had, under Ottoman rule, far greater opportunities for preserving their national character than they would be allowed by Russia, who would seek to absorb and Russianize them:

> Even if Russia were to take our eastern provinces, it would not be to make them autonomous under Armenian rule, but merely to add them to the Russian Empire. They will make the Armenians just a cat's paw for their own desires, and for this there is ample evidence.[31]

The special correspondent of *Manchester Guardian*, Philips Price, who in 1916 spent several weeks in the province of Van, later wrote that from the early days of the war Armenians responded to appeals from the Russian authorities in the Caucasus to cross over and join the Russian military. An underground network was created which enabled recruits to go from eastern Anatolia and enter the czarist army. Thus Armenians sent parties by night to join the Russians, and in this way three Armenian infantry battalions were formed under the command of Generals Andranik and Ishkan, who fought with the Russians all through the campaign.[32]

In several Ottoman towns occupied by the Russians in late 1914 and the winter and spring of 1915 the Armenians joined the invading army. They had prepared themselves for the czarist approach by secretly gathering large stocks of arms and explosives, most of them of Russian origin. All along the line of assault, the Armenian peasants received the Russian troops with enthusiasm and gave provisions to them freely. The *Tribuna* of Rome published at the beginning of November 1914 a Petrograd (as the Germanic-sounding St. Petersburg was renamed on 31 August 1914) dispatch regarding the operations of the Russians in eastern Anatolia. It said that the Russians entered the Ottoman Empire by two routes, one column towards Erzurum and the other striking southward. The dispatch followed: "The Armenians everywhere welcomed the Russians, regarding the war as one of liberation."[33]

Erzurum, 100 kilometers west of the Russian border and the principal fortress in the area, was the solitary bulwark of the Ottoman Empire in Asia. It was situated on the caravan route from the Black Sea at Trabzon to the Persian Gulf and was connected by post roads with the other frontier towns. Since its founding in the fifth century Erzurum had played an important part in all Turkish wars. In 1201 it was captured by the Seljuks and became an important trading center, owing to its proximity to the west branch of the Euphrates River. In 1517 it was taken by the Ottomans and since then had been a part of the Turkish possessions, except for a few months in 1829 and 1878, when it was held by Russian troops. In all of the Muscovite wars with the Ottoman Empire this city had been one of the chief objectives of the Russian campaigns. But save for short periods the Turks had been able to keep the invaders away. The city is built at an altitude of 2,000 meters above sea level and its rugged terrain makes it particularly strong. Possession of that city, the Metz of the Ottoman Empire, would give Russia free access to the interior of Anatolia over a branching system of roads. The Turks possessed no railroads in this section and, though they could muster large armies farther west, the transport both of troops and the heavy supplies necessary to check the Russians would be difficult.[34]

As guides and advance guards, Armenians knew the ways and means of Turks. Some of their leaders knew almost every inch of the territory through which they had to fight Turkish forces. Moreover, they knew the language. Making things worse for the Ottomans, armed and hostile Armenians actively threatened the rear areas of front-line units of the Third Army and its primary supply route. A dispatch received again at the beginning of November 1914 by

The Daily Telegraph of London from Tiflis, capital of the Lieutenancy of Cau-
casia, by way of Moscow, said:

> The Turkish town of Van, 140 miles southeast of Erzerum, Turkish Armenia,
> is being besieged by a detachment of Armenians, who are aiding the Russians.
> The town has a large arsenal. Another Armenian detachment is operating in the
> rear of the Turkish Army.[35]

A dispatch received in Petrograd from Tiflis on November 7 added Armenian
refugees reaching there reported that volunteer bands of Armenians had had
several sharp engagements with the Ottoman garrison at Van.[36]

The supply route of the Fourth Army in Syria and Palestine was equally
threatened by armed Armenian rebellion. In the Dörtyol-İskenderun area, Armenian bands were in direct contact with the British and French fleets. The
prospect of an amphibious invasion, supported by Armenians, was an ever-pres-
ent concern. These also constituted an indirect threat to the logistics posture of
the Sixth Army in Mesopotamia. The Armenian rebellion was a great danger to
the war effort, especially in eastern Anatolia and Cilicia. It was a real threat to
the security of the Ottoman state and came at a very dangerous time. The Allies
landed at Gallipoli on April 25 and in early May the Russians began a major
offensive toward Erzurum supported by Armenians. Armenian agents had come
ashore numerous times at Dörtyol and İskenderun. Armenians living abroad offered to raise a force of 20,000 men to fight the Ottomans in Cilicia.[37]

Russia's ambition, a port on the warm waters of the Mediterranean, would
be fulfilled, said some of the British papers, if it rescued the Armenian nation
from what they termed "the age-long martyrdom at the hands of the Turks," for
the Ottoman Armenians themselves proposed that Russia should either annex or
proclaim a protectorate over the whole of Greater Armenia, which extended to
the shores of the Mediterranean. From a correspondent in Russian Armenia the
Manchester Guardian received a long dispatch recounting the efforts made by
the Catholicos, the head of the Armenian Church and the default political leader
of the Armenians, to use the present opportunity to secure "lasting freedom"
for his people. After explaining why the Ottoman Armenians could act only
through the Catholicos he outlined the ideal for which Armenians should work,
as indorsed by the Catholicos:

> A large and liberal scheme of government, under the protection of Russia, over
> the whole of Greater Armenia and Cilicia down to Alexandretta, on the shores
> of the Mediterranean, is the aim of Armenians pursued by the Catholicos, who
> is hopeful of its realization should the Allies emerge victorious from the pres-
> ent struggle.

These ideas of the Catholicos received the support of such influential Russian journals as the Moscow *Russkoye Slovo*, the Tiflis *Kaffkasski Telegraf*, and even the semiofficial Petrograd *Novoye Vremya*. He then explained that, whatever might come, Armenia could no longer continue under Ottoman rule, and stated the Armenians' ideal for the future of their country:

> The Armenians under any circumstances would prefer simple annexation by Russia to remaining any longer under Turkish dominion; but they recognize that this might be somewhat prejudicial to the preservation of their national type. They would rather see Greater Armenia, with Cilicia down to Alexandretta, placed under the joint protection of the three Great Powers—Russia, France, and England, the former having as its special zone of influence the provinces bordering its provinces, and the latter two the districts bordering on Mesopotamia and the Mediterranean.[38]

The organ of the Catholicos, the Etchmiadzin *Orizon*, hailed the Russian "liberators":

> The Turkish Armenians greet with warm enthusiasm the advance of the Russian army upon Turkish territory, because they are convinced that they will gain their political freedom only through Russia, as was the case of the Christian nations in the Balkans. The Armenians regard the war between Russia and Turkey as a war of liberation.

The Catholicos of Etchmiadzin was the spiritual head of the Armenian Church. He was the source of all orders, and to Armenians everywhere he represented the unity and solidarity of the Armenian people. The *Mshak*, a paper of socialist tendencies published at Tiflis, said:

> With the declaration of war, the status of the Armenian question has changed. Russia drew the sword not for conquests: this war is not an aggressive one, but a war of liberation. There can no longer be a question of Turkish reforms, because a state of war exists. Now the question is, how to put an end to Turkish rule. And, as Russia is not waging an aggressive war, but one of liberation, Armenians can and must express a wish that Turkish Armenians should be given an administrative organization under the protectorate of Russia. We suppose that that will conform also to the political interests of Russia.

Finally, the Petrograd *Ryetch* remarked:

> The question of Turkish Armenia is a very complicated one. Its solution does not depend on Russia alone. France and England are in a measure interested in what the future status of Turkish Armenia shall be. The establishment of autonomy in Turkish Armenia, under the protectorate of Russia, appears to Armenian workers to be a more feasible solution than annexation.[39]

With the support of a recently created Armenian National Bureau 10,000 Armenians voluntarily enlisted in the Imperial Russian Army, where they joined around 100,000 Armenian regulars in hope of liberating historic Armenia from Ottoman rule. In addition, four volunteer units were formed for action across the Ottoman border. Prominent Ottoman Armenians made their way from eastern Anatolia to Tiflis, Baku, or Erivan. The mobilization of Armenians in the Russian Empire, the organization of volunteer units to operate on Ottoman soil, and the tendencies towards pro-Russian sympathies among many of sultan's Armenian subjects alarmed the Ottoman government and provided indications of events to come.[40]

It is worth noticing that Captain John Bennett, British Assistant Liaison Officer at the Ottoman Ministry of War and later head of Military Intelligence 'B' office in İstanbul from 1919 to 1921, in his memoirs in 1962 noted that during the First World War the Dashnak Committee gave much help to the Allies against the Turks. Allies owed a debt to the Dashnaks. Bennett knew what they had done in bringing messages in and out of Kut-al-Amara when Major General Charles Townshend was besieged there, and in helping British prisoners to escape from the Ottoman Empire.[41]

Two days prior to the Allied landing at Gallipoli, William Mitchel Ramsay, who filled the Regius Chair of Humanity in Aberdeen University between 1886 and 1911 and called the leading Latinist in Scotland, wrote in *Manchester Guardian* that on northeastern Anatolia a protected Armenian State was a necessity. He said Armenia must be an autonomous State under European or Russian protection. This was one of the first conditions of peace in Western Asia.[42]

MEASURES TAKEN AGAINST THE ARMENIAN REBELLION

On 24 April 1915, Ottoman Minister of the Interior Talat Paşa issued a cipher-coded circular to the governors of provinces and sanjaks[43] where Armenian rebellious activities were underway. Its contents were as follows:

> Once again, especially at a time when the state is engaged in war, the most recent rebellions which have occurred in Zeytun, Bitlis, Sivas and Van have demonstrated the continuing attempts of the Armenian committees to obtain, through their revolutionary and political organizations, an independent administration for themselves in Ottoman territory. These rebellions and the decision of the Dashnak Committee, after the outbreak of the war, immediately to incite the Armenians in Russia against us, and to have the Armenians in the Ottoman state rebel with all their force when the Ottoman army was at its weakest, are all acts of treason which would affect the life and future of the country.
>
> It has been demonstrated once again that the activities by these committees, whose headquarters are in foreign countries, and who maintain, even in

their names, their revolutionary attributes, are determined to gain autonomy by using every possible pretext and means against the government. This has been established by the bombs which were found in Kayseri, Sivas and other regions, by the actions of the Armenian committee leaders who have participated in the Russian attack on the country, by forming volunteer regiments comprised of Ottoman Armenians in the Russian army, and through their publications and operations aimed at threatening the Ottoman army from the rear.

Naturally, as the Ottoman government will never condone the continuation of such operations and attempts, which constitute a matter of life and death for itself, nor will it legalize the existence of these committees which are the source of malice, it has felt the necessity to promptly close down all such political organizations.

You are therefore ordered to close down immediately all branches, within your province, of the Huntchak, Dashnak, and similar committees; to confiscate the files and documents found in their branch headquarters, and ensure that they are neither lost nor destroyed; to immediately arrest all the leaders and prominent members of the committees, together with such other Armenians as are known by the government to be dangerous; further, to gather up those Armenians whose presence in one area is considered to be inappropriate, and to transfer them to other parts of the province or sanjak, so as not to give them the opportunity to engage in harmful acts; to begin the process of searching for hidden weapons; and to maintain all contacts with the [military] commanders in order to be prepared to meet any possible counteractions. As it has been determined in a meeting with the Acting Commander-in-Chief that all individuals arrested on the basis of files and documents which come into our possession in course of the proper execution of these orders are to be turned over to the military courts, the above-mentioned steps are to be implemented immediately. We are to be informed subsequently as to the number of people arrested, and with regard to the implementation of other orders.

As this operation is only intended to affect the operation of the committees, you are *strongly ordered not to implement it in such a manner as will cause mutual killings* on the part of the Muslim and Armenian elements of the population."[44] [Emphasis added.]

Again on April 24 another ciphered circular order was sent to the same effect to the governors of provinces and sanjaks:

Whereas the Armenian committees have been trying to secure autonomy through their political and revolutionary formations,

Whereas the Dashnak Society after the outbreak of the war made a decision to raise the Armenians of Russia against us and [to order] that for the time being the Armenians of Turkey should await until the Turkish army is exhausted and then assume such an attitude which would affect the life and future of the country,

Whereas this decision and the recent revolutionary movements at Zeytun, Bitlis, Sivas and Van, which took place at a moment when the country was engaged in war, reconfirmed their treacherous aspirations,

Whereas all the Armenian committees, which have their bases in foreign countries, and which by the efforts of their members have prepared a revolution, have formed the opinion that autonomy, which is their objective, may be obtained only by fighting the government,

Whereas the Armenian committees have stored bombs and revolvers, some of which have been discovered at Kayseri and Sivas, have formed volunteer regiments composed chiefly of inhabitants of Turkey and have invaded the country, aiming at threatening the Turkish army from behind, as confirmed by their organization and publications,

Whereas the Turkish government cannot close its eyes and bear any longer the existence of such organizations which form for us a matter of life and death,

Whereas the existence of such committees, which are a source of unrest, cannot still be considered legal,

And whereas an urgent necessity has been felt for the abolition of all these political formations,

We, in agreement with the Acting Commander-in-Chief of the Ottoman army, have promulgated the following decision which you should carry out immediately after you have made the necessary preparations:

The branches of the Huntchak, Dashnak, and similar committees in the provinces should be closed at once and all documents found in these branches should be confiscated without giving them a chance to destroy them.

All the active leaders and members of the committees who are considered dangerous or harmful to the Government should be arrested at once, and those whom you object to remaining at their homes should be concentrated at a convenient place without giving them an opportunity to escape.

Arms should be searched for in suspicious places, but before this is carried out, an adequate force should be prepared through arrangement with the troops, as a precaution against any counteractions.

Exact arrangements securing the thorough execution of this order should be made. All documents found should be investigated, and the persons who are arrested as a result of these investigations should be brought before Courts Martial. The numbers of persons arrested and details of the execution of this order should be constantly reported.

As this order is exclusively a measure against the extension of the Committees, *you should abstain from putting it into a form which might result in the mutual massacre* of the Muslim and Armenian elements [of the population]. Make arrangements for special officials to accompany the groups of Armenians who are being relocated, and make sure that they are provided with food and other needed things, paying the cost out of the allotments set aside for emigrants."[45] [Emphasis added.]

The above documents reflect the kind of intelligence which was flowing into İstanbul relating to the activities of the Armenian revolutionary committees. It provides the background for the first step in the relocation process, that of expelling the known revolutionary ringleaders and their accomplices.[46] In light of actual events, Ottoman anxieties about the movements of Armenian revolutionaries – always present before the war amid earlier nationalist uprisings – were especially justified now that the war was fully underway and Armenian collaboration with the Russian enemy was in plain sight.[47]

To that regard it is interesting to consider the letter delivered by Mgrditch Nercecian, a Huntchakist leader in Sofia, on 18 May 1915 to the British minister there, Henry Bax-Ironside. The former wrote that many thousands of Armenians at the beginning of the European war joined the ranks of the Allies both in France and in the Caucasus against the Ottoman Empire. The letter also said that in the area of Zeytun, the Armenian population had openly revolted against the state authorities. The Huntchak organization in that section was in complete control of the situation, having armed all the male population capable of carrying arms. In Adana, Dörtyol and vicinity, including almost the whole Cilicia, the organization was supreme, according to Nercecian, although the bands which were acting in inaccessible places were in need of assistance.[48]

Arguably, it is also revealing that after the capture of Van by the Russians on 20 May 1915, the Armenians gave a great dinner in honor of General Nicolaiev, commander-in-chief of the Russian army in Caucasus, who made a speech in which he said:

> Since 1826, the Russians have always striven to free Armenia, but political circumstances have always prevented their success. Now, as the grouping of nations has been quite altered, we may hope Armenians will soon be free.

Aram Manoogian, a Dashnak insurgent leader, soon after appointed provisional Governor of Van by General Nicolaiev, replied:

> When we rose a month ago, we expected the Russians would come. At a certain moment, our situation was dreadful. We had to choose between surrender and death. We chose death, but when we no longer expected your help, it has suddenly arrived.[49]

In response to this open insurrection, the Ottoman government pursued a strategy of removing Armenians from strategic zones where they were aiding the enemy and attacking the civilian population. It is particularly instructive to quote the main section of the communication of 26 May 1915 addressed by Minister of the Interior Talat Paşa to Grand Vizier and Minister of Foreign Affairs Said Halim Paşa:

> Recently some Armenians living in areas near the war zones have made difficult movements of the Imperial Army which is busy defending the state. They have blocked the movement of military food and supplies, cooperated with the enemy and joined their forces, made armed attacks in the state on the armed

forces and civilians, assaulted Ottoman towns and killed and robbed and raid-
ed, given supplies to enemy naval forces and turned over plans of fortified
places to help their attacks.

It was necessary to remove these rebellious races from the military zones
and to empty the villages which are their bases of operations and places of
refuge. Through the efforts of the central government as well as local officials, all the Armenians are being removed from the villages and towns in the
provinces of Van, Bitlis, and Erzurum, the sanjaks of Adana, Mersin, Kozan,
Cebelibereket, excluding the cities of Adana, Kozan, and Mersin, the sanjak of
Maraş, excluding the town of Maraş itself, the province of Aleppo, excluding
the city of Aleppo, and the districts of İskenderun, Belen, Cisrulşuğur, and An-
takya, excluding the administrative center of each. They are being transported
to and settled in places chosen and set aside by the government in the southern
provinces, including the province of Musul except for its northern area which
borders the province of Van; the district of Deyrizor; the southern part of the
sanjak of Urfa, excluding Urfa itself; the eastern and southeastern parts of the
province of Aleppo, and the eastern part of the province of Syria.[50]

The foregoing is the key document in explaining the thinking behind the
decision to relocate that segment of the Ottoman Armenian population living
near war zones away from such areas. It is the first basic relocation reference to
actually move Armenian elements from eastern Anatolia and Cilicia on military
grounds. The Ottoman authorities became convinced, following the closure of
the revolutionary headquarters and the confiscation of documents from them
and the revolt at Van, that large-scale Armenian rebellion was a certain risk.

The Ottoman governmental response to the Armenian rebellion at Van was
to adopt on 27 May 1915 the Provisional Law Regarding Measures to Be Taken
by the Military Authorities against Those Who Oppose the Operations of the
Government in Time of War. In time of war, the Army, Army Corps, and Divisional Commanders, and the Independent Commanders, were authorized and
compelled to crush any opposition, armed resistance and aggression by the population. The Army, Army Corps, and Divisional Commanders were authorized
to transfer and relocate the populations of villages and towns, either individually or collectively, in response to any signs of treachery or betrayal.[51]

Such forceful military action was regarded by Armenians and their allies
as massacres, and even at the time, the Ottoman government was aware of the
accusations. It issued an official statement on 4 June 1915 rejecting that massacres had taken place in eastern Anatolia, and protesting against the decision
of the Entente powers to hold it responsible for any alleged atrocities. The government held that the Entente powers themselves, and Russia in particular, had
stirred up trouble in eastern Anatolia, by financing and arming numerous secret
agents, who were to incite the population to revolt. The Ottoman government
said it held documents proving that revolutionary committees, which at present
had their headquarters in Paris, London and Tiflis, enjoyed the protection of the

French, British and Russian governments, and that these documents would be published at an opportune moment. Thanks to the measures adopted by the Ottoman government, the statement continued, the revolutionary movement among the Armenians was suppressed without massacres. Moreover, the Armenian population elsewhere in Ottoman Turkey was unaffected by the forced migrations. Of the 77,835 Armenians in İstanbul only 235 were guilty of participation in the plot, and were arrested, while the rest were left peacefully and enjoyed complete security.[52]

Again the following communication regarding the position of Armenians in the Ottoman Empire in June 1915 had been transmitted from İstanbul by the Wolff bureau and published in the German press:

The imperial (Ottoman) government has taken steps to remove Armenians from settlements where their presence may be considered injurious and dangerous to internal security and calm, and to the national defense. Our opponents have discovered therein a fresh pretext for influencing public opinion against us. Their papers, and those of neutral countries which they have succeeded in winning over to their cause, are endeavoring to obscure the truth by carefully misrepresenting all the facts regarding these measures, and by maintaining that the Armenian element, despite its complete innocence, has been deprived of its most elementary, natural and sacred rights. The urgent necessity for and justice of the attitude which the imperial government has been compelled to take with regard to revolutionary Armenians is, nevertheless unquestionable. Events daily afford our military authorities fresh proofs of the existence of a long prepared and organized plan, which the Armenians continue to execute in detail while fighting on the side of the Russians against us. This illegal and revolutionary movement, which until recently was traceable only at the front and in the districts adjacent thereto, has latterly extended to our lines of communication. Thus on June 2 some 500 armed Armenians, who had been joined by deserters of the same race, attacked the town of Karahissar-Sharki and plundered the houses in the Muhammadan quarter. They barricaded themselves in the citadel of the town, and answered the paternal and conciliatory advice of the local authorities with rifle fire and bombs, with the result that there were 150 casualties among Turkish civilians and soldiers. The last proposal of the government for a surrender met with no success. In these circumstances the authorities were obliged to turn their guns upon the citadel, and thanks to these measures the rebels were mastered on June 20. Similar revolutionary movements which break out here and there are compelling us to withdraw troops from our various fronts for their suppression. In order to avoid this inconvenience and to prevent a repetition of these incidents, which cause regrettable suffering to the innocent and peaceful section of the population as well as to the guilty, the government has taken certain precautionary and restrictive measures against the revolutionary Armenians. In consequence of the execution of these measures Armenians have been removed from the frontier zones, and from the region of our lines of communication. By this means they have been removed from the more or less effective influence of the Russians, and have been rendered incapable of vitiating the defense of the country and of imperiling the security of the state.[53]

In mid-December 1915 a similar statement on Armenian rising was issued from the Ottoman Embassy in Berlin and conveyed to the German press by the Wolff bureau for publication:

> During the night of September 16 the last Armenian bands instituted a revolt. They had barricaded themselves in strong buildings in positions dominating the town of Urfa, and opened fire upon our police patrols, two men of whom fell, while eight were wounded. Our police were everywhere fired at and after the Armenians had gained possession of the settlers' quarters, they continued to fire from behind their shelter there. As these facts proved that the insurgent bands were determined to offer an armed resistance and to take advantage of the inadequacy of the police force available, and as they eventually gained possession of the Muhammadan quarter of the town and were beginning to overpower the inhabitants, several regiments destined for the front were dispatched to Urfa. The refuge of the bands was destroyed, and the insurgents were suppressed on October 3. Twenty soldiers and gendarmes fell in the course of the action, while fifty were wounded. The object of the insurrection was, in the first place, to do damage, to destroy alien settlements, and to attack subjects of states with which Turkey is at war, in order afterwards to represent the Turks as responsible; in the second place, it was intended to compel a portion of the Turkish troops to remain before the fortified place of refuge, and thus to withdraw them from the front. Thanks to the swift and energetic action of the imperial authorities, the insurrection did not have the desired result. It was suppressed without the loss of a single subject of the states with which Turkey is at war, and without any damage being inflicted upon neutrals.[54]

British officers fighting against the Turks were their most staunch defenders against accusations sent broadcast from London by those who accepted Armenian atrocities "verified from Russian sources." In one London periodical an officer wrote: "It is not easy to maintain a 'hate' against the Turk. He is a respectable gentleman who fights well and without malice and accepts captivity with good humor and dignity." Another Britisher wrote:

> One can hardly refrain from admiring the courage of and tenacity shown by the Turkish soldiers in their defense of the Gallipoli Peninsula, and saying a word of praise in their favor for the clean way in which they are fighting. It is a common saying with those long resident in the East whose judgment has not been warped by religious prejudice that the Christian virtues are more widely practiced by the good old Turk than by the so-called Eastern Christians.[55]

Count Bernstorff, the German Ambassador in Washington, on 28 September 1915 sent a communication to the Department of State saying reports of Ottoman atrocities against Armenians were greatly exaggerated and defending the action of the Turks, as having been provoked. While the ambassador's letter did not deny that strong measures had been imposed on Armenians by the Turks, it was stated that attempts to stir up rebellion and revolt and treasonable activity had made the Armenian policy a wartime necessity. And it concluded that since the Ottoman Empire had let it be known that no foreign interference with its Armenian policy would be permitted, the United States would probably avoid the matter as a subject for any formal protest, unless Americans became involved.[56]

Elsewhere there was also support for the Ottoman measures. In 1916, the usually restrained and measured Robert Lansing, United States Secretary of State from mid-1915 to February 1920, wrote to President Woodrow Wilson, who was strongly pro-Armenian, that the mere fact of deportation of civilians from a particular region by military authorities was not reprehensible and he recognized the right of the Ottoman government to displace its Armenian subjects from one locality to another. In the secretary of state's words,

> The well-known disloyalty of the Armenians to the Ottoman government and the fact that the territory which they inhabited was within the zone of military operations constituted grounds more or less justifiable for compelling them to depart from their homes.[57]

The international law expertise of Lansing lends this statement special significance. He drew on long experience as a lawyer with a working knowledge of the finer points and the precedents of international law. He had served as counsel in several international arbitration cases, and by the time of his appointment as secretary of state he possessed enormous practical skills with a great sense of appreciation for diplomacy.[58] The American statesman was one of the first outside the Ottoman Empire to recognize the true cause and nature of the Armenian relocations.

At the ninth and last congress of the Party of Union and Progress, held on 1 November 1918 in İstanbul, Talat Paşa specifically referred to Armenian relocations in a speech:

> The removal of Armenians has given rise, both in the country and more especially abroad, to certain criticisms of war cabinets. I must say that this affair of relocations and massacres has been very much exaggerated. The Armenian and Greek propaganda has worked extremely hard to alienate European and American public opinion, taking advantage of the fact that that the Turks were not well known abroad, or rather of the fact that they were misunderstood there. I do not wish by saying this to assert that abuses were not committed. But the responsibility for them falls first of all on the elements that provoked them. Certainly we can not say that this responsibility falls on all the Armenians. But we must not lose sight of the fact that at a time when the Ottoman Empire

was carrying on a war on which depended its very existence, the responsible government could not allow our armies to be exposed to an attack in the rear. The Armenian bands that were creating difficulties for our troops in the province of Erzurum were receiving all needed help in the Armenian villages. At the least signal, the Armenian peasants seized arms that had been hidden in the churches, and lent their aid to these bands. This was why relocation was above all else a necessity.[59]

An official statement going in detail into nearly every angle of the complex Near East situation was given the *Philadelphia Inquirer Public Ledger* correspondent Clarence Streit on 25 February 1921 by Mustafa Kemal Paşa (later and better known as Kemal Atatürk), president of the Turkish Grand National Assembly, in written answers to questions submitted to him. From his own observation Streit could say Mustafa Kemal Paşa spoke with the authority of a leader who knew his people and enjoyed enormous prestige among them. It should therefore be useful to record here the text of the question and answer regarding the Armenian relocations which ran as follows:

What is the official viewpoint of your government toward the Armenian deportations and massacres during the world war? After making allowance for the enormous exaggerations always made by those who accuse their enemies, the Armenian deportation affair reduces itself to this—the Armenian-Dashnak committee, then in the service of the czar, had caused the Armenian population behind our troops to revolt when the Russian army began its great 1915 offensive against us. Obliged to retreat before the superior numbers and material of the enemy, we found ourselves constantly between two fires. Our convoys of supplies and wounded were pitilessly massacred, roads and bridges destroyed behind us and terror reigned through the Turkish countryside. The bands which committed these crimes, and which included in their ranks Armenians able to bear arms, were supplied with arms, munitions and provisions in Armenian villages where, thanks to the immunities accorded in the capitulations, certain foreign powers had succeeded during peacetime in establishing enormous stocks for this purpose. The world which regards with indifference the fashion in which England in peacetime and far from the battlefield treats the Irish cannot in all justice complain of the resolution we were obliged to take relative to Armenian deportations. Contrary to calumnies spread against us the deportees are alive and many of them would have returned to their homes if the Entente had not forced us to recommence war.[60]

Forced migration of large segments of the population from one area to another was not something which was uniquely Ottoman, or which was new in either the Balkans or the Middle East. It had been a Byzantine policy even before the Turks entered Anatolia in the eleventh century. Banishment was used by the Russians from early times. In the late eighteenth century, for example, the czars periodically moved Muslim Crimean Tatars away from the front lines in time of war.[61]

More recently, beginning in February 1915, the Russian army commanders drove from the zone of military operations to the interior millions of noncombatants in a state of absolute destitution. They were expelled from their homes without provision being made for their shelter, food or ultimate destination. In the words of one group, "We did not want to move, we were chased away. We were forced to burn our homes and crops, we were not allowed to take our cattle with us, we were not even allowed to return to our homes to get some money."[62] The French Ambassador in St. Petersburg, Maurice Paléologue, confided in his diary:

> Everywhere the process of departure has been marked by scenes of violence and pillage under the complacent eye of the authorities. Hundreds of thousands of these poor people have been seen wandering over the snows, driven like cattle by platoons of Cossacks, abandoned in the greatest distress at the stations, camping in the open round the towns, and dying of hunger, weariness, and cold. And to fortify their courage these pitiful multitudes have everywhere encountered the same feeling of hatred and scorn, the same suspicion of espionage and treason.[63]

By the summer of the same year, there was a stream of exiles of all kinds from the empire's large population of ethnic Germans to Russian-subject Jews, Muslims, and others, and the military authorities remained indifferent to their fate. The Russian general staff disposed of sweeping powers to enforce the resettlement of civilians, where this strategy was deemed appropriate. The War Statute of July 1914 had granted the Russian army nearly unlimited control over civilian affairs throughout the entire area declared under military rule. It forced civilian authorities to implement all military orders in the whole zone and it explicitly granted military commanders the right to deport individuals or groups. These actions were justified on the grounds that these noncombatants were actual or potential spies and helpers of the Germans. The displacement of civilians in the Russian empire reached three million in 1915 and may have climbed to as high as seven million by the time Russia left the war in 1917. As Eric Lohr rightly points out, although it was one of the largest cases of forced migration up to the Second World War, the event has received remarkably little scholarly attention. [64]

Nor did the Ottoman Empire establish a precedent of forced migrations. Jurist and historian Samuel Weems remarks that population transfer is much what nations have done to protect themselves from what they perceived as threats from disloyal people for thousands of years. Displacement of populations suspected of disloyalty was a customary war measure throughout human history.[65]

ARMENIAN CONFESSION OF SUPPORT FOR THE ALLIES

During and immediately after the war, the Armenians would make no attempt to hide their contribution to the Allied victory. To the contrary: in a letter to the *Daily News* of London, T. Kouyoumdjian, writing in the spring of 1915 from Moscow, made a vigorous plea for a recognition of the devotion and bravery of the Armenians in the war. After referring to the admiration often expressed at the heroism of Serbia and Belgium, the writer said:

> Every Armenian fully appreciates the heroism of the Serbians and Belgians, and strongly sympathizes with the enormous sacrifices which they have made. But our national honor, our just cause, and even truth and justice, demand that your readers should know that no nation on earth at any time has paid a price for its liberties more than has Armenia. A glance at its history in the fifth century will convince you. In the present war Armenians eagerly took up their shares of the burden for the success of the cause of the Allies, which is also their cause. Armenians from all parts of the world freely contributed materially and with men. At the present moment about 80,000 Armenian soldiers on the western frontier and 40,000 on the Turkish frontier are fighting with their Russian comrades for their Tsar and fatherland. Besides this, more than 6,000 Armenian volunteers are doing heroic deeds on the Turkish frontier, as the reports of the commanders of the Russian army in the Caucasus testify. Several of the heads of the volunteer corps have been decorated with the Order of St. George. The number of volunteers is growing daily. Materially, besides their contribution to the Russian Red Cross, Armenians have equipped and are keeping up the volunteers and are providing food and comfort for the 80,000 Armenian refugees from Turkey and Persia. M. Papadjanian, the member of the Duma, and the president of the Armenian central committee of relief fund in Tiflis, informed me that the committee is spending monthly on the volunteer organization and the refugees about 450,000 roubles, or 45,000 British pounds.

Armenians saw in this war, Kouyoumdjian said in conclusion, their absolute freedom from the Turkish "yoke," and, fully realizing its meaning, were gladly bearing their share of the burden of the war, with the hope that when the hour of peace came the Allies would generously appreciate and satisfy their right demands. In giving what was due to the Armenians, he added, who were regarded as the Belgians of the Near East, Europe would meet its obligation.[66]

Avetis Aharonian, later to become president of the Republic of Armenia, wrote in the summer of 1915 in the Swiss *Journal de Genève* that led by the Dashnaksutiun, the Ottoman Armenians organized themselves into battalions and established their headquarters at Van. Three members of the Dashnak party, Aram Manoogian, Ichkan and Vramian Onnik Dersakian, led the movement. Van was besieged by 10,000 Ottoman regulars, Aharonian continued, but held out, in spite of bombardment, and in a month's time Dersakian managed to repulse the Ottoman troops, threw them back in the direction of Bitlis, and hoisted the Armenian flag over Van. Three days later the Russians entered the city and were welcomed enthusiastically by the Armenian bands and the civilian population. On the other side of the Caucasus, during the winter months of 1915, Russian Armenia was arming and organizing itself for the purpose of coming to the rescue of its kinsmen in the Ottoman Empire. Thousands of young Armenians left schools, colleges and professions and formed a small army of 10,000 which placed itself under the direction of the Russian military commander. They were mentioned, Aharonian added, in the Petrograd and Moscow press for their valor and endurance. With this small army the number of Armenians fighting on various battlefronts in the Great War amounted to over 100,000. In these events the writer of the article saw great hopes for the future of Armenia. They represented, he considered, the end of the Ottoman rule and the emergence of an autonomous country enlarged by the possession of Cilicia which Armenia claimed and which Russia did not seem disposed to refuse it. At any rate the Armenians saw in Russia their hope of salvation and they were expending their strength and resources in fighting for it.[67]

Boghos Nubar, who served the Armenian Catholicos Gevorg V as propagandist and informal diplomat in Paris from 1912 and as president of one of the Armenian delegations at the Paris Peace Conference in 1919, was quick to write to the French Minister of Foreign Affairs Stéphen Pichon on 29 October 1918 to claim the status of belligerent. Between 600 and 800 volunteers, he pointed out, had served on the Western front with the French Foreign Legion. Only forty of them were still alive, some in hospitals. Three Armenian battalions of the Légion d'Orient had been cited by the French commander for zeal and endurance. Their loyalty to the Entente powers had never been denied. General Edmund Allenby, in command of the Allied forces in the Middle East, had also praised them in a telegram to the Armenian National Delegation. Finally, 150,000 Armenians had fought in the Russian army and had held the front in the Caucasus after the Russians had dropped out of the war.[68]

Again, in a letter of 30 January 1919 to the editor of *The Times* of London, Nubar admitted freely that his people had in fact been belligerents, fighting ever since the beginning of the war by the side of the Allies on all fronts. The Armenian spokesman wrote unhesitatingly and he is worth quoting in length:

> The Armenians have been belligerents *de facto*, since they indignantly refused to side with Turkey. Our volunteers fought in the French Légion Etrangère and covered themselves with glory. In the Légion d'Orient they numbered over 5,000 and made up more than half the French contingent in Syria and Palestine, which took part in the decisive victory of General Allenby. In the Caucasus, without mentioning the 150,000 Armenians in the Russian armies, about 50,000 Armenian volunteers under Andranik, Nazarbekoff, and others not only fought for four years for the cause of the Entente, but after the breakdown of

Russia they were the only forces in the Caucasus to resist the advance of the Turks, whom they held in check until the armistice was signed. Thus they helped the British forces in Mesopotamia by hindering the Germano-Turks from sending their troops elsewhere. These services have been acknowledged by the Allied Governments, as Lord Robert Cecil recognized in the House of Commons.

And he urged that the Armenians, by casting their lot with the Allies, would secure their future independence.[69]

Aharonian and Nubar appeared before the peace conference at Paris on 26 February 1919 and as a part of their joint memorandum presented the following on the voluntary participation of the Armenians in the First World War:

> Armenian volunteers fought on all the fronts. In France, in the Foreign Legion, by their bravery they covered themselves with glory. Scarcely one-tenth of their original number now survives. They fought in Syria and in Palestine, in the Legion of the Orient, under French command, where they hurried in response to the call of the National Delegation. In this Legion, the Armenians constituted the largest element, or more than one-half of the entire French contingent. There they took a leading part in the decisive victory of General Allenby, who paid high tribute to their valor. In the Caucasus, where in addition to over 150,000 Armenian men who served in the Russian army on all the fronts, an army of 50,000 men and thousands of volunteers fought throughout under the supreme command of General Nazarbekian. It was with these that, after the breakdown of the Russian army and the treaty of Brest-Litovsk the Armenians, deceived and deserted by the Georgians, and betrayed by the Tartars who made common cause with the Turks, took over the defense of the Caucasus front and, for a period of seven months, delayed the advance of the Turks. They thus rendered important services to the British army in Mesopotamia, as stated by Lord Cecil in an official letter addressed to Lord Bryce and in his response to an interpellation in the House of Commons. In addition thereto, by their resistance against the Turks until the conclusion of the armistice, they forced the Turks to send troops from Palestine to the Armenian front, and thus contributed indirectly to the victory of the Allied Army in Syria. The Armenians have been actual belligerents in this war.[70]

In a Nubar memorandum of 1 December 1920 sent to the Quai d'Orsay, he reminded the French authorities that in October 1916, five months after the conclusion of the Sykes-Picot Agreement partitioning the Ottoman Empire, the French government declared to the Armenian National Delegation that the Armenians should earn the liberation of their country because it furnished volunteers for an expedition into Asia Minor. This was a critical contribution, Nubar said, because at that moment the Western front was then passing through one of its most alarming moments of the war. The Allies, and especially France, could not send even the weakest detachment to the East. The president of the

Armenian National Delegation eagerly accepted the proposition that was put to him, in exchange for which he obtained from the French government a solemn promise to grant after the war the widest possible autonomy under its protection to the Armenian territories.[71]

In response to the French request and promise, an appeal was sent by the president of the Armenian National Delegation to Armenians, who rushed from all sides to enlist. Thus was created the Eastern Legion, later named the Armenian Legion, for it was made up mostly of Armenians. Under the command of French officers and French staffs, the Legion took part in the Palestine-Syria campaign. And in continuing the war for nearly a whole year on the Caucasian front, after the collapse of Russia, the Armenian volunteers prevented the German forces from obtaining oil, according to General Erich Ludendorff. The Armenian volunteers held important Ottoman forces in the Caucasus and prevented them from fighting elsewhere. They thus came to the aid indirectly but very effectively of the Allied troops fighting in Mesopotamia and Palestine and later in the Salonica campaign.

In a statement prepared by the Armenian National Delegation at Paris on 9 December 1920 and signed by its president Nubar, this contribution was asserted clearly: "The Commanding Officer of the French Detachment under whose order the Armenians fought, has brought to light the endurance and the spirit of the Armenian soldiers, whose loyalty to the Allies never faltered."[72]

Most of Aharonian's and Nubar's compelling narratives of what happened in the First World War years are endorsed by David Lloyd George who acted as British Prime Minister from 1916 to 1922. In a similar vein, Aneurin Williams, a longstanding member of the British Parliament and chairman of the British Armenia Committee and of the Armenian Refugees (Lord Mayor's) Fund, draws attention to Armenian support for the Allied war effort. Williams makes it clear several times that the Armenians fought in many zones of the war upon Entente's side.[73]

Henry Morgenthau, American Ambassador to the Sublime Porte between November 1913 and February 1916, in a personal and confidential letter to the Secretary of State Lansing, agrees with Aharonian and Nubar that the losses of the Ottoman army in the Caucasus in 1914-1915 was "greatly due to the assistance rendered to the Russians by the Armenian volunteers who also caused the failure of the Turkish expedition in Azerbaijan."[74] According to Walter George Smith, a commissioner for Near East Relief, formerly the American Committee for Armenian and Syrian Relief, Armenian soldiers held off whole divisions of Turks that would otherwise have been opposing General Allenby in Palestine, and might have delayed or perhaps have prevented his success.[75] Florence Kling Harding, wife of the United States President Warren Harding, in an appeal to the American people for support of the Near East Relief "Bundle Day" on 30 May 1921 praised the loyalty of the Armenians to the Allied cause.[76] Because of their fighting, Armenians became known in the western circles as the "Little Ally." It was on this basis that many promises were made to the Armenian people for future autonomy and independence.

The British paper *Daily Chronicle* had written as early as 23 September 1915:

> Who is our seventh ally? The Armenian nation. The Armenians awaited no one's invitation. They began fighting on the side of the Allies right from the start. Over 100,000 of them are in the Russian army and about 20,000 Armenian volunteers are fighting in the Caucasus, and it is even said that General Michael Alexieff, present commander-in-chief of the Russian army, is an Armenian by birth.[77]

GOVERNMENT INTENTIONS TOWARD THE ARMENIANS

Later in this study, we shall explore the philosophy of Nazi Germany with regard to the Jews, as well as the critical role played by anti-Semitism in Nazi ideology and the rise of Nazi political power. It is important to note, therefore, that the Ottoman government did not at any time undertake such a campaign against Armenian subjects. In fact during the First World War, while the Western allies were using propaganda to make their own people hate the enemy, the Ottoman government stifled news of what Armenian nationalists were doing in order to avoid the racial and ethnic tensions which it knew would result if such agitations became known. While Nazi Germany encouraged and itself carried out attacks on Jews; the Ottoman government on the other hand discouraged such attacks against Armenians, and when they did occur, it tried, convicted and executed those responsible.

The clear intention of the Sublime Porte was to exile the Armenians, not to kill them. The authorities were instructed to protect the refugees against attacks, to provide them with sufficient food and supplies for their journey and to compensate them with new property, land, and goods necessary for their settlement. The circular of 31 May 1915 from the Ottoman Grand Vizier's office to the Ministries of the Interior, War and Finance stipulated:

> When those of the Armenians resident in the aforementioned towns and villages who have to be moved are transferred to their places of settlement and are on the road, their comfort is assured and their lives and property protected; that after their arrival until they are definitely settled in their new homes their food should be paid for out of Refugee Appropriations; that property and land should be distributed to them in accordance with their previous financial situation as well as their current needs and that for those among them who need it the government should build houses, provide cultivators and artisans with

seed, tools, and equipment.[78]

Despite these intentions, there is no doubt that mass deaths did occur. There is abundant evidence that the Ottoman rulers were shocked when they heard what had befallen the Armenians. Of the masses of secret relocation directives seen to date, not one orders murder. Official circulars sent to the governors of the provinces and sanjaks from which Armenians were to be relocated made it clear that the relocation was not intended for the destruction of any individuals or groups; that lives should be protected; that any Ottoman troops engaged in murder, robbery or rape should be severely punished; and that guilty public officials should immediately be removed from office and court-martialed. Strict instructions were indeed issued that the relocations should proceed in an orderly manner and that the persons and property of displaced Armenians should be safeguarded. Official circulars ordering relocations emphasized that care should be taken of vulnerable individuals and protection against attacks, while Armenians left behind should not be taken from their places of residence.[79] Australian historian Jeremy Salt, who has undertaken considerable research on Ottoman Armenians, shows much perspicacity when he asks the relevant question: "If the Ottoman government really had ordered the massacres, why would it send confidential orders to provincial officials instructing them to safeguard the lives of the Armenians during the relocation?"[80]

These orders exist and can be examined and read. Order after order speaks of the need to guard the relocatees and their property and to assure their safety. The Ottoman government through the Ministry of the Interior issued on 10 June 1915 an elaborate thirty-four clause "Decree Regarding the Management of the Property, Building and Land of the Armenians Displaced Due to the War and Extraordinary Political Circumstances." Specially formed commissions and assigned officials were to see that all buildings with furniture and other objects belonging to the Armenians were sealed and taken under protection. The value of the goods taken under protection was to be registered, and the goods themselves were to be sent to convenient storage places. Goods that could spoil were to be auctioned; the result of the sale would be preserved in the name of the owner. Pictures and holy books found at the churches were to be registered and later sent to the places where the population was resettled. The migrants (Muslim refugees) to be resettled in evacuated Armenian villages and houses were to be held responsible for any damage to the houses and fruit trees. Other provisions of the decree regulated the administrative structure of the commissions for abandoned property.[81]

On 11 August 1915, Ottoman Minister of the Interior gave the following specific instructions to his governors on the protection of the property of the relocated Armenians:

Forbid the entry or free circulation of all foreigners and suspicious persons in the localities to be evacuated. If such people are already at the district they should be made to leave at once. If such persons have bought goods of the relocated Armenians at ridiculous prices, measures should be made to annul the sale, restore prices to the proper level, and thus prevent illegal profits from being made. Armenians should be allowed and authorized to take away with them everything they want. If there is found goods not taken away which have deteriorated as a result, sell it by auction. If other merchandise can remain without deteriorating, keep it on behalf of the original owner. Prevent all agreements regarding renting, pawning, attaching or sale or mortgage which is likely to deprive the owner of the property.[82]

The Temporary Law Concerning the Abandoned Goods, Debts and Receivables of the Displaced Persons was promulgated on 26 September 1915.[83] It stipulated that the abandoned goods, debts and receivables of private citizens and corporate bodies displaced in accordance with the Temporary Law of 27 May 1915 were to be liquidated by the tribunals upon presentation of balance-sheets drawn up especially for each person by the commissions established for that purpose. The closed buildings rented to two individuals and the religious endowment grounds belonging to the citizens and corporate bodies would be registered in the name of the Ministry of Religious Endowments; the other estates in the name of the Ministry of Finance. After settlement of the affairs of owners he would be given the balance of the value of his property paid by one of these two ministries. In the lawsuits concerning the estates and similar matters, the adversary would be represented by officials from the Landed Property Department. The ownership could be established by other proofs than the title deeds delivered by the Department of Landed Property, provided there be no question of fraud. If in the acts of transfer and sale consummated by the aforesaid persons during the fifteen days preceding their displacement, misrepresentation, simulation or excessive fraud were adduced, the act would be annulled.

The money in gold, the goods left behind, the receivables and deposits of the above-mentioned people would be gathered and taken by the presidents of the ad hoc commissions, who, at the same time, would carry out the sale of the uncontested abandoned goods. The amounts thus realized were to be deposited with the Ministry of Finance in the name of their owner. A time limit of two months was granted to those who claimed to have rights over the abandoned goods or receivables of the displaced persons to address themselves personally or through a power of attorney to the commissions and have their demands registered. The time limit was extended four months for people living abroad. These must take up their residence in the towns where the commissions sat so that communication with them might be easier. The lawsuits brought after that time limit would follow the ordinary legal procedure.

The commissions would seek proofs of each receivable and debt, accept and register those which they consider well founded and send the creditors to

the competent tribunal after having registered the lawsuits concerning the abandoned goods. Besides, the commissions would draw up the balance-sheets of
the assets and liabilities of each person, and notify the parties of those balance-
sheets by publishing authentic copies thereof; the original were to be sent to the
Attorney General together with the documents belonging to them. The Attorney
General should send these papers to the lower court of the debtor before his displacement, and ask the tribunal to register the documents. The creditors could
object to these adjudications before the competent tribunal during the fifteen
days after the date of publication.

At the end of the above-mentioned limit of time the tribunal was required
to examine the accounts in the presence of the Attorney General and in case
of objections he would summon the person who made the objections and the
president of the commission or his substitute to take note of the demand and
the defense. Then the tribunal would make the changes judged necessary in
the balance-sheets in question, and after having registered them return to the
commissions. When these commissions ceased working, the liquidation commissions and the executive bureaus had to pay the preferred and ordinary debts
of the person in conformity with the final sentence of the tribunal. If all the
goods of the debtor do not suffice to pay the entire amount of his ordinary and
preferred debts the latter had to be paid at the prorata of the assets. Those who
had pending lawsuits against displaced people were free to address themselves
to the commissions or to let the affair to follow its normal course in conformity
with the general provisions.

To the outside observer, therefore, it is no surprise to learn that Oscar Heiz-
er, the American consul at Trabzon, in a note of November 1915, said:

> A commission has been formed at Trebizond by the Governor-General for the
> purpose of taking possession and selling the property of the Armenian pop-
> ulation which has been banished from that province. Persons having claims
> against Armenians are invited to present the same to the commission in order
> that they may be examined, and, if found in order, registered. There were a
> great many Armenian merchants and commission agents in Trebizond; some
> of them had extensive dealings with Europe and England. It is not believed that
> American firms have claims of any great importance. If there are any claims,
> however, an itemized statement, duly sworn to before a notary public and cer-
> tified by a Turkish consul in America, might be sent to the consulate, to be
> presented to the commission.[84]

Beginning in 1915, appointed committees made inquiries into the excesses
committed against the Armenians. On the basis of their reports efforts were
made to restore order and end the killings and deaths and to punish all those
responsible. Under the relevant provisions of the Ottoman Penal Code and Military Penal Code, more than a thousand people belonging to the gendarmerie,

army, judiciary, fiscal and other civil administrations who mistreated the Armenians were tried and condemned—including by execution. Altogether, some 1,376 people were given varying degrees of penalties for offenses that ranged all the way from minor violations of the military code to failure to adequately carry out the requirements to protect the displaced persons.[85]

In the autumn of 1915 the German paper *Frankfurter Zeitung* dwelled on the Armenian relocations. It wrote that it had invariably been Britain's policy to open a door for its intervention in Ottoman politics by its alleged championship of the oppressed, and that in the case in point the Armenian incidents had been grossly exaggerated in order to provide a point of propaganda against Germany. There was no doubt, the paper continued, that the Armenians had suffered hardships, after having organized a revolt at British instigation, but that was not surprising given the nature of Armenian espionage and open revolt.

An official Ottoman white book, dealing with the Armenian revolutionary movements and the government measures, was issued at İstanbul in February 1916. The report stated that the Armenians after the Ottoman-Russian War of 1877-1878 had themselves placed under the protection of Russia by the Treaty of Berlin of 13 July 1878 and later they placed themselves under the aegis of Britain by the Convention of Cyprus of 4 June 1878. The report continued:

> Unfortunately the Armenians saw in the terrible shock caused to the state by defeat in the Balkan War a favorable opportunity for pursuing with great vigor their senseless ambitions. To this end they sought the intervention of the powers by applying to the government of the czar. The European intervention desired by the Armenians took place in fact and assumed a very onerous form. After seven months of negotiations the Sublime Porte found itself obliged to accept inspectors general from a list drawn up by the six great powers. At this point, general war broke out from the Entente. The Armenians shrank from no sacrifice in furtherance of the Entente's military operations. Thus they hoped to hasten and facilitate the formation of an independent Armenia. That they were accessible to the instigations of the aforementioned powers is manifest from letters which have fallen into the hands of the imperial authorities and from the official declarations of statesmen belonging to the Entente group.[86]

The official document continued:

> As regards the reaction which cooperation of the Armenians with armed enemies of the realm was bound to produce, this did not prevent the Armenians, blinded by hatred and false expectations of a Russo-Anglo-French triumph, from resorting to revolutionary activity. Armenian recruits called to arms deserted in great numbers, and having received weapons from Russia joined the armies of the czar. Some remained in the Ottoman Empire, where they formed insurrectionary bands, of which the principal exploit was the massacre of all Muslims in the frontier regions. Under these circumstances the Ottoman com-

mand, to protect the rear, removed the Armenian population to the south. Was it not the evident duty of the imperial government engaged in a desparate war for existence to react with the rigor demanded by the extreme gravity of the times? As to assertions that these measures were taken by the imperial government at the suggestion of certain powers, they are absolutely without foundation. Toward the end of 1914, Armenians fired upon a party of gendarmes on patrol duty in the neighborhood of Van. They cut the telegraph wires connecting the two military centers. Armenian soldiers deserted and formed bands of brigands, which captured the town of Zeitun and massacred Muslim officials and population, irrespective of age. Researches in the town of Kayseri revealed the existence in Armenian churches and cemeteries of bombs, gunpowder, arms, cipher codes, and revolutionary documents and instructions concerning the duties of bands in formation or already formed. It was ascertained that the organizer and director of these treasonable practices was the bishop of suffragan of Kayseri. The accused admitted that the object was the establishment of an independent Armenia.

In the same month Armenians took to arms in the vicinity of the province of Van. This insurrectionary movement spread subsequently to the districts of Gevash and Chatak. It included Van itself, where it took a particularly violent form. An important part of the town was burned and hundreds of soldiers and Muslim citizens were killed. During this episode numerous Armenian brigand bands under the command of Russian officers sought to force the Turkish frontier from Russian to Iranian territory. It was finally decided to remove the Armenian population from the war zone, so the imperial army should not be exposed to interruption in its communications and the Muslim population to massacre. If the Armenians had not extended revolutionary activity to the scene of operations of the imperial army, the imperial authorities would not have gone beyond this measure, but the Armenians suddenly attacked Sharki Karahissar and burned the Muslim quarters of the town. Not content with this, 800 rebels who succeeded in fortifying themselves in an interior fort caused the death of 150 inhabitants, among them the commander of the gendarmerie. It was only natural that the imperial government should have also removed from those regions the Armenian population and dispatched it to inland localities where it could not collaborate with the enemy. On 6 September 1915, Armenian insurgents fortified themselves in Urfa in a quarter commanding the town, and from there fired upon gendarmes on patrol. Having further attacked the Muslim quarters of the locality, and embarked upon a course of massacre, they provoked the expedition of a military force. As a result, their fastness was destroyed and themselves exterminated, but at a price of fifteen gendarmes killed and fifty wounded. Thanks to this prompt and energetic repression, the subjects of foreign powers, neutral as well as hostile, settled in the place, and the establishment escaped destruction.

It is true that in the course of passage of Armenians from one locality to another certain deplorable excesses took place. But which nation in the world can throw a stone at Turkey because the Mussulman population—exasperated by the culmination of Armenian hostility and insurrection and massacre at the time when the empire was engaged in war in defense of its very existence—at last took the law into its own hands and retaliated upon the traitors in their own coin? How could the imperial government immediately and everywhere prevent these not unnatural outbreaks, when the primary duty of the state was to employ all its resources in the defense of the country on three fronts against four great powers? For all this the imperial government did not remain inactive in regard to the protection of lives and property of Armenians. In this connection instructions were issued which were so stringer that a battalion of gendarmerie, entrusted with the task of conveying a batch of Armenians, resisted an attempt made by local Mussulmans to exercise vengeance upon them and lost a considerable number of men in doing so. On the other hand, the Sublime Porte enacted a special law for the protection of the property of displaced Armenians and despatched commissions of capable and upright men to the various localities concerned, with a view of applying the law. Other carefully appointed commissions made inquiries into the excesses committed and are handing over to military courts those found to be guilty in reality for what happened. Here are the contents of a report received from the commission on its inquiries at Sivas. Some fifty-three Ottoman officials belonging to the judiciary, army, gendarmerie, fiscal and other civil administrations were handed over to the military courts on charges of abuse of power in the exercise of their functions. A trial was ordered and fifty-six persons from among the military and civic functionaries and the gendarmerie were condemned to penalties varying from a month in prison to three years at hard labor and the payment of fines for outrages and illegal behavior during the transfer of Armenians from one locality to another.

Many officers and soldiers belonging to the imperial army, as well as a great number of gendarmes, appeared before the military courts on different charges of misconduct. Thirty-four individuals were condemned by the military courts to different forms of penalties, varying from a month's imprisonment and fines to three years at hard labor. In reality, what happened is that the powers of the entente represent the Armenians as victims of deliberate atrocities on the part of the imperial government in the course of their transfer from one place to another. We have proved the falsity of these accusations. To conclude, the measures which the imperial government saw itself obliged to adopt toward the Armenians are nothing but the natural consequences of their own doings and of those who encouraged them. No coercive measures were taken by the Imperial Government against the Armenians until June 1915, by which time they had risen in arms at Van and in other military zones. This was after they had joined hands with enemy.

In mid-1916 fifty-one Turkish soldiers, convicted of mistreating Armenians expelled from the province of Van, had been executed, said Talat Paşa, Ottoman Minister of the Interior. Government employees found guilty of similar abuses had been deprived of their offices and delivered to the military courts for trial. Commissions of investigation had been sent to all centers of trouble not now held by the Russians to investigate. The cabinet minister, next to Minister of War and Acting Commander-in-Chief Enver Paşa, considered the empire's leading statesman, admitted that unfortunately some abuses had occurred. He defended Ottoman Empire's treatment of the Armenians, however, urging that the United States reserve judgment until it had heard from both sides. It was found necessary to relocate Armenians from certain localities, he said, because Armenian secret organizations, encouraged by Russian agencies, had committed treasonable acts.[87]

On 27 September 1917, Grand Vizier Talat Paşa closed the annual congress of the Party of Union and Progress with a long speech justifying Ottoman Empire's entry into the war and its treatment of the Armenians, although he admitted that the relocations of the latter were not executed in a regular way, as gendarmes were incorporated in the army, and that the order desirable could not be maintained. The Ottoman government, he said, had sent several missions of inquiry, and those guilty of misdeeds had been severely punished.[88] On 1 November 1918, at the last congress of the Party of Union and Progress, Talat Paşa again said: "I do not wish to state that Armenian relocations proceeded as it should have done. In many regions, hatred long suppressed was let loose at this time, giving rise to abuses that we had not all desired. Thus numerous innocent Armenians perished, victims of this situation. A punishment of the responsible persons was undoubtedly in order. An inquiry was opened; and it having been proven that in certain places various individuals had acted through hatred or for their own personal interests, these were punished."[89] It should be noted here that the comparison to Nazi Germany is quite telling. While Ottomans who murdered Armenians were prosecuted, those who refused to cooperate in the murder of Jews were prosecuted by Nazi Germany.

Such an observer as Michael Ignatieff has stated:

> Genocide has no meaning unless the crime can be connected to a clear intention to exterminate a human group in whole or in part. Something more than rhetorical exaggeration for effect is at stake here. Calling every abuse or crime a genocide makes it steadily more difficult to rouse people to action when a genuine genocide is taking place.[90]

TOLERANCE TOWARD NON-MUSLIM COMMUNITIES

There is not an equivalent in Ottoman history to the Nazi race-based philosophy or Aryan domination, nor the doctrine of annihilation that followed from it. The tricontinental Ottoman Empire was known instead for its principle of coexistence, represented by the *millets* existing under dynastic Islamic rule. In the Ottoman Empire the term *millet* was used for the organized, recognized, religio-political communities enjoying certain rights of autonomy. The primary basis was religious rather than ethnic. The *millet*, with its own ecclesiastico-civil leader and internal administration, had complete charge of its own affairs. The religious hierarchy was responsible for the spiritual welfare of its particular *millet*, but it also had broad jurisdiction in legal matters affecting two or more parties in the same *millet*, and oversaw social and educational life. This meant that the non-Muslim communities could live under their own leaders in their own way and follow their own religions and customs as they had in the past. It was the beginning of a remarkable system of tolerance for minorities, perhaps best known for its welcome of tens of thousands of Spanish Jews to the Ottoman Empire in the days of the Inquisition.[91] As British specialist Dominic Lieven aptly puts it, "By the standards of many empires and most Christian states in history the *millet* system stands out for its tolerance of religious and ethnic diversity."[92]

Armenians, like all other non-Muslim peoples of the empire, had long enjoyed communal autonomy and lived as a legally protected distinct religious group. They have maintained their religious, cultural, linguistic, and national identity. They did not experience racism for hundreds of years in the diverse and pluralistic Ottoman society. There was no equivalent of Nazi psychological preparation for genocide in the Ottoman Empire.[93]

Marcar Gregory, president of the Armenian United Association of London and the translator of patriarch Malachia Ormanian's book *The Church of Armenia*, in the course of conversation with a representative of *The Christian Science Monitor* in March 1913 pointed out that the great rallying point for Armenians was their church, which commanded their devotion from the earliest times. Their national life was bound up with their religion. The Armenians were jealous of their nationality and of the integrity of their church. The Armenian, he said, would rather endure any form of misgovernment, and any kind of hardship, than do anything which would endanger the continuity of his national church. This was the great fear in regard to Russia. Wherever Russia extended its influence, there was always a tendency for the church of the peoples over which this influence was extended to be swallowed up in the Russian Orthodox Church. Indeed, he went on, this actually happened in Russian Armenia: the decree of 12 June 1903 confiscated church property to the state. In a moment Armenia was roused to action, and in every town and village and throughout the countryside, men and women gathered to resist the theft of church property. The outcry against the act was so great that the Russian authorities found themselves obliged to make restitution.[94]

Harry Jewell Sarkiss, an Armenian-born Professor of History at Findlay College, underlines the fact that the Ottoman government paid little attention, if any, to the internal affairs of the Armenians except to collect taxes and preserve order. Quoting French author Gaston Gaillard, he points out that "from the fourteenth century until 1860 the Armenians had gotten along with their Moslem neighbours, and those who emigrated from Russia found refuge in Turkey. In the course of her history Armenia had been ruled by Romans, Seleucids, Persians, and Arabs. They enjoyed more tranquillity under Turkey than under former rulers." Referring to the proclamation of the Armenian national constitution in 1863, Sarkiss concedes that it was "remarkable that, throughout this period of political convulsion and attempted dismemberment of the Ottoman Empire, the Sublime Porte should have tolerated such democratic progress among her minorities. The three imperial decrees of the Sultan—the *hattı sherif* of Gulhane of 1839, the imperial firman of 1845, and the *hattı humayun* of 1856—are concrete evidences that democracy was making inroads into Turkey itself."[95]

The *Hattı Şerif* (Noble Rescript), which incorporated the reforms, was proclaimed at the Gülhane or the Sultan's Rose Chamber on 3 November 1839 in a solemn ceremony in the presence of the European diplomatic community, ushering in a new political era in the Ottoman Empire. The decree abolished capital punishment without trial; guaranteed justice to all with respect to life, honor and property; ordered the promulgation of a new penal code against which no infringement would be tolerated because of personal rank or influence; ended the system of tax-farming and instituted the collection of taxes by government officials; and, most important of all, stipulated that the provisions of the decree applied to all the sultan's subjects irrespective of religion or sect. A little over sixteen years later, on 18 February 1856, a second decree, *Hattı Hümayun* (Imperial Rescript), reiterated the reforms set out in 1839 and expanded on the process to address reforms in the courts and penal system. Corporal punishment was to be curbed, and torture abolished. The decree sought to regularize the finances of the empire through annual budgets that would be open to public scrutiny. The decree also called for the modernization of the financial system and the establishment of a modern banking "to create funds to be employed in augmenting the sources of wealth" in the empire through such public works as roads and canals. "To accomplish these objects," the decree concluded, "means shall be sought to profit by the science, the art, and the funds of Europe, and thus gradually to execute them." Most of the provisions of the 1856 Imperial Rescript were concerned with the rights and responsibilities of Ottoman Christians and Jews. The decree established for the first time complete equality of all Ottoman subjects regardless of their religion:

> Every distinction or designation pending to make any class whatever of the subjects of my empire inferior to another class, on account of their religion, language, or race, shall be forever effaced from administrative protocol.

The decree went on to promise all Ottoman subjects access to schools and government jobs, as well as to military conscription, without distinction by religion or nationality.[96]

The philosophy that led clearly to greater autonomy for religious and ethnic minorities was supported by a culture that welcomed and acknowledged the diverse communities within the Empire. Victory for the Turks in the First World War was hoped for by Schmarya Levin, a member of the Berlin committee of six and formerly a member of the Russian duma. He was in Chicago in November 1914 to join Louis Brandeis, Boston lawyer, in an attempt to raise 100,000 dollars for Jews in Palestine. "Jews in Palestine have no complaint to make of their treatment by the Turks," said Levin.

> Stories of butchery of Jews by Turks are not true. We hope to see Turkey come of the war with increased strength, for, though there may be laws on the books of that nation of which we do not approve, there are no special laws against Jews. We have been treated fairly and tolerantly by the Turkish government.[97]

The Sephardi community in Palestine during the First World War expressed loyalty to the empire and continued preaching and encouraging the Jews who were foreign subjects to adopt Ottoman citizenship and become Ottoman.[98]

Count Bernstroff, German Ambassador in Washington, issued a statement on 8 March 1915 declaring tolerance toward all religious beliefs had been shown by the Ottoman government. The ambassador's statement followed: "Several times I have published official news, to which I can add today: 'The Government in Constantinople has, since the outbreak of war, strictly adhered to its traditional tolerant attitude toward all religions, and there has never been an anti-Jewish feeling in Constantinople.' "[99] In an interview with Julius Becker, a correspondent of the *Vossische Zeitung* (published 31 December 1917) Grand Vizier Talat Paşa referred to the Ottoman Empire's traditional tolerance of its Jewish citizens; it was the only country in which anti-Semitism was rarely seen. He demonstrated his sincerity by speaking on 5 January 1918 at a conference of leading German Jews in Berlin, called by Emmanuel Carasso, member of the Ottoman Chamber of Deputies and his counterpart in Jewish affairs. Eighteen days later, when returning from Brest-Litovsk, he approved the formation of a Chartered Company to take care of Jewish settlement in Palestine on an autonomous basis.[100] Israeli historian Isaiah Friedman confirms that anti-Semitism was extremely rare in the Ottoman Empire.[101] As a result, of all the Ottoman *millets*, the Jews were the most satisfied and the most loyal. They had good reason to be grateful for Ottoman tolerance and protection. In the nineteenth century their loyalty was unshaken. Awareness of pogroms in Russia and the Christian Balkans, not to mention conflicts with the Greeks within the Ottoman Empire, served to strengthen this loyalty.[102]

Notably, Jews in particular benefited from Ottoman rule. With the rise of nationalism among the various groups of the region, interethnic conflict had started to reach major proportions and the Jews were often at the receiving end. From 1840 onward, blood libel accusations by the Greeks and Armenians emerged with great frequency, followed by riots and mob attacks on the Jews.

The reemergence of this medieval accusation was closely tied to growing economic rivalry between the groups, and fueled by the perception among the Christians that the Jews and the Turks were together opposed to their aspirations. And indeed, it was always the Turkish authorities that intervened to protect the Jewish community in periods of crisis engendered by the blood libel accusations.[103]

No anti-Armenian ideology developed in the writings of the Ottoman leadership. In fact governmental efforts were made to counter the bad feelings held by some Turks against the Armenians as the result of the Armenian revolts and massacres of Turks in eastern Anatolia at the start of the First World War.

NOTES

1. In this regard it is notable that in 1985 no fewer than sixty-nine distinguished American scholars, the great majority of the American academic community with specialized knowledge of the Ottoman Empire and its history, in an open statement emphatically opposed a United States Congressional resolution which said Armenians were victims of "genocide." They publicly declared that current scholarship does not support the seventy-year-old genocide charge. They further expressed that it is historically unjust to focus on the suffering of Ottoman Armenians without viewing it in the context of the overall suffering which the Ottoman citizenry (Muslim and non-Muslim alike) experienced during the First World War. American academic specialists on the region's history spoke as qualified individuals rather than as partisans. See the text of the sixty-nine scholars' statement on House Joint Resolution 192. *The Washington Post* and *The New York Times*, 19 May 1985.

2. Barbara Lerner, "History Speaks: The Moral Case against the Armenian Genocide Resolution," National Review Online, 18 October 2007, p. 2.

3. Joseph Grabill, *Protestant Diplomacy and the Near East: Missionary Influence on American Policy, 1810-1927* (Minneapolis: University of Minnesota Press, 1971), p. 48.

4. J.C. Hurewitz, ed., *Diplomacy in the Near and Middle East: A Documentary Record*, Vol. 1: 1535-1914, (Princeton, New Jersey: D. Van Nostrand Company, Inc., 1956), p. 190. For the full text of the Treaty of Berlin of 13 July 1878 see Great Britain, *Parliamentary Papers*, 1878, Vol. 83, pp. 690-705.

5. Sarkis Atamian, *The Armenian Community: The Historical Development of a Social and Ideological Conflict* (New York: Philosophical Library, 1955), p. 96.

6. Simon Vratzian, "The Armenian Revolution and the Armenian Revolutionary Federation," *The Armenian Review*, Vol. 3, No. 3 (Autumn 1950), pp. 18-19.

7. See William Langer, *Diplomacy of Imperialism: 1890-1902*, Vol.1, (New York: Alfred A. Knopf, 1935), pp. 158 and 164 and Justin McCarthy and Carolyn McCarthy, *Turks and Armenians: A Manual on the Armenian Question* (Washington, D.C.: Assembly of Turkish American Associations, 1989), p. 42.

8. *Aspirations et agissements révolutionnaires des Comités Arméniens avant et après la proclamation de la Constitution Ottomane* (İstanbul: Matbaai Orhaniye, 1917),

p. 305. For the Armenian events of 1909 in Adana see chapter 2.

9. J.A. Zahm, *From Berlin to Bagdad and Babylon* (New York and London: D. Appleton and Company, 1922), pp. 205-206. Reverend J.A. Zahm was member of the Author's Club, La Société Française de Physique, the Arcadia of Rome, and other learned societies in America and Europe.

10. Ibid., p. 207.

11. Ibid., pp. 207-208.

12. Pierre Loti, *La Turquie Agonisante* (Paris: Calman-Lévy, 1913), p. 174.

13. Zahm, *From Berlin to Bagdad and Babylon*, p. 208 fn 17.

14. Ibid., p. 210.

15. Pierre Loti, *Les Massacres d'Arménie* (Paris: Calman-Lévy, 1918), p. 50.

16. Halil Halid, *The Diary of a Turk* (London: Adam and Charles Black, 1903), p. 130.

17. Zahm, *From Berlin to Bagdad and Babylon*, pp. 210-211.

18. Ibid., pp. 211-212.

19. Ahmed Rustem Bey, *La Guerre Mondiale et la Question Turco-Arménienne* (Berne: Imprimerie Staempfli et Cie, 1918), pp. 22-25 and 30-35.

20. See, for instance, ATESE, Birinci Dünya Harbi Koleksiyonu (Collection of the First World War) (henceforth referred to as BDHK), Folder: 2287, File: 12, No. 1-37. Ciphered Telegram from the Fourth Army Command to the Ministry of War on the Revolt in Zeytun, 10 April 1915.

21. Anne Fremantle, *Loyal Enemy* (London: Hutchinson and Co., 1938), p. 280. Anne Fremantle was a British author, art critic, essayist and editor.

22. See, for instance, ATESE, BDHK, Folder: 44, File: 207, No. 2-1, 2-2. Communication from the General Command Headquarters to the Ministry of the Interior on the Revolt in Van, 2 May 1915.

23. Justin McCarthy, *Death and Exile: The Ethnic Cleansing of Ottoman Muslims, 1821-1922* (Princeton, New Jersey: The Darwin Press, Inc., 1995), p. 189. For more details on Armenian destruction and murder in Van see Justin McCarthy, Esat Arslan, Cemalettin Taşkıran and Ömer Turan, *The Armenian Rebellion at Van* (Salt Lake City: The University of Utah Press, 2006), pp. 233-257.

24. Fremantle, *Loyal Enemy*, pp. 280-281.

25. Ibid., p. 281.

26. For an incisive account of this period in the history of the Ottoman Armenians, see Süleyman Kani İrtem, ed., Osman Selim Kocahanoğlu, *Ermeni Meselesinin İçyüzü Ermeni İsyanları Tarihi, Bomba Hadisesi, Adana Vakası, Meclisi Mebusan Zabıtları* (The True Nature of the Armenian Question: History of Armenian Revolts, Bomb Incident, Adana Event, Proceedings of the Chamber of Deputies), (İstanbul: Temel Yayınları, 2004). Süleyman Kani İrtem, a skilled professional administrator, served as governor of several Ottoman districts and provinces from 1896 to 1918. He was governor and mayor of İstanbul in 1918.

27. "Armenians Join Russians and 20,000 Scatter Turks Near Zeitun; Armenians Fighting the Turks," *The Washington Post*, 13 November 1914, p. 3.

28. Nerses Kouyoumjian, "Turkish Soldier Makes His Escape to Boston; With Other Christians He Deserted to Russians," *The Boston Sunday Globe*, 30 May 1915, p. 14.

29. See, for instance, Başbakanlık Osmanlı Arşivleri (Prime Minister's Office Ottoman Archives), İstanbul (henceforth referred to as BOA), Dahiliye Nezareti Şifre Ka-

lemi (Ministry of the Interior Ciphered Correspondence Division) (henceforth referred to as DH ŞFR), No. 48/7. Message to the Governor of Province of Van on the Severing of Telegraph Wires by the Armenian Bands, 15 December 1914 and BOA, DH ŞFR, No. 48/182. Message to the Governor of Province of Van on the Killing of Gendarmes and Civilians by the Armenian Bands, 28 December 1914. The outgoing communication of the Ciphered Correspondence Division was largely confined to the telegrams of the Directorates for the Settlement of Tribes and Immigrants and the Public Security and the Gendarmerie Command.

30. Joseph Pomiankowski, *Der Zusammenbruch des Ottomanischen Reiches: Erinnerungen an die Türkei aus der Zeit des Weltkrieges* (Zürich, Leipzig, Wien: Amalthea Verlag, 1928), pp. 147 and 159-160. Lieutenant Field Marshal Joseph Pomiankowski was military attaché at the Embassy of Austria-Hungary in İstanbul from 1909 to 1918. Also Felix Guse, *Die Kaukasusfront im Weltkrieg: Bis zum Frieden von Brest* (Leipzig: Koehler und Amelang, 1940). Lieutenant Colonel Felix Guse was chief of staff of the Ottoman Third Army during the Caucasian battles in the First World War. For more details on Armenian insurgent attacks on the Ottoman army and population during the First World War, see Garegin Pasdermadjian (trans. Aram Torossian), *Armenia: A Leading Factor in the Winning of the War* (New York: Council for Armenia, 1919) and Gabriel Korganoff, *La participation des Arméniens à la guerre mondiale sur le front du Caucase 1914-1918* (Paris: Massis, 1927). Gabriel Korganoff, a czarist general of Armenian origin, was deputy chief of staff of the Russian Army of the Caucasus in 1914-1917.

31. "The Voice of Turkey," *The Literary Digest*, Vol. 159, No. 24 (12 December 1914), p. 1170. Of the vernacular Turkish press in the Ottoman Empire, beyond question the foremost representative was *İkdam*, a word meaning "the intellectual effort." The war-time editions of this journal ran up to 35,000 copies. A marked influence was exerted by the letters of the proprietor, Ahmed Cevdet, who lived abroad for reasons of health and sent contributions that were frequently of high importance.

32. Philips Price, *A History of Turkey: From Empire to Republic* (London: George Allen and Unwin, 1956), pp. 91 and 115.

33. "Constantinople Called Tzargrad in Russia," *The Boston Globe*, 6 November 1914, p. 3.

34. Yusuf Hikmet Bayur, *Türk İnkılabı Tarihi* (History of the Turkish Revolution), Vol. 3: *1914-1918 Genel Savaşı* (1914-1918 Great War), Sec. 1: *Savaşın Başından 1914-1915 Kışına Kadar* (From the Beginning of the War to the Winter 1914-1915), (Ankara: Türk Tarih Kurumu Basımevi, reprinted, 1991), pp. 260, 352, 356, 358 and 380.

35. "Armenians Lay Siege to Van; Join Russians in Fight Against Turkey," *The Boston Globe*, 7 November 1914, p. 5.

36. "Russians Pursue Turks," *The Boston Globe*, 8 November 1914, p. 17.

37. A multitude of studies in several languages exists on Ottoman Empire's participation in the First World War. For accurate information and analyses see particularly, *Birinci Dünya Harbinde Türk Harbi Kafkas Cephesi Üçüncü Ordu Harekatı* (Turkish War in the First World War: Caucasian Front Operations of the Third Army), 2 Vols., (Ankara: Genelkurmay Basımevi, 1993) ; Fahri Belen, *Birinci Cihan Harbinde Türk Harbi 1914-1918 Yılı Hareketleri* (Turkish War in the First World War: Movements of the Years 1914-1918), 5 Vols., (Ankara: Genelkurmay Basımevi, 1965-1967); Cemal Akbay, *Birinci Dünya Harbinde Türk Harbi* (Turkish War in the First World War), Vol.1: *Osmanlı İmparatorluğunun Siyasi ve Askeri Hazırlıkları ve Harbe Girişi* (Political and Military

Preparations of the Ottoman Empire and Its Entry Into the War), (Ankara: Genelkurmay Basımevi, 1991); Bayur, *Türk İnkılabı Tarihi* 3 Vols. and Maurice Larcher, *La Guerre turque dans la guerre mondiale* (Paris: Chiron et Berger-Levrault, 1926). More recent treatments of the theme are David Nicolle, *The Ottoman Army 1914-1918* (London: Reed International Books, 1996); Edward Erickson, *Ordered to Die: A History of the Ottoman Army in the First World War* (Westport, Connecticut and London: Greenwood Press, 2001); idem, *Ottoman Army Effectiveness in World War I: A Comparative Study* (New York and London: Routledge, 2007) and Stanford Shaw, *The Ottoman Empire in World War I*, 2 Vols., (Ankara: Türk Tarih Kurumu, 2008). Shaw's latest two-volume is the most substantial work on the topic in English and thus offers a very useful gateway to further reading and research. See also Edward Erickson, "The Armenians and Ottoman Military Policy, 1915," *War in History*, Vol. 15, No. 2 (April 2008), pp. 141-167.

38. "The Rebirth of a Nation," *The Literary Digest*, Vol. 50, No. 13 (27 March 1915), p. 682. On the military and naval importance of the district of Alexandretta (İskenderun) during the First World War see Yücel Güçlü, *The Question of the Sanjak of Alexandretta: A Study in Turkish-French-Syrian Relations* (Ankara: Turkish Historical Society Printing House, 2001), pp. 8-13.

39. "The Rebirth of a Nation," p.682.

40. Peter Gatrell, *A Whole Empire Walking: Refugees in Russia During World War I* (Bloomington and Indianapolis: Indiana University Press, 1999), pp. 18-19.

41. John Bennett, *Witness: The Story of a Search* (London: Hodder and Stoughton, 1962), p. 33.

42. William Mitchel Ramsay, "The Future of Turkey," *Manchester Guardian*, 23 April 1915, p. 1.

43. An Ottoman administrative unit meaning county or subdistrict.

44. BOA, DH ŞFR, No.52/94-96. Circular to the Governors of Provinces of Edirne, Erzurum, Adana, Ankara, Aydın, Bitlis, Halep, Hüdavendigar, Diyarbekir, Sivas, Trabzon, Konya, Mamuretülaziz, and Van, and to the Governors of Sanjaks of Urfa, İzmit, Bolu, Canik, Karesi, Kayseri, Niğde, Eskişehir, Karahisarısahib, and Maraş on the Armed Revolts of the Armenian Committees and the Measures to Be Implemented Against Such Acts, 24 April 1915.

45. BOA, DH ŞFR, No.52/96-97-98. Circular to the Governors of Provinces of Edirne, Erzurum, Adana, Ankara, Aydın, Bitlis, Halep, Hüdavendigar, Diyarbekir, Sivas, Trabzon, Konya, Mamuretülaziz, and Van, and to the Governors of the Sanjaks of Urfa, İzmit, Bolu, Canik, Karesi, Kayseri, Niğde, Eskişehir, Karahisarısahib, and Maraş on the Armed Revolts of the Armenian Committees and the Measures to Be Implemented Against Such Acts, 24 April 1915. Text of the circular is also in ATESE, BDHK, Folder: 401, File: 1580, No. 1-2, 26 April 1915. Moreover see Foreign Office Papers, National Archives, Kew/London (henceforth referred to as FO) 371/4141/170751. Ciphered Ottoman Telegrams Captured in Palestine during Operations of Autumn 1918. Admiral John de Robeck (Istanbul) to Lord Curzon (FO), 29 December 1919. Transcripts of Crown copyright records in the National Archives appear by permission of the Controller of Her Majesty's Stationery Office.

46. BOA, DH ŞFR, No.52/102. Ciphered Telegram to the Governor of Province of Ankara on the Transportation of the Detained Ringleaders of the Armenian Revolutionary Committees to Ayaş and Çankırı, 25 April 1915.

47. The historiography on Ottoman Armenian nationalist uprisings from 1894 to

1909 is large, the interpretations diverse, and the scholarly debate vituperative.

48. FO 371/2489/262274. State of Affairs in Eastern Anatolia and Cilicia. Sir Henry Bax-Ironside (Sofia) to Sir Edward Grey (FO), 18 May 1915.

49. Gaston Gaillard, *The Turks and Europe* (London: Thomas Murby and Company, 1921), p.48. A French edition of this book was published at Paris in August 1920. The author makes many sharp observations and insightful remarks that can benefit anyone studying the waning years of the Ottoman Empire.

50. BOA, Babıali Evrak Odası (Records Office of the Sublime Porte) (henceforth referred to as BEO), No. 326758. Communication from the Ministry of the Interior to the Grand Vizier's Office, 26 May 1915.

51. The text of the provisional law of relocations was published in the Official Gazette, *Takvimi Vekayi*, on 1 June 1915. The French translation of original Turkish text of the law in question can be found in the İstanbul daily *La Turquie*, 2 June 1915, p. 1.

52. Esat Uras, *Tarihte Ermeniler ve Ermeni Meselesi* (Armenians in History and the Armenian Question), (İstanbul: Belge Yayınları, 2nd rev. ed., expanded, 1987), pp. 606-610 and "Turkish Statement Regarding Armenia," *The Christian Science Monitor*, 13 July 1915, p. 2.

53. "Turkish Account of Armenian Revolt," *The Christian Science Monitor*, 16 August 1915, p. 2.

54. "Turkish Report on Armenian Rising," *The Christian Science Monitor*, 16 December 1915, p. 2.

55. R. Insley-Casper, "War Adds to the Fame of the Turk as a Fighting Man," *The Boston Sunday Globe*, 26 December 1915, p. 36.

56. "Greatly Exaggerated; Bernstorff So Declares of Reported Atrocities—Defends Course Taken by the Turks," *The Boston Daily Globe*, 29 September 1915, p. 8.

57. Papers Relating to the Foreign Relations of the United States (henceforth referred to as FRUS), The Lansing Papers 1914-1920, Vol. 1, (Washington, D.C.: United States Government Printing Office, 1929), p. 42.

58. Robert Lansing had been continuously engaged in international cases for more than fifteen years. He was also one of the founders of the American Society of International Law, an associate editor of the American Journal of International Law, and author of a textbook on government. See United States Department of State, Office of the Historian, Bureau of Public Affairs, *Principal Officers of the Department of State and United States Chiefs of Mission 1778-1990*, Evan Duncan (comp.), (Washington, D.C.: United States Government Printing Office, 1991), pp. 4-5 and 13 and Daniel Smith, *Robert Lansing and American Neutrality, 1914-1917* (Berkeley, California: University of California Press, 1958).

59. "Talat Paşa's Speech," *Vakit*, 12 July 1921, p. 1. On the ninth and last Congress of the Party of Union and Progress see particularly Şevket Süreyya Aydemir, *Makedonya'dan Ortaasya'ya Enver Paşa* (From Macedonia to Central Asia: Enver Paşa), Vol. 3, (İstanbul: Remzi Kitabevi, 2nd ed., 1995), pp. 453-462 ; Sina Akşin, *İstanbul Hükümetleri ve Milli Mücadele* (İstanbul Governments and the National Struggle), Vol. 1, (Ankara: Türkiye İş Bankası Yayınları, 1998), pp. 34-37 and Mustafa Ragıb Esatlı, ed., İsmail Dervişoğlu, *İttihat ve Terakki'nin Son Günleri Suikastler ve Entrikalar* (The Last Days of the Committee of Union and Progress: Assassinations and Intrigues), (İstanbul: Bengi Yayınları, 2007), pp. 670-688.

60. Clarence Streit, "Turkish Nationalists Put Peace Up to Allies; Mustafa Kemal

Declares for Self-Determination and Just Settlement in Comprehensive Review of Near East Problem," *Philadelphia Inquirer Public Ledger*, 27 March 1921, p. 3.

61. Benjamin Lieberman, *Terrible Fate: Ethnic Cleansing in the Making of Modern Europe* (Chicago: Ivan Dee Publishers, 2006), p. 11.

62. Hans Rogger, *Jewish Policies and Right-Wing Politics in Imperial Russia* (Berkeley and Los Angeles, California: University of California Press, 1986), pp.100-101; Dominic Lieven, "Dilemmas of Empire 1850-1918: Power, Territory, Identity," *Journal of Contemporary History*, Vol. 34, No. 2 (April 1999), p. 170 fn23; Peter Gatrell, "Refugees and Forced Migrants during the First World War," *Immigrants and Minorities*, Vol. 26, Nos. 1-2 (March-July 2008), p. 86.

63. Maurice Paléologue, *La Russie Des Tsars Pendant la Grande Guerre*, Vol. 1, (Paris: Plon-Nourrit, 1921), p. 335.

64. Rogger, *Jewish Policies and Right-Wing Politics in Imperial Russia*, pp. 100-101; Lieven, "Dilemmas of Empire 1850-1918: Power, Territory, Identity," p. 170 fn23; Eric Lohr, "The Russian Army and the Jews: Mass Deportation, Hostages, and Violence during World War I," *Russian Review*, Vol. 60, No. 3 (July 2001), pp. 404 and 407 and idem, *Nationalizing the Russian Empire: The Campaign Against Enemy Aliens During World War I* (Cambridge, Massachusetts: Harvard University Press, 2003), p. 1.

65. Samuel Weems, *Armenia: Secrets of a "Christian" Terrorist State* (Dallas, Texas: St. John Press, 2002), pp. xiv-xv.

66. "Plea Made for Recognition of the Armenians; Communication from Moscow to London Paper Tells of the Part They Are Taking in the Present Conflict," *The Christian Science Monitor*, 2 April 1915, p. 3.

67. "Part Played by Armenians in War," *The Christian Science Monitor*, 24 August 1915, p. 3.

68. James Gidney, *A Mandate for Armenia* (Oberlin, Ohio: The Kent State University Press, 1967), pp. 74-75.

69. Boghos Nubar, Letters, "The Rights of Armenia," *The Times*, 30 January 1919, p. 6.

70. "The Armenian Question Before the Peace Conference: A Memorandum Presented Officially by the Representatives of Armenia to the Peace Conference at Versailles on 26 February 1919," *The Armenian Review*, Vol. 27, No. 3-107 (Autumn 1974), pp. 227 and 231-232. Also see Price, *A History of Turkey: From Empire to Republic*, p.115 where it is stated that one of the leaders of the Armenian Delegation to the Paris Peace Conference in 1919 pointed out with pride to the fact that Armenians in the Ottoman Empire offered to establish and support Armenia legions at their own expense to fight side by side with Russian troops under the Russian generals.

71. John Aram Shishmanian Papers, Hoover Institution, Stanford University (henceforth referred to as Shishmanian Papers). Memorandum from Boghos Nubar to the French Ministry of Foreign Affairs, 1 December 1920. This and the following paragraph are based on this source. Captain John Aram Shishmanian was instructor of Armenian Legion troops on the island of Cyprus and commanding officer of Armenian volunteers in the city of Adana in 1917-1920.

72. Shishmanian Papers, "Cilicia and the War of 1914-1918," Statement of the Armenian National Delegation, 9 December 1920.

73. Consult David Lloyd George, *Armenia's Charter: An Appreciation of the Services of Armenians to the Allied Cause* (London: Spottiswoode, 1918); Aneurin Wil-

liams, "Armenia, British Pledges and the Near East," *The Contemporary Review*, Vol. 121, No. 4 (April 1922), pp.418-425 and Antoine Poidebard, "Rôle militaire des Arméniens sur le front du Caucase après la défection de l'armée russe (décembre 1917-novembre 1918)," *Revue des études arméniennes*, Vol.1, No. 2 (1920).

74. United States National Archives, College Park/Maryland (henceforth referred to as USNA), 867.00/798. Personal and Confidential Letter. Henry Morgenthau (Istanbul) to Robert Lansing (Department of State), 18 November 1915.

75. "The Turks and Armenia; Recently Returned American Says, Despite Defeat, the Same Men Are in Control and Need Is Desperate," *The New York Times*, 4 January 1920, p. 14.

76. "Mrs. Harding Appeals for Near East Relief; President's Wife Urges a Generous Response on 'Bundle Day' to the Call for Help," *The New York Times*, 31 May 1921, p. 15.

77. "Our Seventh Ally," *Daily Chronicle*, 23 September 1915, p. 1.

78. BOA, BEO, No. 326758/Political: 53. Circular to the Ministries of the Interior, War and Finance, 31 May 1915.

79. See, among countless others, BOA, DH ŞFR, No. 54/10. Ciphered Telegram to the Governor of Province of Erzurum on the Necessity of Protecting the Armenians Sent from Erzurum on the Roads and to Punish Those Who Are Involved in Inappropriate Activities, 14 June 1915; BOA, DH ŞFR, No. 54/5. Ciphered Telegram to the Governor of Province of Erzurum on the Assurance of Safety of the Armenians during Their Transfer to Other Places, 26 June 1915; ATESE, BDHK, Folder: 361, File: 1445, No. 3-1. Circular to the Army and Army Corps Commands on the Protection of the Lives and Properties of Armenians, 22 July 1915. Further evidence is found in *Armenians in Ottoman Documents 1915-1920* (Ankara: Başbakanlık Basımevi, 1995), pp. 39-41, 45-49, 55-61, 69-74 and 82-83.

80. Jeremy Salt, "The Narrative Gap in Ottoman Armenian History," *Middle Eastern Studies*, Vol.39, No.1 (January 2003), p. 22.

81. Text of the Decree Regarding the Management of the Property, Building and Land of the Armenians Displaced Due to the War and Extraordinary Political Circumstances issued on 10 June 1915 is in BOA, DH ŞFR, No.53/303 and ATESE, BDHK, Folder: 361, File: 1445, No. 1-3.

82. BOA, DH ŞFR, No.54/381. Circular to the Governors of Provinces of Erzurum, Adana, Ankara, Aydın, Bitlis, Halep, Bursa, Diyarbekir, Suriye, Sivas, Trabzon, Mamuretülaziz, and Musul, to the Governors of Sanjaks of Urfa, İzmit, Karesi, Kayseri, Karahisarısahib, Maraş, Eskişehir, and Niğde, and to the Chairmen of the Commissions of Abandoned Goods of Adana, Halep, Maraş, Diyarbekir, Sivas, Trabzon, Mamuretülaziz, Erzurum, and İzmit on the Protection of the Property of the Relocated Armenians, 11 August 1915.

83. Text of the Temporary Law Concerning the Abandoned Goods, Debts and Receivables of the Displaced Persons is in BOA, Register of Laws No. 28, pp. 245-246. The following description of the law is based on this source.

84. "Effacement of the Armenians Now Revealed," *The Christian Science Monitor*, 12 November 1915, pp. 1 and 10.

85. Among Ottoman sources consult, for example, ATESE, BDHK, Folder: 2287, File: 13, No. 3. Communication from the General Command of Gendarmerie to the Ministry of War on the Investigation Committee relating to the Gendarmes and Officials

Who Abused Their Authority during the Transfer of Armenians, 26 September 1915; BOA, Minutes of the Council of Ministers Meeting (henceforth referred to as MV), No. 199-35. Minutes of the Council of Ministers Meeting on the Establishment of a Committee for Inquiring About the Officials Who Abused Their Authority during the Armenian Relocations, 29 September 1915; BOA, DH ŞFR, No. 58/38. Circular to the Governors of Provinces of Bursa and Ankara, and to the Governors of Sanjaks of İzmit, Karesi, Kütahya, Eskişehir, Kayseri, Karahisarısahib, and Niğde on the Establishment of a Committee for the Prevention of Abuse Against the Armenians during Their Transfer, 16 November 1916; BOA, DH ŞFR, No.66/24. Ciphered Telegram to the Governor of Province of Halep on the Immediate Dismissal of the Officials Who Abused Their Authority during the Transfer of Armenians, 19 July 1916 and *Armenians in Ottoman Documents 1915-1920*, pp.12-15. For the broader context see *Arşiv Belgeleriyle Ermeni Faaliyetleri 1914-1918* (Armenian Activities Through Archival Documents 1914-1918), Vol. 1, (Ankara: Genelkurmay Basımevi, 2005), pp. 132-133 and 139-142.

86. This and the following relevant paragraphs are based on *La Verité sur le mouvement révolutionnaire arménien et les mesures gouvernementales* (İstanbul: Imprimerie Tanine, 1916).

87. "Turks Avenge Armenians; Fifty-one Moslem Soldiers Are Shot for Mistreating Christians," *The Washington Post*, 4 June 1916, p. 2.

88. "War Justified by Talat Pasha," *The Christian Science Monitor*, 29 September 1917, p. 2.

89. "Talat Paşa's Speech," *Vakit*, 12 July 1921, p. 1.

90. Michael Ignatieff, "Lemkin's Word," *New Republic*, No.4493, 26 February 2001, p. 27.

91. There is a vast literature on the unique Ottoman *millet* system. For a general survey, see Halil İnalcık, *Osmanlı İmparatorluğunun Ekonomik ve Sosyal Tarihi (1300-1600)* [Economic and Social History of the Ottoman Empire (1300-1600)], Vol.1, (İstanbul: Eren Yayınları, 2000), p. 54; İlber Ortaylı, "Osmanlı İmparatorluğunda Millet Sistemi" (*Millet* System in the Ottoman Empire), in Hasan Celal Güzel, Kemal Çiçek, Salim Koca, eds., *Türkler* (Turks), Vol.10, (Ankara: Yeni Türkiye Yayınları, 2002), p. 216 and Avedis Sanjian, *The Armenian Communities in Syria under Ottoman Dominion* (Cambridge, Massachusetts: Harvard University Press, 1965), pp. 30-31 and 40-43. A more extensive discussion of the theme can be found in Gülnihal Bozkurt, *Alman-İngiliz Belgelerinde ve Siyasi Gelişmelerin Işığı Altında Gayrımüslim Osmanlı Vatandaşlarının Hukuki Durumu 1839-1914* (The Legal Situation of the Non-Muslim Ottoman Citizens According to German-British Documents and in Light of Political Developments 1839-1914), (Ankara: Türk Tarih Kurumu, 1996) and Benjamin Braude and Bernard Lewis, eds., *Christians and Jews in the Ottoman Empire: The Functioning of a Plural Society*, 2 Vols., (New York: Holmes and Meier, 1982).

92. Dominic Lieven, *The Russian Empire and Its Rivals* (London: John Murray Publishers Ltd., 2000), p. 151.

93. For a fuller discussion of this theme, see İlber Ortaylı, *Osmanlı Barışı* (Pax Ottomana), (İstanbul: Timaş Yayınları, 2007), pp. 135-157. Also Alexander Powell, *The Struggle for Power in Moslem Asia* (New York and London: The Century Company, 1923), pp. 118-119 and Emil Lengyel, *Turkey* (New York: H. Wolff, 1941), p. 187.

94. "Armenia Now Open to Saving by the Great Powers; G. Marcar Gregory Says They Should Annul Turkish Rule, Take the Country as Their Ward and Give It Gover-

nor," *The Christian Science Monitor*, 1 April 1913, p. 3.

95. Harry Jewell Sarkiss, "The Armenian Renaissance, 1500-1863," *Journal of Modern History*, Vol. 9, No. 4 (December 1937), pp. 446-448; Gaillard, *The Turks and Europe*, p. 266. The Armenian national constitution was first written in 1857 and was officially proclaimed by the Armenian patriarch at Kumkapı—a place of importance for the Armenians in the Ottoman Empire, in that it was here that the Armenians first settled in İstanbul after its conquest by Sultan Mehmet II. On demand of the Ottoman government the document underwent a revision, and was finally proclaimed by an imperial decree in 1863. See Kevork Pamukciyan, *İstanbul Yazıları* (İstanbul Writings), Vol. 1: *İstanbul'da Ermeniler* (Armenians in İstanbul), (İstanbul: Aras Yayıncılık, 2002), p. 3 and idem, "Kumkapı Patrikhane Kilisesi Ne Zamandan Beri Ermenilerin Elindedir?" (Since When the Armenians Own the Patriarchate Church at Kumkapı?), *Tarih ve Toplum*, Vol. 14, No. 1 (September 1990), pp. 39-41. Kevork Pamukciyan served at the Armenian Patriarchate in İstanbul as archivist and secretary general from 1967 to 1982. He is thoroughly at home with the extensive Armenian and Turkish sources and has worked up his account from the original materials. For the original text of the Armenian national constitution see BOA, Yıldız Esas Evrakı (Yıldız Palace Main Files), Document No. 112/5, 18 March 1863.

96. For in-depth textual analyses of the *Hattı Şerif* of 1839 and the *Hattı Hümayun* of 1856 see respectively Enver Ziya Karal, *Osmanlı Tarihi Nizam-ı Cedit ve Tanzimat Devirleri (1789-1856)* {Ottoman History: Eras of New Order and Reorganization (1789-1856)}, Vol. 5, (Ankara: Türk Tarih Kurumu, reprinted, 1988), pp. 169-195 and 248-252 and idem, *Osmanlı Tarihi İslahat Fermanı Devri (1856-1861)* {Ottoman History: Era of Reform Rescript (1856-1861)}, Vol. 6, (Ankara: Türk Tarih Kurumu, reprinted, 1988), pp. 1-28.

97. "Denies Turkey Butchers Jews," *The Chicago Daily Tribune*, 21 November 1914, p. 9. Schmarya Levin was a member of the first Russian duma, and when that body was closed by the czar he signed the Viborg protest against the act and, in consequence, was exiled.

98. Abigail Jacobson, "A City Living through Crisis: Jerusalem during World War I," *British Journal of Middle Eastern Studies*, Vol. 36, No.1 (April 2009), p.79. The Sublime Porte did not expel Russian Jews residing in the Ottoman Empire at the period, but permitted them to become naturalized Ottoman subjects. Many of the 70,000 Jews in Jerusalem were immigrants from Russia who, with the remaining part of the Jewish population, had so well adopted themselves to local conditions that they had succeeded in practically monopolizing the greater part of the trade. For details on the subject see Isaiah Friedman, *Germany, Turkey, and Zionism 1897-1918* (Oxford: Oxford University Press, 1977), pp. 191-227.

99. "Blaming the Turks for Disturbance to Jews," *The Boston Daily Globe*, 8 March 1915, p. 8.

100. Isaiah Friedman, *The Question of Palestine British-Jewish-Arab Relations: 1914-1918* (New Brunswick, New Jersey and London: Transaction Publishers, 2nd expanded ed., 1992), pp. 296-297.

101. Friedman, *Germany, Turkey, and Zionism 1897-1918*, p. 143.

102. Lieven, *The Russian Empire and Its Rivals*, pp. 150-151.

103. Aron Rodrigue, "The Sephardim in the Ottoman Empire," in Elie Kedourie, ed., *Spain and the Jews: The Sephardi Experience 1492 and After* (London: Thames and

Hudson, 1992), p. 187.

Chapter Two
The Evidence of Uneven Treatment

A critical element of the definition of genocide is its absolutism: For a geno-cidal regime to be in place, it must view all its potential victims roughly the same – there can be little to no room for exceptions to the rule. Genocide must be complete. And yet in the case of the Armenian tragedy, it was not. There are several important pieces of evidence to support this point.

EXEMPTIONS FROM RELOCATIONS

A critical distinction can also be found in official Turkish policy towards Ar-menian relocations. Whereas in Nazi Germany virtually all Jews were sent to either immediate death or slave labor camps from 1942 to 1945, the Armenians of the Ottoman Empire were not treated uniformly. Many were exempted from relocations: Armenian Protestants and Catholics, together with families of those employed by the Ottoman Railways, General Debt and Tobacco Administra-tions, major foreign banks, soldiers still serving in the Ottoman army, medical doctors and other important professional and managerial groups. All Armenian members of the Ottoman Parliament, with the exception of those who had gone to Russia and joined the Russian army, and Armenian men who were in the employ or under the protection of the foreign diplomats and soldiers were also exempted. There were artisans and master craftsmen retained by the Ottoman military authorities such as tailors, shoemakers, blacksmiths, coach makers, carpenters, woodcutters, cabinet- and furniture makers, ironsmiths, weavers, saddlers, harness makers, tinsmiths, cobblers, draftsmen, and workers in factories that produced goods of public use.[1]

Harry Franck, one of the foremost American travel writers of the first half of the 20th century, says he talked one day with an Armenian who had been for twenty-five years an employee of the Turkish railways. At the time of reloca- tions he was told that he might stay if he wished. He stayed. Nor had he since regretted his decision. This Armenian and his wife were on good social relations with Turkish families of their class.[2]

In his *Fateful Choices: Ten Decisions That Changed the World 1940-1941*, Ian Kershaw takes up this matter. He points out that the German decision in 1942 to simply kill all the Jews of Europe had no precedent. By contrast, the Armenian relocations were replete with exemptions. At the most extreme end, Armenians could avoid forced displacements by converting to Islam – no such option was available to Jews.[3] Kevork Pamukciyan, basing himself on an im- pressive array of authentic Armenian records, estimates the number of Arme- nian men, women, and children conversions reaching 100,000 during the First World War years.[4] These converts were welcomed.[5]

Guenter Lewy notes, as have others, that large Armenian communities in the provinces of İstanbul, Aydın, and Aleppo were left intact. And he remarks: "This would be analogous to Hitler's failing to include the Jews of Berlin, Co- logne, and Munich in the Final Solution."[6] That the Ottoman government did not engage in relocations in these cities could not have been, he points out, the result of an effort to avoid adverse publicity since the knowledge of the forced displacements was widespread.[7] Michael Gunter agrees: "Could any- one conceive of Hitler allowing the Jews to continue living in Berlin while he implemented his genocide against them elsewhere?"[8] The Jews of Berlin were killed, their synagogues defiled and destroyed. The Armenians of İstanbul lived through the war, their churches open. At the sanjak of Kütahya, in western Turkey, the governor Faik Ali (Ozansoy)[9] absolutely refused to carry out his instructions from the Ministry of the Interior and threatened to arrest and put to death any man who laid his hands on the Armenians.[10]

By comparison, the Nazi plans for genocide were all-encompassing. In the Wannsee Conference, where the official Nazi policy of extermination was determined and defined, Reinhard Heydrich, directly subordinate to Heinrich Himmler and head of the SS Reich Security Main Office, noted that the Final Solution would have to deal with eleven million Jews. His target list included 330,000 English Jews, 4,000 Jews from Ireland, and Jews from neutral Sweden (8,000), Switzerland (18,000), Spain (6,000), and the European portion of Tur- key (55,000).[11]

No compromise could be allowed in this biological-metaphysical effort. Stanford University historian Norman Naimark concludes therefore that "the concept of genocide does not fit the Armenian case," nor does "the concept of ethnic cleansing," a phrase that came into common parlance in the spring of

1992 to describe Serbian attacks on the Muslim population of Bosnia. According to him, genocide is "the intentional killing off of part or all of an ethnic, religious, or national group," while ethnic cleansing aims "to remove a people and often all traces of them from a concrete territory," and neither was the case in Ottoman Turkey.[12]

Armenians remained in positions of authority throughout the war – unthinkable in Nazi Germany or Nazi-controlled nations. The first Ottoman Chamber of Deputies, elected during the fall of 1908 included fourteen Armenians. This number remained much the same throughout the remaining years of the empire.[13] The list of thirty-nine senators appointed by the sultan included three Armenians.[14]

Armenians were in practice represented in the Ottoman Parliament—Chamber of Deputies and Chamber of Notables—and Municipal Councils far beyond their proportional share in the population. Under the new regime in 1908[15], superiority of the Armenians in the Turkish language gave them an advantage over their Christian rivals. Young Turks and Armenians had long had mutual sympathies during their exile in Western Europe, and recent demonstrations of fraternity between the two, in deeds no less than in words, were a noteworthy feature of the new order of things. The leadership of the Committee of Union and Progress professed its wish to work hand in hand with the Armenian element for the constitutional regeneration of the Ottoman Empire.[16]

By far, however, the critical difference between the Holocaust and the Armenian case was the example set by many Ottoman officials in preserving, as much as possible, the property, dignity, and life of Armenians. By comparison, the examples of any gentiles assisting Jews facing extermination in Europe are so rare that such individuals are honored individually by Holocaust survivor organizations and Holocaust museums. Moreover, the official Nazi policy was to put to death any who preserved the life of a Jew – and that policy was put into effect often. Official Ottoman policy, as previously noted, was the opposite.

OFFICIAL ACTS OF MERCY

Many Turks helped and protected their Armenian neighbors. Thousands of Turks saved the lives of Armenian men and women and boys and girls by hiding them in their households. Armenian orphans were sometimes taken into Turkish homes for shelter and care—a rare option for Jewish children in Nazi-dominated nations.[17] A former president of Aleppo College, most of whose faculty and students were Armenian, confided in a 31 March 1983 letter to Donald Webster, Assistant Professor of Social Science at International College in İzmir from 1931 to 1934 and a recognized specialist on Near Eastern affairs:

I do want to pass one statement I hear from the lips of Zenope Bezdjian, who was for some years the *vekil* of the Armenian Protestant Community in İstanbul: 'Every Armenian should remember that for every Armenian killed by a Turk, there was another whose life was saved by a Turk.'[18]

Between 1918 and 1922, some of the disunited Armenian women and children reconnected with their families and communities. But women seventeen and over or those married to Turks could choose to stay with their new families, and many did.[19] In several parts of Turkey, many Armenian children were turned over by Turkish families to the Armenian community, but, wrote one well-informed contemporary American journalist, "a large number of these Armenians who had since been given up to the Armenians or the Near East Relief had taken the first opportunity to escape and return for Turkish homes."[20]

Of all examples of Turkish mercy displayed to the Armenians, perhaps none is more noteworthy than that of Cemal Paşa, Ottoman Minister of the Navy and commander of the Fourth Army in Syria and Palestine from 18 November 1914 until 12 December 1917. In his postwar memoirs Cemal Paşa said he did not see any reason to re-tell his efforts of helping Armenian refugees, especially widows and orphans. "It seems to me as though in doing so I am reflecting on the moral value of these actions which were prompted only by feelings of humanity." Cemal Paşa, second only to Enver Paşa (the Acting Commander-in-Chief and Minister of War) in the military hierarchy, and also Governor General for Syria and Palestine, did not allow attacks on the Armenian refugees to take place in his zone and considered it his duty to give stringent orders to this effect.

Cemal Paşa, the military ruler from the Taurus range to Medina, writes that he issued orders that bread be provided for the refugees from the Army depots, and the doctors on the lines of communication look after the sick Armenians. He went himself to Pozantı from Aleppo to oversee efforts to alleviate some of the hardships of the Armenians. He was convinced that relocation to Mesopotamia was bound to cause great distress; and he therefore thought it better "to bring a large number of exiles into the Syrian provinces of Aleppo and Beirut; I succeeded in obtaining the desired permission after I had made vigorous representations to İstanbul." In this way the little understood and often overlooked Ottoman statesman-soldier was actually able to "save 150,000 Armenian emigrants."[21]

Armenian gratitude, at the time, was made clear. Cemal Paşa says Zaven Der Yeghiayan, Armenian Patriarch of İstanbul between 1913 and 1922, visited him in İstanbul in December 1915 at the Pera Palace Hotel and handed him a memorandum thanking him in the name of the whole Armenian nation.[22]

Cemal Paşa was one of three powerful men at the helm of the Ottoman government during the First World War. Bernard Lewis describes him "as a man of high professional competence, personal authority, and responsibility."[23] Frank Chamber writes that "Cemal Paşa had a sense of honor, and there was a streak of

magnificence in him. He was a good patriot, a proud Ottoman, a gifted administrator and a man of his word."[24] The memoirs of such a statesman, consequently,
have a decided historical value. There is not much inquiry on his life and career,
apart from Nevzat Artuç's recent *Cemal Paşa*,[25] the first scholarly biography of
him to appear in any language. Artuç did not consult foreign archives for the
study, but he does cite numerous files from Ottoman repositories and makes effective use of many published sources. The footnotes alone will make an invaluable aid to future researchers. Despite the merits of the book, it suffers from a
number of limitations. For one, the author devotes uneven amounts of attention
to the various phases of Cemal Paşa's professional activities. Resettlement of
Armenians in Syria takes up a mere six pages, and the book tells us very little of
his humanitarian assistance to Armenian exiles.

However, there is much contemporary testimony that corrobates Cemal
Paşa's account of that assistance. George Young, American Consular Agent
at Damascus, on 20 September 1915 informed Ambassador Morgenthau in
İstanbul that Cemal Paşa told him that he was doing everything possible for
the Armenian exiles, furnishing food, tents, and so on. The American official
believed that many of the stories about the relocations that were circulating
were much exaggerated. Young heard of aid extended by Muslims who pitied
the suffering. At Kadem, on the outskirts of Damascus, a hospital for sick Armenians was built. There were practically no deaths among Armenian exiles at
the encampments. The Fourth Army provided food for them. And many exiles
were arriving by train, rather than by foot.[26]

The Bavarian artillery colonel Friedrich Freiherr Kress von Kressenstein,
chief of staff of the Fourth Army in 1915-1916 and an indomitable field fighter,
confirms Cemal Paşa's declaration. Although at times the German chief of staff
and his Ottoman commander were in conflict, both because of their differing
priorities and differing loyalties, the former speaks well of the latter's careful
handling of the Armenian population.[27] Von Kressenstein, who was responsible
for army strategic, operational and tactical planning and had been in daily contact with Cemal Paşa at the command headquarters during the period, notes
that orders were given to distribute food and water as needed and to protect the
exiles. The German officer's memoir, published in 1938, is replete with detailed
references to his Ottoman wartime superior's efforts to provide relief for the
Armenian relocatees.[28]

General Ali Fuad Erden, von Kressenstein's successor in the Fourth Army
in 1916-1917 and a military writer, concurs on this and underscores that through
Cemal Paşa's intervention the lives of a great many of Armenians were saved.
Erden who knew Cemal Paşa intimately and who saw him almost daily during
much of the First World War, records that these Armenians would have starved
to death had it not been for army stores made available by the supreme commander. While the Ottoman army was unable to supply enough food rations,

adequate clothing, decent hygienic conditions, and appropriate medical attention to its Muslim soldiers, efforts were made to provide these to the Armenian
relocatees. Erden states that his former commanding officer's treatment of the
Armenians in Syria during the First World War cannot be forgotten.[29]

Halidé Edib Adıvar, who engaged in educational activities in Syria in 1916-
1918, mentions in her memoirs in 1926 that Cemal Paşa had been as good to
Armenians as it was possible to be in those days. She writes as follows: The
commander of the Fourth Army in Syria took a protective attitude toward the
Armenians exiled there. They were not to be molested in any way in the lands
under his control. He had hanged two notorious outlaws, Cherkess Ahmed and
his companion, for daring to try to start a massacre in Syria. His great dif-
ficulty was the famine, from which the Ottoman army, the native population,
and the Armenians suffered equally. Adıvar stresses that Cemal Paşa helped
all the charitable organizations for children, for Armenians and locals alike,
with what he could spare from the army supplies. The Turkish educator says
she also saw the Armenian orphanages in Damascus, which were opened and
helped by Cemal Paşa, but which were run by Armenians, mostly women. She
recalls that the Armenians considered Cemal Paşa godsend great help, and the
women showed their handkerchiefs with his pictures which they carried around
their necks. Adıvar tells a noteworthy story: After the occupation of Syria by
the French, they brought in a large number of Armenians with them, and one
of them was swearing loudly against Cemal Paşa in the marketplace. A poor
Armenian woman spoke back to him saying, "He was very good to us and gave
us food during the famine and protected our lives when everyone was dying in
the street." To which the man answered, "It is an Armenian's duty to swear at all
Turks, the more so against the good ones, for it is the good ones who make the
world like the Turks."[30]

The German Ministerial Envoy, Baron Max von Oppenheim, in an eight-
page report he sent on 9 August 1915 from Damascus to the Reich Chancellor,
Theobald von Betmann Hollweg, characterized Cemal Paşa as strong-willed
and very determined. Von Oppenheim saw relocations as a measure of defense
and self-preservation against the incidence of the Armenian insurrection.[31]

The German Ministerial Envoy had wide experience in the Middle East as
a diplomat and a scholar. He traveled and studied extensively before the First
World War in Syria, Palestine, and Mesopotamia and knew the region and the
locals well. In 1915 he headed a special information bureau for Middle Eastern
affairs in the Auswärtigen Amtes, that cooperated with the political section of
the army reserve general staff. In that year, he also became the head of the News
Department within the German Embassy in İstanbul. As the representative of
a major power allied to the Ottoman Empire, he was a privileged observer of
developments around him and had direct relations with the Ottoman officials.
Although von Oppenheim and Ottoman authorities did not see eye to eye in

all the war effort, the German diplomat underlined that the Sublime Porte was justified in the measures it took against the Armenian population. He also said Cemal Paşa ordered for the protection and feeding of the relocated Armenians and that these were to be regarded as fellow countrymen and their security guaranteed. The commander of the Fourth Army stipulated daily rations for the relocatees and rules for their safety. The German official added that Cemal Paşa reminded the governors of Aleppo and Adana and the district administrators of Maraş and Deyrizor to treat the Armenians with care.[32]

The correspondence of the diplomatic and consular staff of Germany on the ground, who had longer, direct experience of conditions in the Ottoman Empire, continues to confirm the accounts of Cemal Paşa. Paul Graf Wolff-Metternich zur Gracht, maintaining close contacts with the Sublime Porte through his position as the German Ambassador in İstanbul, wrote on 9 December 1915 to his superiors at Berlin that the commander of the Fourth Army was one of those Turks who expressed disapproval at the way in which the relocations had been carried out. The Ottoman general demanded from his government the alleviation of the lot of the Armenians in the zone of the Fourth Army. Thus, the Armenians in Aleppo were to stay in the area, and those Armenians who were employed by the Baghdad railway management were recalled from the relocation sites.[33]

The veteran German consul in Aleppo, Walter Rössler, informed on 1 April 1915 the Embassy in İstanbul that a circular issued by Cemal Paşa on March 29 had strictly forbidden private individuals to interfere directly or indirectly in the least way with governmental affairs. Anyone who attacked an Armenian for whatever reason would be considered a rioter and face trial by court-martial on the spot.[34] Rössler further reported on 3 January 1916 that the Ottoman commander did not want the Armenians to perish and after the transit camp at İslahiye (north of Aleppo) had been the scene of repeated attacks by brigands and women and children had been killed, he ordered severe measures against the culprits. The Ottoman military ruler was sensitive to such matters and had several brigands hanged who had laid hands on Armenians.[35]

Henry Barby, the French *Journal*'s special correspondent in Armenia, stated in August 1916 that in Cilicia the relocations of the Armenians were smoother than in eastern Anatolia, and that this was due to Cemal Paşa. Barby was not sympathetic to the Turks, so he had no reason to praise Cemal Paşa other than to tell the truth about his actions. In reply to the Armenian catholicos who was imploring him for bread for the Armenian population, Cemal Paşa said if the friends of the Armenians, the French and English, knew what was taking place in other Ottoman territories, and compared the condition of things in Cilicia, they would thank him. Barby notes that Cemal Paşa caught Hasan Çavuş for the killing of Armenians in Cilicia, and had him hanged immediately.[36]

Others also credit the commander of the Fourth Army with saving Armenians. British intelligence operative Aaron Aaronsohn, in a memorandum he presented to the War Office on 16 November 1916, conceded that Cemal Paşa saved the lives of over a hundred thousand of Armenians by shielding them from sufferings and epidemics. The Ottoman commander's interventions on behalf of the Armenians had earned him the nickname "Pasha of Armenia."[37] James Barton, a leading spokesman since 1915 for the missionary and relief groups and president of the Board of Trustees of the Near East Relief organization, forthrightly acknowledged in 1930 that Cemal Paşa was more lenient to the Armenian exiles than were the İstanbul officials. The Ottoman commander permitted them to stop on their march, and allowed those that reached Damascus to remain in the city.[38]

Frederick Bliss, son of the founder of the American College in Beirut, says Cemal Paşa built up a large relief organization in all the centers where Armenians had been gathered: Hama, Damascus, the Hauran, and elsewhere. He had one commission for food; another for clothing. In some cases Armenians themselves were appointed as officers.[39]

Having been a teacher at the American School for Girls (a missionary-supported Protestant educational establishment) at Adana between 1886 and 1930 and friend of the Armenians, Elizabeth Webb had much to say that had deep interest concerning the history of that period. On the relocation of Armenians from the province of Adana in 1915, she observes:

> The exiled Armenians from the Adana district fared much better than most others in Turkey. Many of them on personal application to Jemal Pasha were sent to the Damascus region, reached their destination in safety, and have not been massacred since.

Webb also reported:

> An Adana Armenian woman exiled to the Damascus region was much troubled to find that in the Government register there, she and her husband had been given Turkish names and were recorded as Moslems. On their protesting to the Government, she was told this was something for which she had no concern, that it was purely a matter of Government policy. Later they understood it was done by Jemal Pasha's order for their protection. I wish to give credit where it was due.[40]

The foregoing statements made on Cemal Paşa are solidified by that of an Armenian, Hagop Sarkissian, who had been relocated with his family from Kilis in southeastern Anatolia to Aleppo in 1915. Sarkissian, who later changed his name into James Kay Sutherland in the United States, had served as provincial health care officer and railway station administrator in Aleppo during 1915-1918 and was thus an important eyewitness to the events at the time. In his memoirs *Adventures of an Armenian Boy* published in 1964, Sarkissian provides rare and valuable insights into Cemal Paşa's treatment of the Armenians in Syria. He pays tribute and expresses personal token of appreciation to the memory of the commander of the Fourth Army. Having emigrated from Aleppo to the United States in 1920 at the age of twenty-three, he says the Ottoman general was magnanimous toward the Armenians and refers to him as "a great man," who was "responsible for the saving of half-a-million Armenians in the part of Turkey subject to his control; and consequently, for the large Armenian population flourishing today in Syria, Lebanon and Palestine." He states that also the thousands, who later migrated from those regions to Europe and America, himself among them, were indebted to him.[41]

Sarkissian candidly continues and sums up his impressions about Cemal Paşa as follows:

> I believe he liked the Armenians and tried to avoid their destruction as much as he personally could…As the deportations began, Djemal Pasha acted in what could only have been an attempt to help the Armenians. He sent town-criers through the streets of the city with a message, and I can still hear their high, chanting call: "Djemal Pasha advises you to leave Aleppo and go south, to Beirut or Damascus—anywhere south. Or be driven to Der-az-Zor and suffer destruction." Thousands of Armenians heeded the warning and were transported to the south by trains provided free at Djemal Pasha's order. Even after this, he organized factories to produce military supplies, such as shoes and clothing, by which means many more Armenians were afforded the opportunity to work and thus avoid deportation. From events such as these have I come to the conclusion that Djemal Pasha did all that was practically feasible under the circumstances to give as many Armenians as possible a chance to be saved. In those days we naturally hated the man but he said, "If the Armenians knew what I have done for them, they would make my statue of gold and erect it on the top of their Ararat Mountain." I now believe he was right. The irony of it is that he was shot by Armenians in the Caucasus about a year or two after the Armistice.[42]

Yervant Odian, editor of İstanbul daily *Jamanag*, in his memoirs first published in Armenian in 1919 and translated into English in 2009 notes that generally people in Aleppo spoke well of Cemal Paşa. Odian, who had been in exile in Syria between 1915 and 1919, says thanks to the commander of the Fourth Army many Armenians, especially those from Adana, were taken to Syria and were able to live reasonably comfortable lives, relatively speaking. Individual appeals and requests made to him were often taken into account.[43]

Even Vahakn Dadrian, director of the Zoryan Institute for Contemporary Armenian Research and Documentation and a vocal proponent of the genocide claim , concedes that Cemal Paşa was one of the few leading Unionists who "refused to embrace the secret genocidal agenda of the party's top leadership and whenever they could tried to resist and discourage the attendant massacres."[44]

More important, the British Blue Book of 1916, in a report attributed to Miss M. W. Frearson, a foreign resident in Ayntab who was on her way to Egypt in September 1915 concurs with Cemal Paşa's assertion that no outrages against the relocatees were permitted in the zone of the Fourth Army. The lady missionary tells she met a convoy of Armenian relocatees from Adana and Mersin near Aleppo and saw that they had ox-carts, mules, donkeys, and a few horses and "looked so much better off in every way than any refugees we had been seen that they hardly seemed like refugees at all."[45] At the same time, it would appear of interest to mention the narrative of an Armenian from Aleppo, Hark Toroyan, who visited the American Consulate in Tiflis at the beginning of March 1917. Toroyan, through his ability to pass for a Turk, was employed as a courier by a German officer (Lieutenant Otto Oelmann) during a journey from Aleppo to Baghdad. Toroyan's testimony shows that the Armenians of Cilicia were not molested during the relocations.[46]

Guenter Lewy concludes that Cemal Paşa did much for the Armenian exiles who came to provinces under his jurisdiction. The Ottoman general took steps to prevent violence against the Armenians and actually punished transgressors. He saved thousands of lives by diverting Armenian relocatees to southern Syria and Lebanon and by ordering an effective relief effort.[47]

Fuat Dündar, who strongly opposes the policies of the leadership of the Committee of Union and Progress, in his recent treatment of the subject *Modern Türkiye'nin Şifresi İttihat ve Terakki'nin Etnisite Mühendisliği (1913-1918)*, remains convinced that the lives of thousands of Armenian exiles in Syria were saved thanks to the active efforts of Cemal Paşa.[48]

Striking instances of Cemal Paşa's humanity to peaceful Ottoman Christians and Jews as well as neutral nationals and enemy subjects were constantly in evidence in Syria and Palestine during the First World War. He preached tolerance and friendship among Muslims and non-Muslims. In this regard it is worth recalling that soon after his arrival at Damascus to assume the command of the Fourth Army, Cemal Paşa proclaimed to the peoples of these regions that it was their duty to establish and maintain cordial relations and indissoluble ties among all the Ottoman elements. The smallest act that might cause injury to such amicable relations would be severely punished. He therefore ordered the Muslims, who formed the majority, to make proof of their patriotic sentiments by cordial relations with the Christian and Jewish elements of the population. The nationals of the allies of the Ottoman Empire and those of friendly and neutral States, who were living in Syria and Palestine, were to be treated as their respected guests. At a time when the Ottoman Empire was engaged in a life and death struggle, Muslims lived under an obligation to be more cordial to others.[49]

The sympathetic approach of Cemal Paşa towards Armenians and other non-Turks and non-Muslims was particularly notable in the region under his domain. Syria and Palestine had been practically under siege ever since the

Ottoman Empire entered the war. The Levantine coast had been blockaded by the Allies. The resources of the region had always been scant owing to its lack of rainfall and low agricultural productivity. Meanwhile, able-bodied men of all creeds had been drafted for the army and sent to the fronts. A plague of locusts had spread all over Syria and Palestine in the spring of 1915, eating up the harvest and every green thing. The commandeering of cattle and wheat by the military authorities, wherever they could find them, had added to the misery of the inhabitants. All mules and horses had been requisitioned by the army. Cemal Paşa was attentive to these conditions and he took charge of the even distribution of what little provision there was in the stricken country between the troops, native population and the Armenian exiles.[50]

Cemal Paşa's relations with the American College in Beirut form an interesting chapter in the history of that missionary-founded institution. At the beginning of the war, he secured the exemption from relocation of three British professors in the Medical School, who continued their positions all through the war. He allowed the students of belligerent nations, including those of military age, to remain at their studies. He welcomed to Southern Palestine an American Red Cross Unit, sent under the auspices of the College and Mission. He permitted the College to obtain provisions at Army rates, at the risk of provoking bitter opposition from Germans and others. Without this concession, which was continued by his successor, it would have been impossible for the large College community to have held together. At a time when travel was extremely difficult, he facilitated the departure to America of members of the Faculty and their families.[51]

All matters, civil and military, in Syria and Palestine were under absolute control of Cemal Paşa. He ruled these lands with authority and discipline and frequently declined to comply with wishes or decisions of İstanbul. The Sublime Porte said it only sent him recommendations, not instructions.[52] Morgenthau wrote privately to Lansing:

> Repeatedly, when I have asked Enver to do something for me in that district [Syria and Palestine], he told me that he would recommend it to Djemal and if he had no objection thereto, my request would be granted. I have begged Enver several times to order it done, and he said that he could not do so as military means might still exist which would justify Djemal to object thereto.[53]

Cemal Paşa's work of humanitarian relief and reconstruction when he was governor of the province of Adana in 1909-1911 should also be added to his credit.[54] In April and May 1909, Turks and Armenians in the area engaged in violent communal clashes in which around 20,000 people were killed. Many buildings had been destroyed by fire. The tension between them had been on the breaking point for several months since the reintroduction of the constitution on 23 July 1908. The Armenians benefited in many ways by the greater liberty

allowed to them by the establishment of the constitutional government and bus-
ily imported arms and ammunition in an aggressive and self-assertive vein of
enthusiasm, which led them to discourse on the great destinies of the Armenian
nation and on the eventual setting up of an Armenian principality. The more
they armed the more they talked, the more they aroused the anxiety and alarm
of the Turkish population. The relations of the two peoples worsened.[55]

On 12 April 1909, an Armenian in Adana shot one of his opponents dead
and wounded two others. This Armenian escaped to Mersin and took passage
by sea. After two days the Turkish-Armenian outbreak erupted. Agents of the
Armenian revolutionary societies had been at work in the province of Adana for
months past and had aggravated the already strained relations between Turks
and Armenians.[56] The report of the judicial authorities had concluded that Armenians had provoked the outbreak.[57] Cemal Bey (as he was called prior to 3
January 1914)[58] was detailed to the area to restore order.

This soldier-governor did not allow religious prejudices to interfere with
the impartial manner in which he treated Muslims and Christians. Not only had
he introduced reforms throughout his province, but Cemal Bey had begun to
reestablish confidence amongst the inhabitants of his province—a confidence
which was conspicuous by its absence when he took over the governorate from
Mustafa Zihni Paşa in August 1909.[59]

Cemal Paşa's memoirs show that when he was appointed to the governorship of Adana the Sublime Porte placed a sum of 200,000 Turkish liras at his
disposal. Divided into two equal parts, the first 100,000 was a present from the
country and was utilized to give immediate relief, supply shelter for the homeless, establish a reserve fund to be devoted to setting up tradesmen and small
farmers, and pay for work for the destitute. The other half was to be lent, on
low-interest terms, to the Armenian traders, artisans, and farmers to enable them
to resume business. The loans were not to be paid back for ten years. A building committee was established in Adana and Cemal Bey took the chairmanship
himself. The committee consisted of several foreigners, such as William Nesbitt
Chambers, who was the resident missionary for the American Board of Commissioners for Foreign Missions in Adana, and a large number of natives, the
majority being Armenians. Thanks to the steps Cemal Bey took, four months
after his arrival, all the Armenian houses in the province had been built and in
the city of Adana itself there was not a single small family house which had not
been finished. In brief, within five or six months the Armenians had resumed
their trade, agriculture, and industry.[60]

Commander Herbert Adam of the British warship *Barham*, after a visit to
Adana in October 1909, reported to London:

> The new Vali, Dhjemal Bey, has a very good reputation, and His Britannic
> Majesty's Acting Vice Consul has a high opinion of him. He is young, active,
> and is doing all in his power with the relief work. The Relief Camp has been

abolished, and the Armenians have been housed in various parts of the town. The financial relief is in the hands of an International Committee, with Vali as President, and appears to be working well. They are advancing money for Armenians to open shops and start work generally; and a new plan of the ruined portion of the town is being made and will be completed in a month; and after that re-construction of houses will be commenced by the Turkish Government, and when they are built, it is proposed to let Armenian families live in them for two years rent-free.[61]

Cemal Bey wrote that the Armenians themselves have fully recognized all the efforts he made in their behalf, and the restoration of their property while he was governor of Adana. Many foreigners—Americans, British, French, and Russians—who came to the city were witnesses of his work, and congratulated him upon it. The great orphanage he had built for the reception and bringing up of the children orphaned in the Adana affair was still in existence. [62]

Cemal Bey's qualities, combined with firm principles, made him a formidable provincial governor in Adana. Andrew Ryan, who served at the British Embassy in İstanbul in various consular and diplomatic positions from 1897 to 1922 and who dealt with the Sublime Porte in all day-to-day matters, expressed with confidence: "It is fair to say that Jemal Bey gained much credit in that post."[63] Ryan further commented: "He did well as governor at Adana."[64]

The Young Turk governor devoted his energies to restoring order and quiet through the country and reconciling Christian and Muslim elements. Some 8,000-10,000 of the 12,000-15,000 Christians who left Adana after the 1909 incidents had returned by February 1910.

The governor traveled to Hacin, a district of Adana, in March 1910, to try to improve the condition of the people in the area. British Ambassador Sir Gerard Lowther, in his annual report on the Ottoman Empire for the year 1910, noted: "High hopes were entertained as to the vali's administration. His attitude was energetic and highly commendable and the economical situation of the vilayet was distinctly improving."[65]

Historian Dikran Mesrob Kaligian acknowledges that "his generally fair treatment of the Armenian population had allowed them the freedom to restore much of their prior prosperity." In April 1911 Cemal Bey published, under his own name, an article in a local newspaper in which he promised harsh punishment for any disturbances of the public order. [66]

American Major-General James Harbord, who led a fact-finding mission to Turkey and Trans-Caucasia in September-October 1919, notes that American testimony in Adana was that while governor there Cemal Bey saved many Armenians from death, erected the orphanage which now housed hundreds of orphans, and built a dike to protect the city from the annual river flood, as well as other good works.[67]

William Nesbitt Chambers confesses that this Ottoman administrator made a deep impression on him. The American missionary writes that soon after the Turkish-Armenian communal fighting of 1909 at Adana, Cemal Bey organized commissions of relief and reconstruction on which the various communities were represented, both Muslim and Christian. He obtained large grants from the central government which were economically and efficiently administered for the relief of the Armenians. He made grants for food and rebuilding of burned houses. He made loans at low interest and long, easy terms to enable large numbers to begin business again and for villagers to reconstruct their farm work. This was a very great boon to the Armenians. The relief was confined to the Christians who had suffered. But his most spectacular and radical undertaking, Chambers goes on, was the organization of courts for the trial and punishment of those guilty of massacre.[68]

According to Chambers, in the prosecution of relief work there were two enterprises that Cemal Bey organized and put forth every endeavor to establish on a permanent basis. One was an orphanage for which he raised, largely by voluntary subscription, between thirty and forty thousand dollars. It was to be open for all the communities. However, it was filled with roughly 200 Armenian children orphaned by the fighting. The government financed it and it was entirely in the hands of Armenians appointed by the government. The other enterprise was industrial relief for women and girls for which a commission was appointed composed of a Turk, a Syrian, three Armenians and an American missionary. Cemal Bey, Chambers maintains, showed his confidence in the American missionaries and his sympathy for their ideals in that he made the head of Adana station of the American Board of Commissioners for Foreign Missions president of the commission and so placed in his hands a sum of about 17,000 dollars (4,000 Turkish gold liras) to be expended in the work.[69]

With the object of further assisting the women of the Adana region Mrs. Shepard (the wife of the well-known American missionary doctor), who some eighteen years ago had so successfully founded an embroidery industry at Ayntab, was invited by Cemal Bey to establish a branch of her work in Adana. Owing to the initiative of the governor, a liberal allowance was made by the Government Relief Committee in order to allow this industry to be started.[70]

Zeeneb Charlton says Cemal Bey's transference to Baghdad, in the dual capacity of governor and military commander, was deeply regretted.[71] In the fall of 1911 Chambers noted sadly:

> I was sorry on my return [from annual leave] to find His Excellency Djemal Bey gone from Adana. He had much to do still in the reconstruction of the province. The man that succeeds him has a difficult place to fill.[72]

Dorothea Chambers Blaisdell, the daughter of William Nesbitt Chambers, in her memoirs *Missionary Daughter Witness to the End of the Ottoman Empire* published in 2002 writes that Cemal Bey put all his energy and idealism into the task ahead of him, that of rebuilding a once thriving city, and reassuring the Armenian population of a good faith which had been badly shaken. More immediate was the care of homeless groups and wounded and sick refugees. According to Blaisdell, the cooperation of missionary and military foreigners was at Cemal Bey's service immediately and the Ottoman governor found both Major Charles Doughty-Wylie, British consul at nearby Mersin, and Chambers a type of person who was only too glad to work with him. Cemal Bey had the perspicacity to avail himself of this willing cooperation. When an inadvertent remark of his showed Cemal Bey that Chambers was contemplating a trip through the villages, he begged him not to go just then. "I desire your help and advice. Perhaps we shall make the trip together." And they did. Blaisdell tells that twin pictures of Cemal Bey and Chambers on horseback in front of a fountain in the countryside were interesting reminders of this intelligent, sympathetic cooperation of Ottoman governor with American missionary.[73]

There is not one example of a single German military commander exerting the kind of humanity towards Jews as Cemal Paşa showed the Armenians. And Cemal Paşa, while extraordinary, was not alone. Ara Sarafian says many Ottoman officials, including governors, subgovernors, military personnel, police chiefs, and gendarmes saved thousands of Armenians. And he adds: "Most Armenians from the province of Adana, for example, were not killed. This very basic fact is elided in the works of prominent Armenian historians. There are other examples too."[74] This is a critical distinction.

ARMENIAN POWER WITHIN THE OTTOMAN ELITE

Some important figures in the Committee of Union and Progress were Armenians, including Bedros Halladjian, who twice acted as minister of commerce and public works in the cabinets formed by Hüseyin Hilmi Paşa and Hakkı Paşa respectively in 1909-1910 and 1911. This ministry held tenders for the construction of new and extension of old railways, for the building of highways, for the installation of telephones and electric lighting and power plants, and for the electrification of tramways. It also made decisions to develop the natural resources of the country, expand its commerce, establish industries, and enhance the purchasing power of the people.[75]

Halladjian became Second Vice President of the Chamber of Deputies on 18 May 1912 and also served as head of public works commission in the Chamber. After the restoration of the constitution on 23 July 1908 (declared in 1876 and suspended in 1877) he was elected deputy for İstanbul in all the three elections of 1908, 1912 and 1914 under the auspices of the Committee of Union and Progress and played an important role in the introduction and passage of legislation designed to bring about the modernization and economic revival of the empire. Even those persons whose political principles were diametrically opposed to those of the Young Turk government or those of the "Committee Reign" were forced to admit that he was master of his subject, and that he spoke with extraordinary precision and logic on many matters. He rose in the councils of the party and gained influence in the higher echelons of the government. [76]

Prior to the First World War, Halladjian succeeded in being elected to the thirteen-member Central Committee of the Committee of Union and Progress, the highest decision making organ of the empire. Every fortnight the Central Committee met at the Nuruosmaniye office at İstanbul under the chairmanship of Talat Paşa. The men of the first rank took their resolutions, plans and schemes to the meeting for consideration and approval. Comments were made there, criticisms were expressed and things presented to the meeting were voted. His colleagues often heeded Halladjian's views. [77]

Again, the distinction with the Nazi era is clear. Under the Nazis Jews were immediately excluded from the civil service and prohibited from holding public office. Shortly after Hitler's appointment as Chancellor on 30 January 1933, the Reichstag began to institute a series of anti-Jewish decrees. According to the Law for the Restoration of the Professional Civil Service of 7 April 1933, civil servants who were not of Aryan descent were to be retired. Law Regarding Admission to the Bar of 7 April 1933 stipulated that persons who were of non-Aryan descent might be denied admission to the bar. Jews were denied the right to vote and to speak freely. They were banned from the practice of medicine and dentistry in state institutions, from teaching in universities, from writing for publication and from working as artists, actors or musicians before an Aryan audience. The Jews were almost immediately isolated from the rest of the society.

For this reason, the scholarly disinterest in Halladjian is curious. The life and career of an Armenian statesman, who, during the period in question promoted Ottoman patriotism, or Ottomanism, would certainly be fruitful areas for scholarly inquiry.

Halladjian attended university in Paris and held a doctorate in jurisprudence and political and economic sciences from Sorbonne. He spoke French and English in addition to Armenian and Turkish, and before 1908 was chief of legal section of the Ottoman Public Debt Administration, an agency representing foreign creditors with extensive control over the Sublime Porte's tax revenues. [78]

In the introduction to his electoral platform presented in a speech delivered in the Hasköy quarter of İstanbul on 27 September 1908 Halladjian argued that through the organization of liberty, the existence of duty, and civilization advancement, the Ottoman nation would become one of the most prosperous nations on earth. Article 1 of his platform stated Armenian deputies of the Parliament would protect completely and totally the equality of right of all the elements and the individuals, and on that basis, they would protect also the unity and the integrity of the Ottoman Empire totally and completely. His second article was on the establishment of relationships between the different forces of the state that must exist in a truly constitutional country. Halladjian's main point here dwelled on the position of the sultan, as he argued that there were articles within the Ottoman constitutional law which were irreconcilable with the principal of the unaccountability of the sultan. He contended that by protecting the sultanate which was a great and useful force for the Ottoman land, it was necessary to amend the Ottoman constitution according to the principles of democratic constitution. By this Halladjian meant to confine the power of the sultan.[79]

Article 3 of Halladjian's platform dealt with protecting the special legal position of the Armenian nation. However, he refused to use the word "privileges" in describing the status of the Armenians:

> In order to express these special positions the word privilege is used. It is said that the Armenian nation is enjoying privileges. This is completely wrong. The Armenian nation does not have any kind of privileges. The Armenians are simply found in special conditions in the different religious, educational and legal issues, as are other elements, which are the result of their racial and religious differences in a country where an official religion exists, in which many legal issues have religious particularity, and in which races and languages are extremely different.

He argued that the preservation of religious and national privileges would not contradict with the political system of the Ottoman Empire. For this aim he brings the cases of France and the United States to further explain:

> Let us see the United States in which besides the English race, there are huge numbers of Germans, French, Italians, Polish, and other national elements. Therefore, in that huge country, which recently looks a lot like our beloved country, the English, German, French, Italian, the Polish, together by maintaining their national existence, language, religions, glories with complete liberty, they are honorable Americans. We also, together, by being Armenians, we are sincerely Ottomans, we are completely enemy to any separatist idea, completely ready to preserve Ottoman unity and integrity by sacrificing our life and property, under the glorified Ottoman flag.[80]

Halladjian supported the idea of administrative decentralization but rejected political decentralization, and advocated a limited extension of responsibility within certain limits:

> Hence, we see that in addition to demanding local extension of responsibility for the Ottoman Empire, it is necessary to define its measure and condition after examining the willingness of the country and its civilizational condition, and taking into consideration that premature extension of administrative discretion can cause extremely bad consequences on the economic condition of

the country and indirectly, but surely, on the political condition.

These were the major points that Halladjian addressed in his political platform. In addition, he raised other points such as mandatory teaching of Turkish in the Armenian schools, military service for Muslims and non-Muslims, finding remedy for the confiscated lands during the past thirty years, insuring the properties of the Armenian nation, encouraging trade, profession and farming, improving the taxation system by abolishing harmful taxes, establishing a new taxing system, and abolishing the Hamidiye regiments. Halladjian concluded his political platform saying:

> Hence, let the Armenian members of the Ottoman Parliament, with their plans and with their parliamentary tactic and method give new proof to the Armenian nation, of being an inseparable part of the Ottoman fatherland, let them work effectively for the strength and growth of the Ottoman fatherland.[81]

Halladjian was a man of moderate views, and worked in harmony with the Turks. Being modern and businesslike, he was positive and self-assertive as regards the vindication of Ottoman national rights.[82] He was an authority on international law in its wide and perplexing ramifications. He had had a tremendous amount of actual, practical experience in his practice of that particular branch of jurisprudence. The Unionists hoped to use his legal expertise to further their own program of reform and progress.[83]

On 9 September 1909, the İstanbul daily *İttihad* hailed the nomination of Halladjian to the post of minister of commerce and public works. The paper said:

> The new face at the Cabinet table is a welcome one. It is a wise appointment, and one which will commend itself in the most diverse quarters. Professionally, he comes to his new duties with the prestige of his acknowledged ability and his exceptional technical training. Exceptional it has been, for none of the recent ministers of commerce and public works has come to that office with any special preparation for the post.

The post had strategic importance, and was vital to Turkey's long-term future. The construction of roads and railways in the interior would show the people of the country, and especially those of eastern Anatolia, that the New Regime was really doing something, and that they themselves were going to gain real advantages from it. According to *İttihad*, Halladjian had proven himself intelligent and up to the task.[84]

It speaks volumes that the British Ambassador to the Sublime Porte Gerard Lowther in his annual report on the Ottoman Empire for 1910 observed that alongside Talat Paşa, Minister of the Interior, and Cavit Bey, Minister of Finance, Halladjian represented the views of the Committee of Union and Progress in the cabinet in 1909-1910. The Armenians were among the brains of the Ottoman Empire. They managed great financial concerns in the country; in science, art, and literature they were preeminent.[85] It is also notable at this juncture that the British statesman Winston Churchill respected the motives and admired the courage of the Young Turks, who sought to establish a Europeanized regime. In September 1910 he had spent five days in İstanbul, and there he met several Ottoman ministers, including Talat Paşa and Cavit Bey.[86]

In 1916, in the middle of the First World War years, Halladjian presided the special committee formed at the Ministry of Justice with a view to modify and reform the Ottoman Code of Commerce, to bring it up to date and to adapt it to the exigencies of modern conditions. The committee began its work on 29 May 1916, after a speech by Halil Bey (Menteşe)[87], Minister of Foreign Affairs and Acting Minister of Justice, setting forth the aim and importance of the reform which was undertaken. Halladjian provided expert opinion when matters related to his legal expertise were discussed in the meetings. Armenians Krikor Sinapian, former Minister of Agriculture, Mines and Forestry, and Stepan Karayan, former member of the Court of Cassation, were among the members of the committee.[88]

Hüseyin Cahit Yalçın, by common consent the best journalist Turkey had produced during the first half of the twentieth century, pays a high tribute to Halladjian's political sagacity, progressive instincts, loyalty to his country, and high character. Yalçın wrote of Halladjian in one of his memoir books *Tanıdıklarım* (My Acquaintances): "Halladjian proved to be true to the hopes that were based on him. He remained loyal to the Committee of Union and Progress till the last minute and did not deviate from the policy of Ottomanism."[89] Ottomanism was basically the concept of an identity and allegiance embracing all imperial subjects irrespective of their religion or of ethnic origin in a single Ottoman nation inhabiting the Ottoman fatherland. Halladjian was committed to the continuation of the empire as a political entity in which all elements would live harmoniously and in which Turks and Armenians, bound by the links of a recreated Ottomanism, would jointly cooperate in its government. He wisely felt that unity, not divided nationalities, should be the country's strength. He was certainly an Armenian, but as much an Ottoman. He was able to equate the identification with the ethnoreligious community with the more secular, western European concept of the state.[90]

Halladjian was a particularly close associate of Talat Paşa, in whom he saw an authentic Ottoman leader. Although from different backgrounds, he and Talat Paşa forged a friendship. The two frequently dined together.[91] Talat Paşa and Halladjian held a rally on 4 October 1912 about Ottoman entry into the Balkan War, after which they led several hundred İstanbul University students marching to the Sublime Porte. The Grand Vizier was called on to make his appearance. Gazi Ahmed Muhtar Paşa asked for a delegation to visit him, but the crowd refused to accept this proposal. The Grand Vizier and his son Mahmud Muhtar finally appeared, and were saluted with shouts of "Down with the Government!" "We Want War!"[92] They also demonstrated before the residence of Gabriel Noradounghian, Minister of Foreign Affairs, who appeared at a window and declared that all the necessary measures had been taken and that the rights of Ottomans would be safeguarded.[93]

On 23 January 1913 Halladjian told Colonel G.E. Tyrell, the military attaché of the British Embassy in İstanbul, that the whole army was with the Committee of Union and Progress in its determination not to accept peace with dishonor. Halladjian said the Ottoman army would sacrifice itself and fight to the death, but whatever happened, order would be preserved in İstanbul and complete tranquillity would reign.[94]

Halladjian was an example of a broader presence of Armenians within the upper echelons of the Ottoman leadership structure. As mentioned earlier, always considered the most trustworthy Christian subjects of the empire, Armenians were referred to in the Ottoman lexicon as *milleti sadıka* (loyal community) in recognition of the great devotion they had shown to the State. When the Ottoman Empire moved to modernize in the middle of the nineteenth century, the first Christians to enjoy the benefit of full citizenship were the Armenians. The first Christian Ministers and high dignitaries in the government were Armenians. During the times of the four great standard-bearers of reform and modernization, Reşid, Ali, Fuad, and Midhat Paşas, the chancery of the Ministry of Foreign Affairs were almost continously led by Armenians. So, too was the imperial bureau of translations, where political and diplomatic documents were translated into and from Turkish.[95]

Armenian liberals such as Krikor Odian played an influential role among Ottoman constitutionalists during the 1860s and 1870s. A close confidant of Mithat Paşa, Odian participated in drafting the first Ottoman constitution of 1876. After the Greek revolt of 1821 the Armenians began to occupy far more positions in the state bureacracy than their share of the overall population, and did so almost to the end of the Ottoman Empire. Increasingly active in government after the proclamation of the pro-democracy Imperial Edict of Reform of 1856, Armenians succeeded in reaching significant positions of power and influence in the Ottoman land. Cyrus Hamlin, the missionary-educator founder of Robert College in İstanbul, said in 1898: "The Armenians had always been loyal and useful until influence from abroad had changed the complexion of affairs. They had lived amicably with the Turks. The sub-departments of all the high offices were filled with Armenians."[96]

There existed many Armenian Cabinet members, Under Secretaries of State in the Ministries, members of Council of State (the highest administrative court in the realm), Ambassadors, Provincial Governors and Mayors in the late Ottoman period. Armenians were reserved one portfolio in each cabinet.

To name a few Armenian ministers will be illustrative. Krikor Agaton was the first non-Muslim achieving full ministerial rank in the Sublime Porte. He became Minister of Public Works in 1868. Garabed Artin Davud Paşa, who was successful in managing the construction of the Roumelian railway, later occupied the same ministerial post for a time. In 1877 Ohannes Chamich was Minister of Commerce and Agriculture. Krikor Sinapian, an Armenian Catholic, who had long been known as a lawyer of skill and reputation, joined the Cabinet as Minister of Agriculture, Mines and Forestry on 4 October 1911. Sinapian was for many years the legal advisor of the ministry, and had therefore a good deal of technical knowledge. He continued as Minister of Public Works in 1912. Stambulian, who was named Minister of Posts and Telegraphs on 6 July 1911, was an Armenian judicial inspector and a member of the lay council of the Gregorian church. Examples could be multiplied.

Gabriel Noradounghian played an important role in Ottoman politics and government after the proclamation of the constitution. Although he was a committed monarchist, Noradounghian approved of the Unionists' success in forcing Sultan Abdülhamid II to restore the constitution of 1876, which had not been in effect for thirty years, and to recall the Parliament, which had been dissolved in 1877. In 1908 he entered the Ottoman Party under the leadership of Amasya deputy İsmail Hakkı Paşa. In 1911 he joined the Party of Liberty and Entente which was composed of opposition senators and deputies, and some breakaway members from the Committee of Union and Progress. This party was initiated under the auspices of the well-known dissident former Colonel Sadık Bey. Noradounghian was a member of the Armenian National Assembly in 1908, and became its president in 1914.[97]

Noradounghian was also senator between 1908 and 1916, and served as minister of commerce and public works in 1908-1909.[98]

On his ministerial appointment, Noradounghian declared that roads and railways would have his first attention. Throughout the month of November 1908 in İstanbul he represented the Sublime Porte in the negotiations with the Bulgarian delegates in view of the discussion of the financial matters concerning the Public Debt, the payment of financial compensation to the Ottoman Empire over the Roumelian railways, and the religious endowment properties in Bulgaria. He was named permanent member of the Arbitration Tribunal at The Hague by the government on 21 January 1909.[99]

The Grand Vizier, Said Paşa, on 7 October 1911 summoned him to the Sublime Porte and, it is reported, offered him the portfolio of Foreign Affairs.[100]

Noradounghian became minister of foreign affairs in the grand cabinet formed by the decorated war hero and president of the Senate, the very popular Field Marshal Gazi Ahmed Muhtar Paşa, on 22 July 1912 to reestablish understanding among all Ottoman elements. The Cabinet of Grey-beards, as they were called, which kept strong links with the Liberty and Entente Party, received an enthusiastic welcome from the press, after restoring freedom of speech and announcing a general amnesty for all political crimes. Noradounghian continued to act as minister of foreign affairs in the cabinet of the experienced statesman Kamil Paşa in the critical years of 1912-1913. After arranging the Treaty of Ouchy of 15 October 1912 which formalized the loss of the Ottoman province of Tripolitania to the Italians in a bid to concentrate on the danger closer to home, the Armenian statesman proceeded to conduct the Ottoman diplomacy of the First Balkan War. [101]

On 4 November 1912, he presented to the Ambassadors of the European powers in İstanbul the request of the Sublime Porte for their mediation between the Ottoman Empire and the Balkan states of Montenegro, Serbia, Bulgaria, and Greece.

According to the American Ambassador to the Sublime Porte in 1911-1913, William Rockhill, the post of the minister of foreign affairs was offered by Mahmud Şevket Paşa in the subsequent Cabinet, not once but several times, to Noradounghian who refused.[102] The Armenian papers in İstanbul announced that the portfolio of Foreign Affairs was again offered on 24 January 1913 to Noradounghian, who refused it. [103] It is also reported that Talat Paşa requested him to take office in the new cabinet as minister of public works, Noradounghian declining the proposal.[104] There is no explanation available for his decision.

Armenians made up about one-third of the bureaucracy of the Ministry of Foreign Affairs by 1897. Ohannes Kuyumdjian was Under Secretary of State for Foreign Affairs between 1909 and 1912 in succession to Azarian Efendi. Kuyumdjian had occupied many important posts and amongst others that of Counselor of the Embassy in Rome for ten years. Said Bey, Kuyumdjian's successor at the ministry of foreign affairs, was the first Muslim to occupy the post for a long series of years, a fact due to the appointment having been made when a Christian, Noradounghian, was minister.

During the years of the First World War, Hrant Abro, an Armenian, was legal advisor of the Ottoman Ministry of Foreign Affairs and he accompanied Talat Paşa, Grand Vizier, and Ahmed Nesimi Bey, Minister of Foreign Affairs, at the Brest-Litovsk peace negotiations with Soviets which led to the signing of a treaty on 3 March 1918 restoring the districts of Kars and Ardahan, annexed from the Ottoman realm in 1878, and surrendering the Russian claim to capitulary privileges in the Ottoman Empire. Abro had earlier represented the Ottoman government in a variety of other diplomatic missions abroad. [105] For instance, Reşit Bey, Under Secretary of State for Foreign Affairs, and Abro had proceeded in March 1916 to Berlin to arrange details with the German government on the conclusion of a treaty for the establishment of a Deferential Tariff in the Turkish Customs, a treaty for new Consular Conventions, which not only abolished the Capitulations, but went far beyond the normal limits in giving the Ottomans rights over foreign subjects and a treaty for a Judicial Convention.[106]

Until the very end of the Ottoman Empire, Armenians were able to maintain the important positions they had held.[107] Again, the distinction with the case of the Jews living in Nazi Germany could not be more different.

Norman Stone, who taught at Cambridge and Oxford in Britain for thirty years before retiring early from the chair of modern history, in his most recent work *World War One: A Short History* recalls that in 1914 Boghos Nubar was offered a place in the government (he refused on the grounds that his Turkish was not up to the task).[108] As indicated earlier, Nubar was at the time touring Europe on behalf of his Armenian compatriots and acting in the name of the Catholicos of Etchmiadzin, the head of the Armenian Church all over the world.

Oskan Mardikian was minister of posts and telegraphs at the entry of the Ottoman Empire in the First World War on 29 October 1914. Because he believed entering the war was against the interests of the State, he resigned with three other ministers from the cabinet on November 2. There was no guarantee of a German victory, they argued, and in the event of defeat, the Entente powers would sweep the Ottoman Empire off the map. In retrospect, their prediction proved to be quite prescient.[109]

Halil Bey, Minister of Foreign Affairs, in an interview with the Associated Press representative on 25 October 1916, said the position of the Ottoman government on the Armenian question was never fully understood. And he went on:

> I wish to say that the Young Turks have always looked upon the Armenians as a valuable asset to the Ottoman Empire. The fact is, we needed them. The country's commerce was largely in their hands, and as farmers the Armenians have a great value. We did not look upon them as valuable chattels, however. We were willing to give them an equal share in the Government, which we did, as is shown by the fact that before the outbreak of war we had a large number of Armenians in the Chamber of Deputies and also several Senators and a Minister. Nearly all the Vice Ministers were Armenians, because we recognized the ability of the Armenians and were ready to give them their political rights in the tenancy of a proportionate number of public offices.[110]

The last dragoman of the British Embassy in the Ottoman Empire, Andrew Ryan, said that after the First World War most of the İstanbul Armenians were "quite ready to fit into a new Turkey, as they had fitted into the old system, in which they had played an important part, providing among other things many of the most capable officials in the administration."[111] Not surprisingly, Mustafa Kemal Paşa had an Armenian aide-de-camp in 1919.[112]

Under the Republic of Turkey, the Armenian community (like the Greek and Jewish communities) enjoyed autonomy in matters of personal and civil law in which their rites differed from those of Islam. Articles 37 to 45 of the Treaty of Lausanne of 24 July 1923, the founding document of the modern Turkish state, perpetuated these special privileges for minority communities, but the Armenians relinquished them on 29 October 1924 in favor of full Turkish citizenship. After considerable debate in February 1926 the Jewish community's leadership also renounced the rights to special personal status that they would have been accorded under the Treaty of Lausanne. The Jews professed their loyalty to Turkey and expressed full confidence that Turkish law would protect them. Marriage and divorce became civil matters, and practicing Judaism was a private concern. The republican administrations saw to it that the Armenian, Greek, and Jewish communities were represented in the parliament.[113]

In his annual report on Turkey for 1938 the British Ambassador at Ankara, Percy Loraine, wrote:

> The Turkish government is not anti-Semitic. It treats its Jewish and Christian minorities with moderation and has taken advantage of the anti-Jewish campaign in Europe in 1938 to allow entry into Turkey of a number of Jewish and other non-Aryan specialists.[114]

Here the comparison with the Holocaust is again revealing. After the Second World War, Europe's surviving Jews chose, almost without fail, to leave the continent of their birth and move to what was then the British Mandate of Palestine, the United States, or Canada. Most did so consciously, as they felt that Europe no longer had a Jewish future. Clearly, Armenians living within the Turkish Republic felt otherwise, and continue to feel that way, as evidenced by their ongoing citizenship.

Given the distinct treatment afforded Armenians prior to, during, and after the tragedy associated with their relocation, it is critical to look at the forced displacements and determine whether they pose a comparable event to the concentration and elimination of European Jews. That is to say, if Armenians in general received uneven treatment by the Ottoman Turks – with some suffering terribly but many others unaffected at all or treated with great care, how does that compare to the case of the Jews?

This is critical to the issue of defining the event. We understand the Holocaust as a genocide, because as University of Aberystwyth historian William Rubinstein defines it, genocide is "the deliberate killing of most or all members of a collective group for the mere fact of being members of that group." The Holocaust clearly falls into that definition. Rubinstein is not convinced the Armenian tragedy of 1915 meets the same definition. It is, he said, "difficult to fit into any typology, and much about it, especially on detailed analysis, remains rather mysterious: unlike the Jewish Holocaust, it is anything but straightforward." Rubinstein also rejects another term used to describe the tragedy: "Nor is it really accurate, except in hindsight, to term the Armenian deportations an example of ethnic cleansing, since Armenians were moved from one part of the Ottoman Empire to another while not all Armenians were deported."[115]

Moreover, the nature of those relocations is quite relevant. Whereas Jews were first concentrated in ghettos and then sent to death or slave labor camps with an expressed purpose of having them killed, Armenians were generally moved only when they posed a risk or record of insurrection. Rubinstein points out that the relocation of the Armenians was accomplished at a time of grave national crisis, with the existence of the state clearly hanging in the balance, akin to the context preceeding the internment of Japanese Americans in special camps following the imperial Japanese attack on Pearl Harbor.[116]

According to Rubinstein, an even clearer analogy is with Stalin's expulsion of Crimean Tatar, Kalmyk, Chechen-Ingush, Balkar and Karachai populations in whole or in part from their natal territories on the Soviet Union's southern borderlands to areas of "internal exile" in deep Uzbekistan, Kazakhstan, Kirghizia and Siberia on the charge of collective treason after the retreat of the German army from November 1943 to June 1944 and from July to December 1944. The chief motive of Stalin's policy was primarily strategic – the removal of potentially disruptive ethnic groups on its sensitive southern border -- rather than the pursuit of ethnic or religious purity. The Nazi destruction of the Jews, by comparison, was driven by a unique ethnoracist ideology, demanding national purity. Jews did not represent a strategic risk – they represented an affront to the metaphysical worldview of Nazi Germany.[117]

Bernard Lewis also explored the contrasts between the Jewish and Armenian cases:

> Unlike the persecution of the Jews, the suffering of the Armenians was limited both in time and place—to the Ottoman Empire and even there only to the last two decades of Ottoman history. More important, it was a struggle about real issues; it was never associated with the demonic beliefs or the almost physical hatred which inspired and directed anti-Semitism in Europe and sometimes elsewhere.[118]

By "real issues," he refers to wartime considerations which justified the Armenian relocations. The fact of Armenian revolts in the provinces of eastern Anatolia and Cilicia astride the main trunk roads and railways posed a significant military problem in the real sense. The Sublime Porte sought to counter this danger by removing the Armenian population from the route of the invading Russian armies and the threatening British navy.[119]

Lewis later advocated similar themes in his engaging and erudite *The Middle East A Brief History of the Last 2,000 Years*. He notes that in the spring of 1915, when Armenian rebels had gained control of Van, the British were at the Dardanelles, the Russians attacking in the east, and another British force advancing on Baghdad, the Ottoman government decided on the relocation of the Armenians. Lewis declines to call the Armenian tragedy a genocide.[120]

In response, Shayke Weinberg at the United States Holocaust Memorial Museum asked Lewis to expound on his thinking. On 11 October 1991 Lewis

wrote in reply. The Princeton professor said no one could doubt that the Ottoman Armenians, in 1915 and after, underwent appalling hardships and suffered
terrible loss of life. Nor could there be any doubt about the searing effect of
these experiences on the consciousness of Armenians there and elsewhere. Yet,
in spite of this, Lewis said the term "genocide" would be misleading, for the
following reasons:[121]

First, what happened to the Armenians did not happen to all Armenians.
Relocations were limited to certain areas. Some were relocated harshly, some
not. Armenians living elsewhere in the Ottoman Empire—in İstanbul and other
cities away from the areas of relocation—were unmolested except for the few
cases when specific criminal charges were brought against individuals.

Secondly, there was in the Ottoman Empire no equivalent to anti-Semitism,
a searing and historic ideology of hatred. There was no anti-Armenian ideology
or propaganda comparable with the Nazi doctrines and teachings that preceded
and accompanied the Holocaust, and which were used to justify it. There was
no attempt to assert that Armenians were inferior or noxious. The Turkish complaint about Armenians was quite specific—that they were disloyal to the Ottoman Empire and were sympathizers or active supporters of Russia, with which
the Empire was at war. The Turks saw them as a security risk, and therefore
decided to remove them, at whatever the cost, from strategic and vulnerable
areas in the Russian line of advance.

Thirdly, what happened in the small towns and villages of Turkey in Asia
was not one-sided. While a number of relocatees were innocent civilians, some
were active in an Armenian separatist movement and were seeking to achieve
independence from Ottoman rule. In an attempt to take advantage of the war
situation, Armenian bands operated behind the Ottoman lines, and attacked Ottoman installations, some of which were not of a military nature. These bands
were armed, trained, and in part directed by the Russians, and their activities
preceded, and to some extent caused, the relocation.

In addition, Lewis points out, there is great debate whether the death of
great numbers of Armenians was due to a deliberate policy of genocide on the
Ottoman side, or to the effects of a badly planned, badly-executed relocation in
a harsh terrain and in poor conditions. In the case of the Holocaust, there can be
no such disagreement.

Lewis said it is not easy to reconstruct what happened in remote mountain
areas almost a century ago, and these issues will no doubt be debated for a long
time to come. He also suggested that historians looking to distinguish the two
should not be charged with historical denial, as the historians seeking to define
genocide in a limited way should not be treated on the same level as those so-
called "historical revisionists" of the pro-Nazi lunatic fringe.

Lewis has not altered his view in the decades since. In a statement made in
response to a question asked of him in a 14 April 2002 appearance on Book TV

on the C-SPAN2 network, Lewis again clearly distinguished the Armenian case from the Holocaust. The question was,

> The British press reported in 1997 that your views on the killing of one million Armenians by the Turks in 1915 did not amount to genocide and this report in the *Independent* of London says that a French court fined you one franc in damages after you said there was no genocide. Have your views changed on this whether the killing of one million Armenians amounts to genocide and your views on this judgment?

He answered:

> The point that was being made was that the massacre of the Armenians in the Ottoman Empire was the same as what happened to Jews in Nazi Germany and that is a downright falsehood... To make this, a parallel with the Holocaust in Germany, you would have to assume the Jews of Germany had been engaged in armed rebellion against the German state, collaborating with the allies against Germany. That in the deportation order the cities of Hamburg and Berlin were exempted, persons in the employment of state were exempted, and the deportation only applied to the Jews of Germany proper, so that when they got to Poland they were welcome and sheltered by the Polish Jews. This seems to me a rather absurd parallel.[122]

Lewis' position has been buttressed by a number of specialists—including Patrick Brogan, who has spent over twenty-five years as a foreign correspondent on assignment for *The Times* of London, the New York *Daily News*, and *The Observer* on many international conflicts. Brogan points out that in 1915 when the Armenians were actively helping the Russians in eastern Anatolia and the British were at the gates of İstanbul, "Turkey's object was its own security, not genocide. There were no gas chambers."[123]

German historian Hans-Walter Schmuhl of Bielefeld University also examines the question of Armenian tragedy comparatively and posits that the history of the Holocaust presents only very superficial points of comparison. According to Schmuhl, Ottoman policies regarding the Armenian forced migration were not the result of a religious confrontation but instead followed a strategic calculation.[124]

Such German staff officers as General Friedrich Bronsart von Schellendorf, Chief of the Ottoman General Staff, Lieutenant Colonel Felix Guse, chief of staff of the Ottoman Third Army, Lieutenant Colonel Otto von Feldmann, head of operations division in the Ottoman General Staff and Lieutenant Commander Hans von Humann, naval attaché at the German Embassy in İstanbul had all recognized during the First World War years that the Armenian population displacements were justified by military necessity. They believed in freeing the rear of the army from Armenians. Further General Otto Liman von Sanders, head of the German military mission in the Ottoman Empire from December 1913 to the end of the First World War and the only German officer with ex officio command power, had testified at the 1921 trial of Talat Paşa's Armenian assassin that military necessity caused the relocations.[125]

NOTES

1. See, among others, BOA, DH ŞFR, No. 55/20. Circular to the Governors of Provinces of Erzurum, Adana, Bitlis, Halep, Bursa, Diyarbekir, Sivas, Trabzon, Konya, Mamuretülaziz, and Van, and to the Governors of Sanjaks of Urfa, İzmit, Canik, Karesi, Karahisarısahib, Kayseri, Maraş, Niğde, and Eskişehir on Non-relocation of Protestant Armenians, 15 August 1915; BOA, DH ŞFR, No. 54-A/252. Circular to the Governors of Provinces of Adana, Ankara, Bitlis, Halep, Diyarbekir, Sivas, Trabzon, Mamuretülaziz, and Van, and to the Governors of Sanjaks of Urfa, Canik and Maraş on Non-relocation of Catholic Armenians, 3 August 1915; BOA, DH ŞFR, No. 54/221. Circular to the Governors of Provinces of Erzurum, Adana, Ankara, Bitlis, Halep, Hüdavendigar, Diyarbekir, Sivas, Trabzon, Konya, and Van, and to the Governors of Sanjaks of Urfa, İzmit, Canik, Karesi, Karahisarısahib, Kayseri, Maraş, Niğde, and Eskişehir on Non-relocation of Armenian Officials of Major Foreign Banks and General Debt Administration and Their Families, 28 June 1915; BOA, DH ŞFR, No. 54/287. Circular to the Governors of the Provinces of Trabzon, Sivas, Diyarbekir, and Mamuretülaziz, and to the Governor of Sanjak of Canik on Non-relocation of Armenian Merchants and Craftsmen and Their Families, 4 July 1915; BOA, DH ŞFR, No. 56/176. Circular to the Governors of Provinces of Erzurum, Ankara, Adana, Bitlis, Halep, Hüdavendigar, Diyarbekir, Trabzon, and Konya, and to the Governors of Sanjaks of Urfa, İzmit, Canik, Sivas, Kayseri, Karahisarısahib, Karesi, Maraş, Niğde, and Eskişehir on Non-relocation of Armenian Medical Doctors and Their Families, 26 September 1915; ATESE, BDHK, Folder: 1329, File: 396-806, No. 1-43, 24 August 1915. Circular to the Army and Army Corps Commands on Non-relocation of Families of Armenian Army Officers and Soldiers, 15 August 1915; BOA, DH ŞFR, No. 55/48. Circular to the Governors of Provinces of Adana, Ankara, Aydın, Beyrut, Halep, Hüdavendigar, Suriye, and Konya, and to the Governors of Sanjaks of İzmit, Deyrüzzor, Karesi, Kudsi Şerif, Karahisarısahib, Eskişehir, Niğde, and Kütahya on Non-relocation of Armenian Railway Officials, Workers and Employees and Their Families, 17 August 1915.

2. Harry Franck, *The Fringe of the Moslem World* (New York: Grosset and Dunlop Publishers, 1928), pp. 297-298.

3. Ian Kershaw, *Fateful Choices: Ten Decisions That Changed the World 1940-1941*(New York: The Penguin Press, 2007), pp. 432-433. For a similar analysis with more nuance see the Hebrew University of Jerusalem professor Robert Wistrich, *Hitler and the Holocaust* (New York: Modern Library, 2001), p. 238.

4. Kevork Pamukciyan, *Ermeni Kaynaklarından Tarihe* Katkılar (Contributions to History from the Armenian Sources), Vol. 3: *Zamanlar, Mekanlar, İnsanlar* (Times, Places, Men), (İstanbul: Aras Yayınları, 2003), p. 292. This four-volume set is a treasure trove for anyone interested in the history of the Ottoman Armenians. On Armenian conversions see also BOA, DH ŞFR, No. 54/100. Circular to the Governors of Provinces

and Sanjaks of Van, Trabzon, Erzurum, Bitlis, Mamuretülaziz, Diyarbekir, Sivas, and Canik regarding the Armenian Adoption of Islam, 22 June 1915 and BOA, DH ŞFR, No. 58/146. Ciphered Telegram to the Governor of Karahisarısahib regarding the Armenian Women's Adoption of Islam, 25 November 1915.

5. Richard Hovannisian, "The Question of Altruism During the Armenian Genocide of 1915," in Pearl Oliner, Samuel Oliner, Lawrence Baron, Lawrence Blum, Dennis Krebs, and Zuzanna Smolenska, eds., *Embracing the Other: Philosophical, Psychological, and Historical Perspectives on Altruism* (New York and London: New York University Press, 1992), p. 295.

6. Lewy, "The First Genocide of the 20th Century?," p. 51. On the areas to be evacuated by the Armenian population see BOA, MV, No. 198/24. Minutes of the Council of Ministers Meeting, 30 May 1915.

7. Lewy, *The Armenian Massacres in Ottoman Turkey*, p. 251.

8. Michael Gunter, *"Pursuing the Just Cause of Their People": A Study of Contemporary Armenian Terrorism* (Westport, Connecticut: Greenwood Press, 1986), p.23.

9. According to the law of 2 July 1934, all Turks assumed a family name. For the earlier, family names which are later adopted will be given in parentheses on the first appearance of the particular person.

10. "Rapport provenant du Service des Renseignements anglais au Ministère de la Guerre" in Arthur Beylerian, ed. and comp., *Les grand puissances, L'Empire Ottoman et les Arméniens dans les Archives Françaises (1914-1918)*, (Paris: Université de Paris I, Panthéon-Sorbonne, 1983), p. 208. On Faik Ali Ozansoy's governorship of the sanjak of Kütahya and the Armenians see Ömer Çakır, "Birlikte Yaşamak: Faik Ali Bey ve Kütahya Ermenileri" (Living Together: Faik Ali Bey and the Armenians of Kütahya), in Metin Hülagü, Şakir Batmaz, Gülbadi Alan, Süleyman Demirci, eds., *Hoşgörü Toplumunda Ermeniler* (Armenians in the Society of Tolerance), Vol.3, (Kayseri: Erciyes Üniversitesi Yayını, 2007), pp. 475-488 and Sarkis Seropyan, "Vicdanlı Türk Valisi Faik Ali Ozansoy"(Conscientous Turkish Governor Faik Ali Ozansoy), *Toplumsal Tarih*, Vol. 4, No. 23 (November 1995), pp. 46-50.

11. Nora Levin, *The Holocaust Years: The Nazi Destruction of European Jewry, 1933-1945* (Malabar, Florida: Krieger Publishing Company, 1992), pp. 238-242; Michael Berenbaum, *The World Must Know: The History of the Holocaust as Told in the United States Holocaust Memorial Museum* (New York: Little, Brown and Company, 1993), p. 105.

12. Norman Naimark, *Fires of Hatred: Ethnic Cleansing in Twentieth-Century Europe* (Cambridge, Massachusetts: Harvard University Press, 2001), pp. 3 and 35-36.

13. William Rubinstein, *Genocide: A History* (Harlow: Pearson Education Ltd., 2004), pp. 132-133. This important book adopts an explicitly comparative approach to its theme. The author identifies the broad contextual as well as immediate political factors that led to the developments in each of the cases he examines in detail.

14. Aliyar Demirci, "İkinci Meşrutiyet Birinci ve İkinci Yasama Döneminde (1908-1914) Osmanlı Ayan Meclisinin Ermeni Üyeleri ve Faaliyetleri" (Armenian Members of the Ottoman Chamber of Notables and Their Activities in the First and Second Legislative Terms [1908-1914] of the Second Constitutionalism), in Şenol Kantarcı, Kamer Kasım, İbrahim Kaya, Sedat Laçiner, eds., *Ermeni Araştırmaları Birinci Türkiye Kongresi Bildirileri* (Communications Presented at the First Turkish Congress on Armenian Studies), Vol.1, (Ankara: Avrasya Stratejik Araştırmalar Merkezi Ermeni Araştırmaları

Enstitüsü Yayınları, 2003), pp. 309-311.

15. The Young Turk Revolution of 1908 is described in much detail in British Parliamentary Papers, Accounts and Papers (1909), CV, (Cd. 4529), pp. 943-1082.

16. Feroz Ahmad-Dankwart Rustow, "İkinci Meşrutiyet Döneminde Meclisler 1908-1918" (Chambers in the Period of Second Constitutionalism 1908-1918), *Güney-Doğu Avrupa Araştırmaları Dergisi,* Nos. 4-5 (1976), pp. 245-284 and Recep Karacakaya, "Meclis-i Mebusan Seçimleri ve Ermeniler 1908-1914" (Chamber of Deputies Elections and the Armenians 1908-1914), *Yakın Dönem Türkiye Araştırmaları,* No. 3 (2003), pp. 135-140.

17. Ahmed Emin Yalman, ed., Erol Şadi Erdinç, *Yakın Tarihte Gördüklerim ve Geçirdiklerim* (What I Have Seen and Experienced in Recent History), Vol. 1: 1888-1922, (İstanbul: Pera Turizm ve Ticaret A.Ş, reprinted, 1997), p. 400; Fethiye Çetin, *Anneannem* (My Grandmother), (İstanbul: Metis Yayınları, 2005); İrfan Palalı, *Tehcir Çocukları Nenem Bir Ermeniymiş* (Children of the Relocations: My Grandmother Had Been An Armenian), (İstanbul: Su Yayınları, 2005); Baskın Oran, ed., *"M.K." Adlı Çocuğun Tehcir Anıları 1915 ve Sonrası* (Relocation Reminiscences of a Child Called "M.K." 1915 and Beyond), (İstanbul: İletişim Yayınları, 2005); Erhan Başyurt, *Ermeni Evlatlıklar Saklı Kalmış Hayatlar* (Armenian Adopted Children: Hidden Lives), (İstanbul: Karakutu Yayınları, 2006); Alice Clark, *Letters from Cilicia* (Chicago: A.D. Weinthrop and Company, 1924), p. 119.

18. Letter from Donald Webster to George Deukmejian, Governor of California, Claremont/California, 25 April 1983.

19. BOA, DH ŞFR, No. 96/75. Circular to the Governors of Provinces and Sanjaks on the Reconnection of Armenian Women and Children with Their Families and Communities, 21 October 1918. Also see the instructions sent to the Governor of the Province of Adana on the same subject BOA, DH ŞFR, No. 94/56, 4 December 1918; Naimark, *Fires of Hatred,* pp. 35-36 and 42. For an insightful analysis of the plight of the disunited Ottoman Armenian women and children see particularly İbrahim Ethem Atnur, *Türkiye'de Ermeni Kadınları ve Çocukları Meselesi* (The Question of Armenian Women and Children in Turkey), (Ankara: Babil Yayınları, 2005) and idem, "Kadınlar ve Çocuklar" (Women and Children), in Hikmet Özdemir, ed., *Türk-Ermeni İhtilafı Makaleler* (Turkish-Armenian Conflict: Articles), (Ankara: Türkiye Büyük Millet Meclisi Kültür, Sanat ve Yayın Kurulu Yayınları, 2007), pp. 305-325. İbrahim Ethem Atnur's research, drawing upon sources untapped by previous historians, clearly surpasses its predecessors in scope and authority.

20. Clair Price, "A Defense of Young Turkey," *The New York Times Book Review and Magazine,* 3 July 1921, p. 34. Turks often adopted Armenian and Greek children, and few could recognize them as any but good Muslim Turks afterward. See Franck, *The Fringe of the Moslem World,* p. 299.

21. Djemal Pasha, *Memories of a Turkish Statesman 1913-1919* (New York: George Doran Company, 1922), pp. 277-279 and idem, "Zur Frage der Greuel in Armenien: Eine Rechtfertigungsschrift," *Franfurter Zeitung,* 3 September 1919, p. 1. See also Celalettin Yavuz, "Göçmenler ve Cemal Paşa" (Emigrants and Cemal Paşa), in Özdemir, ed., *Türk-Ermeni İhtilafı Makaleler,* pp. 277-303.

22. Djemal Pasha, *Memories of a Turkish Statesman 1913-1919,* p. 301.

23. Bernard Lewis, *The Emergence of Modern Turkey* (London: Oxford University Press, 2ⁿᵈ ed., 1968), p. 226.

24. Frank Chambers, *The War Behind the War 1914-1918: A History of the Political and Civilian Fronts* (London: Faber and Faber Limited, 1939), p. 60.

25. Nevzat Artuç, *Cemal Paşa* (Ankara: Türk Tarih Kurumu, 2008).

26. USNA, 867.4016/212-554. Cemal Paşa's Aid to the Armenian Exiles. Henry Morgenthau (Istanbul) to Robert Lansing (Department of State), 22 October 1915.

27. Friedrich Freiherr Kress von Kressenstein, "Zwischen Kaukasus und Sinai," *Jahrbuch des Bundes der Asienkämpfer*, Vols. 1 and 2 (1921-1922). These two articles are summarized in the *Journal of the Royal United Service Institution*, Vol. 67 (February 1922), pp. 503-513, as "The Campaign in Palestine from the Enemy's Side."

28. Friedrich Freiherr Kress von Kressenstein, *Mit den Türken zum Suezkanal* (Berlin: Vorhut-Verlag, 1938), pp. 127-129 and 132-137. This work is translated into Turkish by Mazhar Besim Özalpsan, *Türklerle Beraber Süveyş Kanalına* (İstanbul: Askeri Matbaa, 1943).

29. Ali Fuad Erden, ed., Alpay Kabacalı, *Birinci Dünya Harbinde Suriye Hatıraları* (Recollections of Syria in the First World War), (İstanbul: Türkiye İş Bankası Kültür Yayınları, reprinted, 2003), pp. 148-155. There is no biography of Ali Fuad Erden. His memoir, *Paris'ten Tih Sahrasına* (From Paris to the Tih Desert), (Ankara: Ulus Basımevi, reprinted, 1949), is the single best source of information on his early life and his experiences in the First World War.

30. Halidé Edib Adıvar, *Memoirs of Halidé Edib* (Piscataway, New Jersey: Gorgias Press, reprinted, 2004), pp. 389, 391, 406-407 and 428. See also idem, *House with Wisteria: Memoirs of Halidé Edib* (Charlottesville, Virginia: Leopolis Press, 2nd ed., 2003), pp. 321 and 335-336. A prominent novelist, social activist, and journalist Halidé Edib Adıvar was one of Turkey's leading feminists in the Second Constitutional and early Republican period. *Memoirs of Halidé Edib* was first published in New York and London by The Century Company in 1926.

31. USNA, T-137/24/0766-69. Microcopy of the German Foreign Ministry Archives, 1867-1920 (T-137), Reel (24), Frame (0766-69). Max von Oppenheim (Damascus) to Theobald von Betmann Hollweg (Berlin), 9 August 1915.

32. Wolfgang Gust, ed., *Der Völkermord an den Armeniern 1915/16 Dokumente aus dem Politischen Archiv des deutschen Auswärtigen Amts* (Springe: Zu Klampen, 2005), pp.271-277. This 675 page volume is a selection of some 218 telegrams, letters and reports from German diplomatic and consular officials in the Ottoman Empire to the Ministry of Foreign Affairs in Berlin on the Armenian events of 1915-1916. On Max von Oppenheim's intimate knowledge of the Ottoman Empire in 1915 see his *Die Nachrichtenstelle der Kaiserlich Deutschen Botschaft in Konstantinopel und die deutsche wirtschafliche Propaganda in der Türkei* (Berlin: Reichsdruckerei, 1916) and FO 371/2489/262274. Pan-Islamic Mission of Baron Max von Oppenheim. Sir Rennell Rodd (Rome) to Sir Edward Grey (FO), 29 May 1915; FO 371/2489/262274. Mark Sykes Reporting Departure of Baron Max von Oppenheim from Istanbul to the Interior. Albert Wratislaw (Salonika) to Sir Edward Grey (FO), 1 July 1915.

33. Gust, ed., *Der Völkermord an den Armeniern 1915/16 Dokumente aus dem Politischen Archiv des deutschen Auswärtigen Amts*, pp.396-397.

34. Ibid., pp. 134-135.

35. Ibid., pp. 418-419.

36. "Resistance to Turkish Orders," *The Christian Science Monitor*, 17 August 1916, p. 3.

37. "Rapport d'un habitant d'Athlit, région du mont Carmel (Syrie) sur les massacres d'Arméniens," in Beylerian, ed. and comp., *Les grandes puissances, L'Empire Ottoman et les Arméniens dans les Archives Françaises (1914-1918)*, pp. 286-290; Yair Auron, *The Banality of Indifference: Zionism and the Armenian Genocide* (New Brunswick, New Jersey: Transaction Publishers, 2003), pp. 377-378.

38. James Barton, *Story of Near East Relief (1915-1930): An Interpretation* (New York: The Macmillan Company, 1930), p. 72. James Barton, secretary of the American Board of Commissioners for Foreign Missions, had been for years a resident in the Ottoman Empire and was a member of the Board of Trustees of several American colleges there.

39. Frederick Bliss, "Djemal Pasha: A Portrait," *The Nineteenth Century and After*, Vol. 136, No. DX14 (December 1919), p. 1152.

40. Papers of the American Board of Commissioners for Foreign Missions (henceforth referred to as ABCFM), Houghton Library, Harvard University. 87/257, Unit 5 (ABC 16.9.5) Reel 672. The Exiling of the Armenians of the Adana District, Elizabeth Webb. To this report is attached a statement by James Barton, who affirmed that Elizabeth Webb was thoroughly familiar with the Ottoman Empire and that her testimony was worthy of credence and confidence. For the same testimony see also USNA, Inquiry Documents: Special Reports and Studies, 1917-1919, Document 819, Elizabeth Webb, "The Exiling of the Armenians, Adana District," 1 June 1918.

41. James Kay Sutherland, *The Adventures of an Armenian Boy: An Autobiography and Historical Narrative Encompassing the Last Thirty Years of the Ottoman Empire* (Ann Arbor, Michigan: Ann Arbor Press, 1964), p. 146.

42. Ibid., pp. 147-148.

43. Yervant Odian (trans. Ara Stepan Melkonian), *Accursed Years: My Exile and Return from Der Zor, 1914-1919* (London: Gomidas Institute, 2009).

44. Vahakn Dadrian, *The Key Elements in the Turkish Denial of the Armenian Genocide: A Case Study of Distortion and Falsification* (Toronto: Zoryan Institute, 1999), p. 54 fn 64.

45. Great Britain. *The Treatment of Armenians in the Ottoman Empire 1915-1916*, Parliamentary Papers Miscellaneous No. 31 (London: Joseph Causton, 1916), p. 543. Also James Bryce and Arnold Toynbee, eds., *The Treatment of Armenians in the Ottoman Empire 1915-1916* (Princeton, New Jersey: Gomidas Institute, Uncensored Edition, 2000).

46. USNA, 867.00/797-785. Political Situation of the Ottoman Provinces Adjacent to the Caucasus. David Francis (Petrograd) to Robert Lansing (Department of State), 4 June 1917.

47. Lewy, *The Armenian Massacres in Ottoman Turkey*, pp. 112, 192, 194-195 and 218-219. Interestingly, according to the Turkish journalist and writer Falih Rıfkı Atay, who was chief of the second division in charge of political and administrative affairs at the headquarters of the Fourth Army in 1915-1917, Cemal Paşa conceived that the Armenians would not create any political or social problem in Syria—to the contrary, they would serve as a buffer against the emergent Arab nationalist movements. See Falih Rıfkı Atay, *Zeytindağı* (Mount of Olives), (İstanbul: Bateş Yayınları, reprinted, 1981), pp. 65-66. This biographical account was first published in 1932.

48. Fuat Dündar, *Modern Türkiye'nin Şifresi İttihat ve Terakki'nin Etnisite Mühendisliği (1913-1918)* [Cipher of Modern Turkey: Ethnicity Engineering of the

Committee of Union and Progress (1913-1918)], (İstanbul: İletişim Yayınları, 2008).

49. "Proclamation to the Peoples of Syria and Palestine," *The Orient*, 20 January 1915, p. 1.

50. On Cemal Paşa's distribution of provision from army stores to Armenians in Syria see, among many others, BOA, DH ŞFR, No. 56/123, 22 August 1915; BOA, DH ŞFR, No. 64/116, 23 May 1916; BOA, DH ŞFR, No. 53/317, 6 November 1916. For the background, development, significance and consequences of the First World War famine in Syria and Palestine see Linda Schatkowski Schilcher, "The Famine of 1915-1918 in Greater Syria," in John Spagnolo, ed., *Problems of the Modern Middle East in Historical Perspective* (Reading: Ithaca Press, 1992), pp. 229-258.

51. Bliss, "Djemal Pasha: A Portrait," p. 1152.

52. USNA, 367.11/1470. Internal Situation in the Ottoman Empire. Abram Elkus (Istanbul) to Robert Lansing (Department of State), 27 November 1916; USNA, 867.00/809. Report on the General Situation in the Ottoman Empire. Frederick Wirth, Jr. (Berne) to Robert Lansing (Department of State), 5 December 1917.

53. USNA, 867.00/797. Personal and Confidential Letter Concerning the Conditions in the Ottoman Empire. Henry Morgenthau (Istanbul) to Robert Lansing (Department of State), 4 November 1915.

54. Cemal Paşa was nominated to governorship of Adana on 1 August 1909 and his term of duty had terminated on 14 June 1911. See BOA, Dahiliye İradeleri (Formal Decrees of the Ministry of the Interior) (henceforth referred to as İ. DH), 1 August 1909 and BOA, İ. DH, 14 June 1911.

55. Bayram Kodaman and Mehmet Ali Ünal, eds., *Son Vakanüvis Abdurrahman Şeref Efendi Tarihi İkinci Meşrutiyet Olayları (1908-1909)* {History of the Last Chronicler Abdurrahman Şeref Efendi: Events of Second Constitutionalism (1908-1909)}, (Ankara: Türk Tarih Kurumu, 1996), pp. 71-81. The tome contains an exhaustive survey of the subject. See also Mehmet Asaf (İsmet Parmaksızoğlu {ed.}), *1909 Adana Ermeni Olayları ve Anılarım* (1909 Armenian Incidents of Adana and My Reminiscences), (Ankara: Türk Tarih Kurumu, 1982); FO 195/2363. Annual Report on Turkey for the Year 1909. Sir Gerard Lowther (Istanbul) to Sir Edward Grey (FO), 7 February 1910 and William Nesbitt Chambers, *Yoljuluk: Random Thoughts on a Life in Imperial Turkey* (London: Simpkin Marshall Limited, 1928; republished, Paramus, New Jersey: Armenian Missionary Association of America, 1988), pp. 78-79.

56. "On Adana Incidents," *Tanin*, 11 May 1909, p. 2; Charles Woods, *The Danger Zone of Europe: Changes and Problems in the Near East* (London: T. Fisher Unwin, 1911), pp.133-134; Papers of the ABCFM, Library of Congress Manuscript Division 87/257 Unit 5 (ABC 16.9.5), Reel 665, Letter from Stephen van Trowbridge to William Peet, Bible House, Istanbul, 23 April 1909, Adana.

57. Kodaman and Ünal, eds., *Son Vakanüvis Abdurrahman Şeref Efendi*, pp. 104-116.

58. Colonel Cemal Bey being promoted to the rank of Brigadier General on 3 January 1914 was thenceforth called Cemal Paşa. See BOA, Harbiye İradeleri (Imperial Decrees of the Ministry of War), 3 January 1914.

59. Woods, *The Danger Zone of Europe*, pp. 194-195.

60. Djemal Pasha, *Memories of a Turkish Statesman 1913-1919*, pp. 261-262. Adana was a station of the ABCFM, with a working force of five missionaries and twenty-two native workers. The city was an out-station of the synod of the Reformed Presby-

terian church of North America and a Bible depot and sub-agency family Bible society.

61. FO 371/780. Affairs in the Levant: Report from H.M.S. "Barham." Herbert Adam, Commander to Admiralty, 13 October 1909.

62. Djemal Pasha, *Memories of a Turkish Statesman 1913-1919*, p. 262.

63. Andrew Ryan, *The Last of the Dragomans* (London: Geoffrey Bles, 1951), p. 66.

64. Ibid., p. 85.

65. FO 195/2363. Annual Report on Turkey for the Year 1910. Sir Gerard Lowther (Istanbul) to Sir Edward Grey (FO), 14 February 1911.

66. Dikran Mesrob Kaligian, *Armenian Organization and Ideology under Ottoman Rule 1908-1914* (New Brunswick, New Jersey and London: Transactions Publishers, 2009), p. 71.

67. James Harbord, "Investigating Turkey and Trans-Caucasia," *The World's Work*, Vol.15 (May 1920-October 1920), p. 41. James Harbord had commanded American troops at Soissons and Château-Thierry in France, and served as chief of staff under General John Pershing in 1917-1918.

68. Chambers, *Yoljuluk*, pp. 91-93.

69. Ibid., p.94.

70. Woods, *The Danger Zone of Europe*, p.142.

71. Zeeneb Charlton, "Six Ottoman Patriots," *The Nineteenth Century and After*, Vol. 124, No.CCCCXLII (December 1913), p. 1227. See also Lucy Cavendish, "The Peril of Armenia," *The Contemporary Review*, Vo l. CIII, No. 1 (January 1913), p. 39.

72. "Situation in Cilicia," *The Orient*, Vol. 2, No. 28 (25 October 1911), p. 3.

73. Dorothea Chambers Blaisdell, *Missionary Daughter: Witness to the End of the Ottoman Empire* (Bloomington, Indiana: 1ˢᵗ Books Library, 2002), p. 76.

74. On Ara Sarafian's statement, see "Study the Armenian Genocide with Confidence, Ara Sarafian Suggests," *The Armenian Reporter*, 18 December 2008, p. 1.

75. Nuri Akbayar, Raşit Çavaş, Yücel Demirel, Bahattin Öztuncay, Mete Tunçay, eds., *İkinci Meşrutiyetin İlk Yılı 23 Temmuz 1908-23 Temmuz 1909* (The First Year of the Second Constitutionalism: 23 July 1908-23 July 1909), (İstanbul: Yapı Kredi Yayınları, 2008), pp. 167, 344 and 360; Lütfi Simavi, *Osmanlı Sarayının Son Günleri* (The Last Days of the Ottoman Court), (İstanbul: Hürriyet Yayınları, reprinted, 1973), pp. 96-98; Galip Kemali Söylemezoğlu, *Hariciye Hizmetinde Otuz Sene* (Thirty Years in the Service of the Ministry of Foreign Affairs), Vol. 1: 1892-1922, (İstanbul: Şaka Matbaası, 1949), p. 210 and Anahide Ter Minassian, "The Role of the Armenian Community in the Foundation and Development of the Socialist Movement in the Ottoman Empire and Turkey: 1876-1923," in Mete Tunçay and Erich Zürcher, eds., *Socialism and Nationalism in the Ottoman Empire 1876-1923* (London: British Academy Press, 1994), p. 140.

76. For Bedros Halladjian's biographical details see *Türk Parlamento Tarihi* (History of the Turkish Parliament), *Birinci ve İkinci Meşrutiyet* (First and Second Constitutionalism), Vol. 2, (Ankara: Türkiye Büyük Millet Meclisi Basımevi Müdürlüğü, 1998), p. 402; Yervant Gomitas Çarkcıyan, *Türk Devleti Hizmetinde Ermeniler 1453-1953* (Armenians at the Service of the Turkish State 1453-1953), (İstanbul: Kesit Yayınları, reprinted, 2006), p. 151 and Pamukciyan, *Ermeni Kaynaklarından Tarihe Katkılar*, Vol. 4: *Biyografileriyle Ermeniler* (Armenians With Their Biographies), p. 238.

77. For Halladjian's membership of the Central Committee of the Committee of Union and Progress consult Hüseyin Kazım Kadri, ed., İsmail Kara, *Meşrutiyetten*

Cumhuriyete Anılarım (My Reminiscences from the Constitutionalism to the Republic), (İstanbul: Dergah Yayınları, reprinted, 2000), p. 134.

78. FO 195/2363. Annual Report on Turkey for the Year 1908. Turkish Ministers and Other Leading Politicians: Bedros Halladjian. Sir Gerard Lowther (Istanbul) to Sir Edward Grey (FO), 17 February 1909. Since 1881, the European-dominated Ottoman Public Debt Administration had control of all revenues raised through customs and tax collection in the empire, from monopoly duties on salt, silk and tobacco production to sales taxes on alcohol and stamps. No less than four-fifths of the revenues collected from these duties went to payment of interest on the Ottoman debt.

79. Bedross Der Matossian, Ethnic Politics in Post-Revolutionary Ottoman Empire: Armenians, Arabs, and Jews during the Second Constitutional Period (1908-1909), doctoral dissertation, Columbia University, 2008, pp. 310-311.

80. Ibid., p. 311.

81. Ibid., p. 312.

82. Feroz Ahmad, "İkinci Meşrutiyet Döneminde Jön Türk-Ermeni İlişkileri 1908-1914" (Young Turk-Armenian Relations in the Period of Second Constitutionalism 1908-1914), in Metin Hülagü, Şakir Batmaz, Gülbadi Alan, Süleyman Demirci, eds., *Hoşgörü Toplumunda Ermeniler*, Vol. 2, p. 185.

83. Feroz Ahmad, "The Special Relationship: The Committee of Union and Progress and the Ottoman Jewish Political Elite, 1908-1918," in Avigdor Levy, ed., *Jews, Turks, Ottomans: A Shared History, Fifteenth Through the Twentieth Century* (Syracuse: Syracuse University Press, 2002), pp. 215-216.

84. "The New Minister of Public Works," *İttihad*, 9 September 1909, p. 1.

85. FO 195/2363. Annual Report on Turkey for the Year 1910. Sir Gerard Lowther (Istanbul) to Sir Edward Grey (FO), 14 February 1911; British Documents on Foreign Affairs: Reports and Papers from the Foreign Office Confidential Print, eds., Kenneth Bourne and Donald Cameron Watt, Part 1: From the Mid-Nineteenth Century to the First World War, Series: B: The Near and Middle East, 1856-1914, Vol. 20: The Ottoman Empire under the Young Turks, 1908-1914 (Frederick, Maryland: University Publications of America, 1985), pp. 64-65, 116, 131, 141, 170 and 182.

86. Martin Gilbert, *Winston S. Churchill*, Vol. 3: *1914-1916 The Challenge of War* (Boston: Houghton Mifflin Company, 1971), pp. 188-189.

87. There is no biography of Halil Menteşe. His career may be followed in İsmail Arar, ed., *Osmanlı Mebusan Meclisi Reisi Halil Menteşe'nin Anıları* (Memoirs of the President of the Ottoman Chamber of Deputies Halil Menteşe), (İstanbul: Hürriyet Vakfı Yayınları, 1986).

88. "Modernization of Ottoman Legislation," Editorial, *Osmannischer Lloyd*, 27 June 1916, p. 1; "Transformation of Turkish Law," *Levant Trade Review*, Vol. 6, No. 1(June 1916), p. 82.

89. Hüseyin Cahit Yalçın, ed., Cemil Koçak, *Tanıdıklarım*, (My Acquaintances), (İstanbul: Yapı Kredi Yayınları, reprinted, 2001), p. 156. Hüseyin Cahit Yalçın's memoir books are an indispensable source of information about the leading personalities of the Committee of Union and Progress period. See also his *Talat Paşa* (İstanbul: Yedigün Neşriyat, 1943) and idem, ed., Rauf Mutluay, *Siyasal Anılar* (Political Reminiscences), (İstanbul: Türkiye İş Bankası Yayınları, reprinted, 2000). For a comprehensive study on Hüseyin Cahit Yalçın see Hilmi Bengi, *Gazeteci, Siyasetçi ve Fikir Adamı Olarak Hüseyin Cahit Yalçın* (Hüseyin Cahit Yalçın As Journalist, Politician, and Intellectual),

(Ankara: Atatürk Araştırma Merkezi, 2000).

90. Cavit Bey, ed., Osman Selim Kocahanoğlu, *Felaket Günleri Mütareke Devrinin Feci Tarihi* (Days of Disaster: Tragic History of the Armistice Period), Vol. 1, (İstanbul: Temel Yayınları, 2000), pp. 297-298 and Vol. 2, pp. 35, 76, 119-120, 248-249, 301-302, 306-307, 314, 332 and 337.

91. Talat Paşa, *Hatıralarım ve Müdafaam* (My Reminiscences and Defense), (İstanbul: Kaynak Yayınları, reprinted, 2006), p. 61; Hüseyin Cahit Yalçın, ed., Osman Selim Kocahanoğlu, *İttihatçı Liderlerin Gizli Mektupları* (The Secret Letters of the Unionist Leaders), (İstanbul: Temel Yayınları, 2002), pp. 145-146; Arsen Avagyan and Gaidz Minassian (trans. Ludmilla Denisenko and Mutlucan Şahan), *Ermeniler ve İttihat ve Terakki İşbirliğinden Çatışmaya* (Armenians and the Committee of Union and Progress: From Cooperation to Conflict), (İstanbul: Aras Yayıncılık, 2005), pp. 126, 192 and 197. I wish to thank Professor Şükrü Hanioğlu, Garrett Professor in Foreign Affairs and head of Near Eastern Studies Department at the Princeton University, for making available to me copy of a personal handwritten note of 1909 by Talat Paşa addressed to Halladjian calling him brother.

92. Hasan Babacan, *Mehmet Talat Paşa 1874-1921* (Ankara: Türk Tarih Kurumu, 2005), p. 69; "Constantinople Letter," *The Near East*, Vol. 3, No. 76 (18 October 1912), p. 623.

93. "Yesterday's Meetings," *The Levant Herald*, 5 October 1912, p. 1.

94. FO 195/2451. Coup d'état in Istanbul. Colonel G.E. Tyrell (Military Attaché) to Sir Gerard Lowther (Ambassador), 23 January 1913.

95. Minassian, "The Role of the Armenian Community in the Foundation and Development of the Socialist Movement in the Ottoman Empire and Turkey: 1876-1923," p. 117.

96. Cyrus Hamlin, "The Genesis and Evolution of the Turkish Massacre of Armenian Subjects," *Proceedings of the American Antiquarian Society*, April 1898, pp. 288-289.

97. A biography of Gabriel Noradounghian has yet to be written. On his political background see Aykut Kansu, *Politics in Post-Revolutionary Turkey 1908-1913* (Leiden: E.J. Brill, 2000), pp. 56, 87, 130, 136, 153, 210, 396 and 437 and Naim Turfan, *Rise of the Young Turks: Politics, the Military, and Ottoman Collapse* (London and New York: I.B. Tauris Publishers, 2000), pp. 202-203, 205, 207-208 and 309. On Party of Liberty and Entente see Ali Birinci, *Hürriyet ve İtilaf Fırkası* (Party of Liberty and Entente), (İstanbul: Dergah Yayınları, 1990.)

98. Gabriel Noradounghian was nominated to senatorship on 15 December 1908. See BOA, Dosya Usulü İradeler (Dossier Method Formal Decrees [DUİT]), 5/6-1-1, 15 December 1908. On his activities in the Ottoman Senate or the Chamber of Notables see Demirci, "İkinci Meşrutiyet Birinci ve İkinci Yasama Döneminde (1908-1914) Osmanlı Ayan Meclisinin Ermeni Üyeleri ve Faaliyetleri," pp. 309-311. On Noradounghian, as minister of commerce and public works, consult Nuri Akbayar, Raşit Çavaş, Yücel Demirel, Bahattin Öztuncay, Mete Tunçay, eds., *İkinci Meşrutiyetin İlk Yılı*, pp.167 and 302 ; Söylemezoğlu, *Hariciye Hizmetinde Otuz Sene*, pp. 209-210 and Edwin Pears, "The Turkish Revolution," *The Contemporary Review*, Vol. 154, No. 3 (September 1908), p. 296.

99. Edwin Pears, "The Baghdad Railway," *The Contemporary Review*, Vol. 154, No. 5 (November 1908), p. 591 and "Les Travaux Publics," *The Levant Herald*, 9 Sep-

tember 1909, p. 1.

100. "The Ministry for Foreign Affairs," *The Levant Herald*, 8 October 1911, p. 1.

101. For Gabriel Noradounghian's ministerial posts see *Türk Parlamento Tarihi* (History of the Turkish Parliament), *Birinci ve İkinci Meşrutiyet* (First and Second Constitutionalism), Vol. 1, (Ankara: Türkiye Büyük Millet Meclisi Basımevi Müdürlüğü, 1997), pp. 284, 287, 290, 292 and 309; Çarkcıyan, *Türk Devleti Hizmetinde Ermeniler 1453-1953*, pp. 131-132; Pamukciyan, *Ermeni Kaynaklarından Tarihe Katkılar*, Vol. 4: *Biyografileriyle Ermeniler*, p. 324 and Basri Danışman, *Artçı Diplomat Son Osmanlı Hariciye Nazırlarından Mustafa Reşit Paşa* (The Rearguard Diplomat: From the Last Ottoman Ministers of Foreign Affairs Mustafa Reşit Paşa), (İstanbul: Arba Yayınları, 1998), p. 59.

102. USNA, 867.00/467-379. Internal Political Situation in the Ottoman Empire. William Rockhill (Istanbul) to Philander Knox (Department of State), 30 January 1913.

103. "The New Cabinet," *The Levant Herald*, 25 January 1913, p. 1.

104. "Capture of the Sublime Porte," *The Near East*, Vol. 4, No. 91 (31 January 1913), p. 351; "The Coup d'Etat; An Uncensored Despatch," *The Times*, 27 January 1913, p. 6.

105. Emin Ali Türkgeldi, "Brest-Litovsk Hatıraları" (Brest-Litovsk Reminiscences), *Belgelerle Türk Tarihi Dergisi*, Vol. 3, No. 13 (March 1986), pp. 46-53.

106. See War Office Papers, National Archives, 157/702. General Headquarters (Cairo), Egyptian Expeditionary Force. Turkey: Report on Istanbul. Intelligence Summary, 30 March 1916.

107. Söylemezoğlu, *Hariciye Hizmetinde Otuz Sene* , pp. 54-55; Çarkcıyan, *Türk Devleti Hizmetinde Ermeniler 1453-1953*, pp. 147-150.

108. Norman Stone, *World War One: A Short History* (London: Allen Lane, 2007), p. 59.

109. Oskan Mardikian was earlier a ranking official in the Ministry of Finance and a member of the Macedonian Financial Commission of Ottoman Europe. On the development of his career see Sinan Kuneralp, *Son Dönem Osmanlı Erkan ve Ricali 1839-1922 Prosopografik Rehber* (The Late Period Ottoman Statesmen and Officialdom 1839-1922: Prosopographical Guide), (İstanbul: İSİS, 1999), p. 114 and Çarkçıyan, *Türk Devleti Hizmetinde Ermeniler 1453-1953*, pp. 137-138.

110. "Blames Armenians for All Their Woes; Halil Bey, Turkish Foreign Minister, Says He Gave Them Fair Warning Against Rebellion; Regrets Loss to Turkey; Insists That the Young Turks Have Always Been Friendly to Armenians; Sees Victory for Teutons," *The New York Times*, 28 October 1916, p. 9.

111. Ryan, *The Last of the Dragomans*, p. 140.

112. James Harbord, "Mustapha Kemal Pasha and His Party," *The World's Work*, Vol. 15 (May 1920-October 1920), p. 179.

113. George Gruen, "Turkey," in Reeva Spector Simon, Michael Menachem Laskier and Sara Reguer, eds., *The Jews of the Middle East and North Africa in Modern Times* (New York: Columbia University Press, 2003), p.305. Treaty of Lausanne was the only freely negotiated treaty to follow the First World War, and the only one to survive until this day. The Turkish Republic, in a sense, grew out of the Lausanne settlement. Full text of the Lausanne Treaty in League of Nations Treaty Series, Vol.28, No. 1-4 (1924), pp. 11-114.

114. FO 1214/1214/44. Annual Report on Turkey for the Year 1938. Sir Percy Lo-

raine (Ankara) to Lord Halifax (FO), 11 February 1939.

    115. Rubinstein, *Genocide: A History*, pp. 2, 127 and 138.

    116. Ibid., p. 137.

    117. Ibid., pp. 137-138.

    118. Bernard Lewis, *Semites and Anti-Semites: An Inquiry into Conflict and Preju-dice* (New York and London: W.W. Norton and Company, 1986), p. 21.

    119. BOA, DH ŞFR, No. 53/94. Ciphered Telegram to the Fourth Army Command regarding the Areas to Be Evacuated by Armenians, 23 May 1915.

    120. Bernard Lewis, *The Middle East: A Brief History of the Last 2,000 Years* (New York: Scribner, 1995), pp. 339-340.

    121. Letter from Bernard Lewis, Professor of Near Eastern Studies at Princeton University, to Shayke Weinberg, director of the United States Holocaust Memorial Museum, Princeton/New Jersey, 11 October 1991. The account of the views of Lewis relates to this source.

    122. See www.bookstv.org.

    123. Patrick Brogan, *World Conflicts: Why and Where They Are Happening* (London: Bloomsbury Publishing Limited, 1989), p. 550.

    124. Hans-Walter Schmuhl, "Der Völkermord an den Armeniern 1915-1917 in vergleichender Perspektive," in Fikret Adanır and Bernd Bonwetsch, eds., *Osmanismus, Nationalismus, und der Kaukasus: Muslime und Christen, Türken und Armenier im 19. und 20. Jahrhundert* (Wiesbaden: Reichert Verlag, 2005), p. 287.

    125. Isabel Hull, *Absolute Destruction: Military Culture and the Practices of War in Imperial Germany* (Ithaca, New York and London: Cornell University Press, 2005), pp. 274-278.

Chapter Three
A Comparison to the Holocaust

By comparison to the case of the Armenians, the Jews of Europe were wholly different. They were uninvolved in the causes of the Second World War, and would not have benefited from one side's victory or the other – as the Armenians clearly did. While Jews were loyal German subjects and had no secessionist aspirations, many Armenians were involved in armed hostilities against their government. The Jews were set upon for strictly ideological, non-military reasons: to fulfill the Nazis' aim of "purifying" Europe by the wholesale annihilation of the Jewish people. Moreover, though Hitler did engage in a policy of forced mass migration, he was not trying to relocate Jews to other territories to achieve a military goal. Rather, his goal was genocidal from the very beginning. The Nazis created a large bureaucracy to round up the Jews everywhere they could be found, exploit them economically, murder them and dispose of the corpses. This was all done systemically. Some of the most critical individuals and organizations in German science, technology and government administration were devoted over a period of years to the planning and execution of this effort. Herein lay the unique horror of the Holocaust, the traits that distinguish it from the many other atrocities in human history. The difference between that effort and the forcible mass migrations orchestrated by the Ottoman Turks is obvious. And importantly, the difference begins with the simple fact that while Europe's Jews were largely innocent of any accusation of disloyalty or armed resistance, the same cannot be said of the Armenian community.

The Armenians were not the Jews of the First World War. The analogy simply does not fit. The Jews were never a threat to the German national interest either from within or without. On the contrary, Jews probably could have helped Germany economically and militarily. There was also no state in Europe or elsewhere that attempted to use Jewish communities in Europe for political or military ends – in fact, those Jews who attempted to join resistance forces were often rejected. They were scapegoats, not enemies. Yet the full force of a modern state was mobilized to slaughter the helpless. The circumstances of the Armenians were wholly different.

There was no counterpart in the Ottoman Empire, regarding the Armenians or any other minority, to the Nazis' murderous ideology of anti-Semitism. There was never an attempt by an Ottoman government to create a religious or ideological justification for the annihilation or ruination of any of the empire's minority groups. There was no history of physical or verbal attacks on the Armenian (or any other minority) community in the Empire that corresponds to the history of anti-Semitic depredations against the Jews in Christian Europe. Even during the First World War, there was no policy against Armenians as such.

Arthur Grenke, who works as a historical researcher at the Archives of Canada and for many years has dedicated his studies to genocide and expulsion, maintains that the Ottoman view of the Armenians was different from the Nazi view of the Jews. The goals of the Young Turks were specific. They did not see Armenians as being some sort of disease or vermin that had to be eradicated so that the Ottomans could thrive, Grenke argues. The Young Turks wanted to punish them for their support of the Russians. He concludes that the Armenian events of 1915 were not a holocaust because of Armenian disloyalty to the Ottoman Empire in the wake of the czarist military threat. Nor was the killing of Armenians an effort at extermination, as in the cases of some mass population displacements in history. For the reader familiar with genocide studies, Grenke's thinking has much to offer in the way of different analyses from those given in other works.[1]

A mere glance at the history of Turkish-Armenian relations in the past proves that the two nations lived on good terms with each other for several centuries without a conflict of any magnitude. In the *Spiritual and Political Revolutions in Islam*, written with great skill, Felix Valyi contends that all national conflicts within the Ottoman Empire were the creation of the foreigner, without whose interference the various nationalities would have lived side by side in peace. He posits that the agreements reached between Sultan Mehmet II and the nations which Byzantium left as a legacy to the newly-formed Ottoman Empire prove the truth of this hypothesis; these agreements were not brutally "imposed," as is generally believed, but were the result of prolonged negotiations between the Turks and the conquered peoples. It is important to recall that the Turks were greeted as liberators from the yoke with which the Byzantine clergy had oppressed the people, and yet Sultan Mehmet II allowed the Christians freedom of conscience, which until then had been a thing unknown in the whole of Europe. The Christians of Asia Minor were delighted to find themselves delivered from the tyranny of the Byzantine clergy. Valyi is also convinced that many centuries of Turkish-Armenian collaboration should be weighed against thirty or forty years of national conflict.[2]

The British author E.F. Knight, in his *The Awakening of Turkey: A History of the Turkish Revolution* wrote that it had often been claimed by the enemies of the Turk that his Muslim "fanaticism" made his continued occupation of any portion of Christian Europe undesirable. But in justice to the votaries of the Muslim creed, Knight maintained, one ought to bear in mind, in the first place, that early Mohammedanism never persecuted the Christian religion in the ferocious fashion that Christianity persecuted Mohammedanism, as for example in Spain. When the Turks conquered the territories of the Christians they did not massacre the Christians, nor enslave them, nor interfere with their religion. Under the more equitable Muslim rule the conquered Greeks found themselves less heavily taxed and generally better off than what they had been under the rule of the emperors of the decaying Byzantine Empire. To Jews also, as being worshippers of the one God, they extended a similar level of tolerance; and it was to the Ottoman Empire that the Jews fled when they were driven out of Spain by the persecutions of Ferdinand and Isabella.[3]

The comparison of the Armenian tragedy with the attempted eradication of European Jewry under the Third Reich has also often brought vigorous criticism from Jewish studies scholars. Many believe that the Holocaust must be treated as a unique event, and support the study of the Holocaust on its own, without comparison to other genocides or significant mass death events. Some disagree with the view that both the Holocaust and the Armenian events of 1915 are equal in scale and scope, or should even both be considered genocides. They also differentiate the experience of the Armenians in the Ottoman Empire from that of the Jews in Nazi-controlled Europe.

To give a notable example of the views of Judaic studies scholars, Steven Katz, Professor of Jewish History and Religion and Director of the Elie Wiesel Center for Judaic Studies at Boston University, explored the nature and the extent of the Armenian tragedy of 1915, comparing them to the Holocaust in his masterful 1994 work, *The Holocaust in Historical Context*. The Holocaust, he argued, represented "a phenomenological and historical novum" and "an event without real precedent or parallel in modern history." "The Holocaust," he said "is phenomenogically unique by virtue of the fact that never before has a state set out, as a matter of intentional principle and actualized policy, to annihilate physically every man, woman, child belonging to a specific people ... Only in the case of Jewry under the Third Reich was such all-inclusive, noncompromising, unmitigated murder intended."

Katz refused to use the term genocide to apply to the Armenian tragedy. In his 1,000-plus page treatise, resting upon a solid foundation of archival and published sources, Katz writes specifically on the Armenian tragedy: "My understanding of its causation, unfolding, and consequences, not least in terms of its demographic proportions, does not support a fully genocidal reading of this event."[4]

In an earlier publication, which had won the national Jewish Book Award in 1984, Katz undertook a similar comparative analysis of the Jewish and Armenian cases and reached the same conclusion. He emphasized that the intention of the Turks in regard to the Armenians was not parallel and comparable to the intention of the Nazis toward the Jews. The Ottoman government's intention was essentially political in character, he concluded. As a consequence, Katz said:

> The anti-Armenianism of the Turks takes on a different character than the anti-Semitism of the Nazis. For example, anti-Armenianism is not expressed in the language of metaphysical evil in which the Turks are the manifestation of the God and the Armenians the Devil Incarnate, as was the case of Nazi theorizing about their struggle with the Jews. Again, the anti-Armenian crusade was not explicated and advanced in terms of a pseudo-scientific racism that, in itself, was yet another kind of nonsensical metaphysics. Instead, the rationale almost universally cited by Turks as a justification of their behavior is political, e.g. the Armenians were secessionists, revolutionaries, Russian spies, fifth-columnists, and divisive nationalists against the Turkish people's revolution, and the like.[5]

Katz concluded that to the Turks, the Armenians were fundamentally a political threat. The Ottoman government had no argument with Armenians per se, or the ethnographic characteristics of "Armenianism." For example, the Ottoman government had no qualms with the Armenian populations living in Russia, the United States, or even İstanbul. Rather it objected to Armenians in eastern Anatolia, seeing them as a vital source of the betrayal of Turkish destiny and integrity. This differs markedly from the international scope of the Nazi outlook and policy which aimed at discovering, uprooting and destroying all Jews everywhere. For Nazism, Jews were not a local problem.[6]

Katz further pointed out that the Ottoman policies of relocation, though harsh, were distinct from those of the Nazi's. The principle of relocation allowed for continued life at the journey's end and indeed several hundred thousand Armenians survived such journeys. Had the Ottomans intended an Armenian genocide, the manner of the relocations, as well as their destinations, would have been different. Certainly, the example of the Nazi program of extermination, whereby Jews were sent to Auschwitz and other death camps from all corners of Europe—Germany, Poland, Russia, Holland, France, Greece, Hungary and elsewhere—with a single purpose: To be murdered upon arrival, or within a few weeks of arrival. Such a plan suggests a perverse methaphysical view, not something framed by political or even strategic expediency.[7]

What Katz calls genocide is the intent to bring about the total annihilation of a group. He employs the notion of genocide as applying to the "actualization of the intent, however successfully carried out, to murder in its totality any national, ethnic, racial, religious, political, social, gender or economic groups, as these groups are defined by the perpetrators, by whatever means."[8] For Katz, not only is the issue of motivation crucial to genocide but the case of the Holocaust is the only one in which he can discern it.[9]

The United Methodist theologians Alice and Roy Eckardt, who in 1979 served as special consultants to President Jimmy Carter's Commission on the Holocaust, carry the Katz argument a step further, when they argue for the "uniquely uniqueness" of the Holocaust in their seminal work *Long Night's Journey Into Day: A Revised Retrospective on the Holocaust.* For them, the Jewish catastrophe is a category apart from even those historical events one would also classify as unique. In their book, the Eckardts said:

> The Holocaust contains its own peculiarities—such as the truth that never before in human history was systematic genocide conducted by a government in the name of a pseudoscientific doctrine of race and to the end of final blessedness.

They added: "Again the intent of the Holocaust was unparalleled in human history, most especially the intent to eradicate human compassion."[10]

Scholars favoring the Armenian position have generally affirmed that the Armenian tragedy and the Holocaust should be viewed as co-equals of human suffering and examples of genocide.

The Armenian writer Pierre Papazian questioned the uniqueness of the Holocaust and suggested numerous ways in which it paralleled the events of 1915. In response, the Jewish monthly *Midstream* published contributions to a symposium arguing the opposite. Lucy Dawidowicz accused Papazian of turning "the subject into a vulgar contest about who suffered more."[11]

RELOCATIONS AS A MODEL FOR THE "FINAL SOLUTION"

There is no evidence at all that Nazi potentates and their eliminationist organs— the SS, the SD (Sicherheitsdienst) and the Einsatzgruppen—took the Armenian relocations as a model for a European-wide "Final Solution." In *The War Against the Jews 1933-1945*, historian Lucy Dawidowicz shows the uniqueness of the Final Solution: "The Final Solution transcended the bounds of modern historical experience. Never before in modern history had one people made the killing of another the fulfillment of the ideology, in whose pursuit means were identical with ends." She concludes that "the Final Solution was a new phenomenon in human history."[12] In a later work when Dawidowicz reiterates her position on the same subject by arguing that "(N)ever before in human history had a state and political movement dedicated itself to the destruction of a whole people," she had the cases of the Ottoman Empire and the Committee of Union and Progress in mind as a possible, but in the end inadequate, comparison.[13] Philip Rutherford, in his in-depth study of the German atrocities committed in Poland during the first two years of the Second World War, also stresses that "Nazi perpetrators' mission was indeed unprecedented: never before had a nation attempted to eradicate an entire ethnoreligious group of human beings as a matter of governmental policy, using all means at its disposal to do so."[14]

And it is noteworthy that on the question of the responsibility of the Nazi Holocaust in *Eichmann in Jerusalem: A Report on the Banality of Evil*, the prominent German-American political philosopher and theoretician Hannah Arendt dismisses outright the Armenian case as "pogroms" — a term derived from the Russian word for riot. Jews were killed only because they were Jews. Arendt thought that only the Jewish people were exterminated in a way that would be defined as genocide.[15]

THE MATTER OF JUSTICE: LEGAL REVIEWS OF THE TRAGEDY

The Holocaust and the Armenian tragedy must be considered on their own terms. International law honors this distinction. By trials before an international body of jurists at Nuremberg, a long array of individuals have been found guilty of participation in Hitler's genocide and sentences were carried out in accordance with agreed-upon procedures. Subsequent tribunals made similar determinations for Rwanda and for Srebrenica in the former Yugoslavia. By contrast, the First World War victors exonerated the Malta detainees—144 Ottoman statesmen and officials who were alleged to have been responsible for the maladministration of the Armenian relocation policies. Not a single Turk has ever been found guilty of what later to be articulated as genocide or its equivalent in a genuine court of law, although the victorious powers of the First World War enjoyed both the incentive and opportunity to do so if incriminating evidence existed.

After the First World War, the Ottoman capital was under Allied occupation and all state archives were under the control of the British authorities. The prisoners were held in Malta for twenty-eight months while the British, French and Americans searched for evidence of centrally arranged large-scale murders. If there were any credible witnesses or evidence regarding the alleged Armenian massacres, they should have been found in that period of time. However, as a matter of fact, no evidence could be found to support the charge that the Ottomans had planned a mass slaughter of the Armenians. The British had appointed an Armenian, Haig Khazarian, to conduct a thorough examination in the Ottoman archives, yet he was unable to discover evidence of government complicity or premeditation in the killings of Armenians. The British High Commission at İstanbul was unable to forward any legal evidence to London. There was also nothing in the British state archives that corroborated the accusations of the Armenians. When the tireless and unimpeded investigations concluded, the British Procurator-General determined that it was "improbable that the charges would be capable of proof in a court of law" and released all detainees. In short, the accusations were exhaustively probed, investigated, and studied, with the Allies agreeing that the charges could not hold.

A member of the British Embassy staff in Washington D.C. also visited the United States State Department on 12 July 1921 regarding the matter. He was permitted access to reports from American Consuls on the Armenian events. There was nothing there that could be used as evidence against the Turks who were being detained for trial at Malta. The reports seen gave no concrete facts that could constitute satisfactory incriminating evidence. The reports in the possession of the State Department did not appear under any circumstances to contain evidence against the detained Turks at Malta. The case was closed beyond reasonable doubt.

One must add that on 13 February 1919, Mustafa Reşit Paşa, Ottoman Minister of Foreign Affairs, in a diplomatic communication appealed to five neutral European countries, Switzerland, Denmark, Sweden, The Netherlands and Spain, and invited them to appoint two legal assessors or magistrates to a Turkish Commission already constituted for investigating the alleged abuses in connection with the relocation of the Ottoman subjects of different race and religion. Although the British occupation authorities in İstanbul attempted to prevent the local missions of the neutral governments from transmitting the appeal to their capitals, the messages got through. The British response from that moment forward was to thwart the neutral commission at all costs. The British Foreign Office, for example, informed the Spanish Ambassador on 4 March 1919 that "the acceptance of the Turkish invitation might, and probably would, run counter to the arrangements made at the [Paris] Peace conference, and could cause serious complications." Similarly, the British delegate at the Paris Peace Conference, on 25 March 1919 suggested to the Foreign Secretary in a note that the Spanish government should be discouraged from appointing any legal assessor to the Turkish Commission. Facing the intense opposition of the British government, Spain, and then the other neutral governments declined the invitation of the Sublime Porte either to take part actively in the process, or to act as independent observers.[16]

It is also worth noting that the İstanbul daily *Vakit* editorialized on 17 November 1921 regarding the safeguarding of the rights of the Christian minorities in Turkey:

Turkey since the time of Mehmet II has passed through many revolutions and great crises; but the tranquility and the well-being of the Christians have not been disturbed for a single moment. Absolutely the contrary; their number has increased, their economic prosperity has grown; and this state of things continued up to the time when the idea arose of the protection of the Christians of the East by Russia. The Christians thus served as instruments for the policy of Russia. The greatest benefit that can be rendered to the Christians of the East is, not to liberate them from the Turks, but to liberate them from the yoke that makes of them instruments for propaganda in the Balkans.

The *Vakit* also said:

At the moment when the Washington Conference seems to open up a fresh page in the history and destinies of the world we ought to give proof of our goodwill and invite the Powers to send to Turkey a commission of experts to study the situation of the Christians among us. In order to get exact ideas on this point the commission should compare the situation of the Christians of Turkey with that of the Muslims of Crete, Thessaly, Macedonia, and Thrace. If that course is adopted many responsibilities will fall upon us but what are these compared with the calumnies with which we are overwhelmed? We do not at all fear a judicial and impartial inquiry. The Carnegie commission as well as the other international bodies which have already made inquiries in the İzmir region have reported in our favor. Every European authority who looks into the question in detail never fails to become our friend. We do not think there could be a better way to clear the air and to acquit us than the appointment of such a commission.[17]

Not surprisingly, the appeal went unheeded.

Notes

1. Arthur Grenke, *God, Greed, and Genocide: The Holocaust through the Centuries* (Washington, D.C.: New Academia Publishing, 2005), pp.128-130, 133-134 and 136. See also Robert Spector, Review of Grenke's aforesaid book in *European History Quarterly*, Vol. 39, No. 1 (January 2009), pp. 142-143.

2. Felix Valyi, *Spiritual and Political Revolutions in Islam* (London: Kegan Paul, Trench, Trubner and Company Ltd., 1925), pp. 149-150 and 152-153. Felix Valyi was the Hungarian-born editor of a French journal of opinion, *La Revue politique international*.

3. E.F. Knight, *The Awakening of Turkey: A History of the Turkish Revolution* (London: John Milne, 1909), pp. 9-10.

4. Steven Katz, *The Holocaust in Historical Context*, Vol.1: *The Holocaust and Mass Death before the Modern Age* (New York and Oxford: Oxford University Press, 1994), pp. 22, 24 and 28. This work, which was selected as the outstanding book in

philosophy and theology for the year 1994 by the American Association of University Publishers, should become a primary point of reference for future scholarship concerning the Armenian relocations and its implications for the study of the Holocaust. Also see idem, "The Uniqueness of the Holocaust: The Historical Dimension," in Alan Rosenbaum, ed., *Is the Holocaust Unique? Perspectives on Comparative Genocide* (Boulder, Colorado: Westview Press, 1996), pp. 19-38 where Armenian relocations is dismissed, since Armenians were killed for being "secessionists," not because they were the victims of a "totalistic" ideology of hate, based on their destruction. In idem, *Historicism, the Holocaust and Zionism: Critical Studies in Modern Jewish Thought and History* (New York and London: New York University Press, 1992), especially in chapter 7 pp. 162-192 identical opinions are expressed.

5. Steven Katz, *Post-Holocaust Dialogues: Critical Studies in Modern Jewish Thought* (New York and London: New York University Press, 1983), pp. 302-303. Also see idem, "The Unique Intentionality of the Holocaust," *Modern Judaism*, Vol. 1, No. 2 (September 1981), pp. 173-174. Many historians agree with Katz on the point that the anti-Semitism against the Jews was without parallel in Ottoman feeling toward the Armenians. See, for instance, Merrill Peterson, *"Starving Armenians" America and the Armenian Genocide, 1915-1930 and After* (Charlottesville and London: University of Virginia Press, 2004), p. 160.

6. Katz, *Post-Holocaust Critical Studies*, p. 303. Idem, "The Unique Intentionality of the Holocaust," p. 174.

7. Katz, *Post-Holocaust Critical Studies*, p. 305. Idem, "The Unique Intentionality of the Holocaust," pp. 174-175.

8. Katz, *The Holocaust in Historical Context*, p. 131.

9. On this point, see for instance, Mark Levene, "Is the Holocaust Simply Another Example of Genocide?" *Patterns of Prejudice*, Vol.28, No.2 (April 1994), pp. 3-26.

10. Alice Eckardt and Roy Eckardt, *Long Night's Journey Into Day: A Revised Retrospective on the Holocaust* (Detroit, Michigan: Wayne State University Press, 1988), p.55. See also Roy Eckardt, "Is the Holocaust Unique?" *Worldview*, Vol. 17, No. 9 (September 1974), pp. 31-36 and Roy Eckardt and Alice Eckardt, "The Holocaust and the Enigma of Uniqueness: A Philosophical Effort at Practical Clarification," *The Annals of the American Academy of Political and Social Science*, Vol.450 (July 1980), pp. 165-178.

11. Pierre Papazian, "A 'Unique Uniqueness'?" and "Was the Holocaust Unique? Responses to Pierre Papazian," *Midstream*, Vol. 30, No. 4 (April 1984), p.20 and passim; Peter Novick, *The Holocaust in American Life* (Boston and New York: Houghton Mifflin Company, 2000), pp.192-193.

12. Lucy Dawidowicz, *The War Against the Jews 1933-1945* (New York: Holt, Rinehart and Winston, 1975), pp.xvi-xvii and passim.

13. Lucy Dawidowicz, *The Holocaust and the Historians* (Cambridge, Massachusetts and London: Harvard University Press, 1981), p. 20.

14. Philip Rutherford, *Prelude to the Final Solution: The Nazi Program for Deporting Ethnic Poles, 1939-1941* (Lawrence, Kansas: University Press of Kansas, 2007), p. 10.

15. Hannah Arendt, *Eichmann in Jerusalem: A Report on the Banality of Evil* (New York: The Viking Press, rev. and enlarged ed., 1975), p. 265.

16. *Armenians in Ottoman Documents 1915-1920*, pp. 195 and 245.

17. "Editorial," *Vakit*, 17 November 1921, p. 1. The report of the international commission sent into the Balkan Peninsula by the Carnegie Endowment for International Peace to investigate the charges and countercharges of atrocities made by all sides during the wars of 1912 and 1913 filled 200 book-pages and had a preface by Nicholas Murray Butler, president of Columbia University. It was signed by the following members of the commission: Joseph Redlich, professor of public law in the University of Vienna, Austria; Baron d'Estournelles de Constant and Justin Codart, lawyer and member of the Chamber of Deputies of France; Walther Schucking, professor of law at the University of Marburg, Germany; Francis Hirst, editor of *The Economist*, and H.N. Brailsford, journalist, of Britain; Professor Paul Miloukov, member of the Russian Duma, and Samuel Dutton, professor in Teachers' College, Columbia University. For further details see "Carnegie Report on the Balkan Atrocities," *The Literary Digest*, Vol. 158, No. 22 (30 May 1914), p. 1302.

Chapter Four
Adolf Hitler and the Armenian Tragedy

For those who analogize the Armenian tragedy to the Holocaust, creating a clear line of connection between Adolf Hitler and the reputed actions of the Ottoman Empire is essential. It is not enough to merely suggest Hitler's actions were akin to those of the Ottomans. The argument is made that Hitler was himself inspired by the Ottomans, and that he modeled his own plans on the actions of the Ottoman Empire.

There are two major problems with this argument. First: The actions of Nazi Germany bore no resemblance to those of the Ottoman Empire. As previously argued, the Ottoman efforts to remove Armenians from the region of Anatolia where they were deliberately undermining the Empire's efforts to defend themselves was conducted with an intent to preserve life and property; the Nazi efforts to remove Jews from Europe were almost always deliberate in their efforts to deprive Jews of life and property. The methods were completely different, and intent completely different.

Second: What Hitler knew about the Armenian tragedy is not known, and is surmised solely through circumstantial evidence. Some scholars surmise that Hitler learned of the Armenian massacres through wide publicity and through his close association with Max Erwin von Scheubner-Richter, the former German Vice Consul in Erzurum in 1915, who later became a co-founder of the Nazi Party. Von Scheubner-Richter was one of Hitler's most trusted and revered colleagues, and his death in a Munich putsch in 1923 was deemed a total loss by Hitler. Given their close relationship, some scholars believe it is unthinkable that von Scheubner-Richter's own experience witnessing the destruction of an ethnic group would not have been kept from Hitler, especially given Hitler's ambitions to destroy the Jews.[1] Evidence to support such an actual conversation, however, is lacking.

Other scholars still suggest that many German civilian officials and army officers, like Constantin von Neurath, Count Friedrich Werner von der Schulenburg, Franz von Papen, Hans von Seeckt and Karl Dönitz who had been in the Ottoman Empire during 1914-1918, and who witnessed the Armenian tragedy, later became collaborators of Hitler in the Nazi Party, and organized the Nazi crimes.

The prime piece of alleged evidence, for those who analogize between the Armenian tragedy and the Holocaust, is a report of Adolf Hitler's two and a half hour address to the three supreme commanders of the three branches of the armed forces (Army, Navy, Air Force), as well as the commanding generals bearing the title commanders-in-chief at his mountain headquarters at Obersalzberg in the Bavarian Alps on 22 August 1939, ten days prior to the invasion of Poland and the start of the Second World War in Europe. He is alleged to have said, in this speech: "Who, after all, speaks today of the annihilation of the Armenians?" The words are frequently cited as fact, and even appear on the wall of the United States Holocaust Memorial Museum. Yet the veracity of this quote is questionable at best. Princeton professor Heath Lowry has clearly demonstrated that there is no proof that Hitler ever made such a statement[2]; nor did the International Military Tribunal at Nuremberg accept during its 23 November 1945 session, or in any other session, the above-mentioned quotation. Its publication, in a *The Times* of London article, "Nazi Germany's Road to War," on 24 November 1945, followed its publication in *What About Germany?* by Louis Lochner, the Associated Press of America's Berlin bureau chief in 1921-1942. Lochner, like *The Times* author, never disclosed his source.[3]

The Nuremberg investigation explored German documents of Hitler's address, as it was a critical proof point for Nazi German's war ambitions. The tribunal examined and then rejected Lochner's third-hand version of Hitler's address. Instead, the tribunal entered into evidence two official versions of the 22 August 1939 address found in captured German military records quoting those who were present at Obersalzberg. These bear document numbers US-29/798 PS and US-30/1014 PS. Neither document contains any reference to Armenians, nor to Jews. Instead, Hitler's address was an anti-Polish invective.[4]

Scholars generally doubt or do not believe that Hitler could possibly have uttered the statement. They contest the historical use and authenticity of the quotation. For example, Norman Naimark notes: "We cannot be absolutely certain that Hitler referred to the Armenians at all on this occasion."[5] Cherif Bassiouni, Professor Emeritus of Law at DePaul University, agrees.[6]

Robert John, a historian and political analyst, who is of Armenian descent said in August 1984 at the Orwellian Symposium at Baden-Baden, West Germany that the quotation was a forgery and should not be used. He had discussed it with Brigadier General Telford Taylor, who had said, "I know the document you mean, I don't know its provenance, and I have not used it in my own work." "We all believe that violence breeds violence," said John. "There has been an increase in Armenian violence since this false inflammatory statement was given publicly." He briefly traced the history of Armenian atrocity propaganda, particularly from the British and American view. John's view that real atrocities occurred lends special credibility to his concern that deliberate fabrications – especially of quotes by historical figures – would undermine the cause of memory and contribute to seething ethnic tensions for decades. "Hate hurts the hater and the hated. We are still living in the haze of distortions and actual horrors which occurred so long ago," he commented. "The Armenian... should not damage its development with a continual conditioning of hate, neither should spurious guilt be visited upon others. These negative preoccupations and obsessions are obstructing our evolution."[7]

In a follow-up letter of 8 June 1985 to the editor of *The New York Times*, John argues that the reference to Hitler's remark is a dubious one. The Armenian scholar suggests that those who produced it did so with a deliberate intent to deceive the world. As he tartly observes:

> One must suspect that the document was released to create a climate of hate and revulsion to stifle the protests of eminent American jurists such as Senator Robert Taft and Chief Justice Harlan Fiske Stone, who criticized the Nuremberg trials. Those who issued the document did not do it in good faith. I wrote to Louis Lochner, inviting him to tell for the record what he knew about the material, but he did not reply and died soon after. Much later in the trial, the German defense lawyers were able to introduce the most complete account of Hitler's address, taken down by Admiral Hermann Böhm, which runs twelve pages in translation. There is no mention of the Armenians or the rest of the quotation.[8]

The Obersalzberg meeting was not a secret one, though the conversations were not to be made public, and there was no official stenographer. Ian Kershaw, the most recent British biographer of Hitler, mentions particularly that no minutes were taken during the gathering. Those listening were explicitly told not to make any record of the proceedings. Not even Hitler's adjutant, Colonel Rudolf Schmundt, was taking the address down. But not all respected this injunction and a few of those present thought what they heard was so important that they quickly compiled a summary of what had gone on that day.[9]

There are various versions of what Hitler said. Admiral Wilhelm Canaris, chief of the Abwehr, Intelligence and Clandestine Warfare Service of the German High Command, and a member of the military opposition, had stayed in the background during the speech so that, despite the prohibition against taking notes, he was able to furtively scribble down. He only caught scraps of what

was said. Canaris worked his notes into a digest of Hitler's address and presented it to a meeting of his departmental chiefs next day. Canaris evidently hoped
to feed the text to the British, perhaps in language that was more colorful and
alarming, in order to alarm the British or anti-Nazi German military officials
into taking action against Hitler. Canaris' fiercely anti-Nazi deputy, Lieutenant
Colonel Hans Oster, head of the coordinating section in the foreign intelligence,
got his superior to give him a copy of his transcript of Hitler's speech—for
his "collection," as he put it. What happened to this copy is uncertain, but it is
known that Oster and his confederates produced a version of it, which bore only
a remote resemblance to the original.[10]

This new version was greatly rewritten to underline the brusqueness of Hitler's expressions. It teemed with insults of world leaders: He is alleged to have
called Turkish leaders after Atatürk's death "cretins and half idiots," Edouard
Daladier and Neville Chamberlain were called "poor worms," the Italian mon-
archy a "nitwit of a King and the treacherous scoundrel of a Crown Prince,"
the Japanese Imperial leader Hirohito a "weak, cowardly, undecided emperor,"
King Carol of Romania "the corrupt slave of his sexual instincts," and so on.

Other quotations were equally dubious, given their content: "After Stalin's
death—he is a very sick man—we will break the Soviet Union. Then there
will begin the dawn of the German rule of the earth." Clearly, such a statement
would be dubious, considering Hitler and Stalin had formed a mutual non-ag-
gression pact that paved the way for Germany and the Soviet Union to carve up
eastern Europe. The text also included some annotations that rendered it highly
suspicious, such as a description of Hermann Goering's reaction to Hitler's
speech, "Goering, beside himself with excitement, jumped on to the long table
in the salon and gave bloodthirsty thanks and bloody promises. He danced like a
savage."[11] British author Leonard Mosley suggests that it seems most unlikely;
it would have been out of character. Besides, according to Mosley, Goering's
mood was hardly ecstatic.[12]

Ludwig Beck, former chief of the German Army's General Staff, and Hermann Maass, an anti-Nazi and former Social Democratic youth leader, vol-
unteered to pass the text to Lochner. The latter showed it confidentially to an
American diplomat, who was too terrified of it to hold on to it, so Lochner
turned over the document to George Ogilvie-Forbes, Counsellor at the British
Embassy in Berlin and second-in-command, who on August 25 forwarded it
with great haste to London. The United States journalist reported that the transcript came from a German staff officer "who had it from a general present at
the (Obersalzberg) meeting." The general had been shocked and hoped that "the
madman" – Hitler – would be restrained by Britain, but the transcript, which
was on plain paper and unsigned, failed to impress its recipients.[13]

Lochner told British Lieutenant Colonel William Byford-Jones at Nuremberg in 1946 how he was responsible for the delivery of one of the most sen-

sational of the innumerable documents to prove the Nazi conspiracy. This document purported to be the record of a secret conference between Hitler and his commanding generals on 22 August 1939 at Obersalzberg. It was given to Lochner by a confidant of Colonel General Beck.[14]

This particular copy differed substantially from the text of Canaris' careful version. The likely author was Oster. Yet Anthony Cave Brown, in his minutely and expansively researched *Bodyguard of Lies*, tells another story of how Hitler's address was leaked to the West. He posits that Canaris drove directly from Obersalzberg to the Vier Jahreszeiten Hotel in Munich, and there he made some notes and handed them to Oster. Canaris' deputy took the night express to Berlin, and shortly after the train left the Munich station, he met a man in civilian clothes in the corridor outside his sleeper—Major Gijsbertus Jacob Sas, an assistant military attaché at the Dutch Embassy in Berlin, who had been a friend of Oster's for many years. Oster gave him Canaris' notes and by the evening of August 23 a report of Hitler's speech was on the desk of Major Francis Foley, the resident of the British Secret Intelligence Service at Berlin, as well as the desks of all other intelligence services friendly to Dutch. In this version, however, Hitler had not posed the rhetorical question "Who, after all, speaks today of the annihilation of Armenians?" Instead, he is reported to have urged the most savage treatment of the enemy: "Thus for the time being I have sent to the East only my Death Head Units, with the order to kill without pity or mercy all men, women, and children of Polish race and language." The presumed author of the adulterated version, Oster, understood that the planned attack for 1 September 1939 was linked to mass human destruction.[15]

Hermann Böhm, Chief of the German High Seas Fleet, also took notes during Hitler's speech and transcribed them on the same evening in the Vier Jahreszeiten Hotel in Munich. The correctness of the copy was certified by the International Military Tribunal at Nuremberg. The original was in the handwriting of Böhm and he himself identified it with no reservation. The defense lawyers in the trials of German Major War Criminals called Böhm as a witness and he confirmed that the speech was made in this form.[16]

The post-1945 memoirs of Grand Admiral Erich Raeder, Commander-in-Chief of the German Navy between 1928 and 1943, have also been illuminating on this issue. He, too, being one of those present at the Obersalzberg harangue, was of the opinion that there was no doubt that Böhm's notes were an accurate record not only of the form and content of Hitler's speech, but also of the impression of those present gained from it.[17]

A record of what Hitler said at the Obersalzberg meeting can also be found in the notebook of Colonel General Franz Hadler, which consists of extracts written personally by him in the Gabelsberger system of shorthand not only from day to day but from hour to hour during the day. It is a unique source of information and contains a voluminous running account of what he heard and did as Chief of the General Staff of the German Army from 14 August 1939 until his dismissal on 24 September 1942. Halder's notebook provides an extraordinary insight into the private thoughts of Hitler on the eve of and during the Second World War. Halder's notes and testimony provide a historical document of major worth.[18]

On August 22, Halder took notes while Hitler spoke, and then summarized them after the meeting was over. His notebook does not also include the Armenian reference.[19] As Telford Taylor points out, the two documents seized in the High Command of the German Armed Forces files, Böhm's account and Halder's notebook "correspond very closely both as to sequence and content, and are all certainly authentic."[20]

William Shirer, who had watched and reported on the Nazis for about two decades and achieved great success as a journalist, concurs with Taylor and in his still popular book *The Rise and Fall of the Third Reich: A History of Nazi Germany* states that "all three versions are similar in content and there can be no doubt of their authenticity. In piecing together Hitler's remarks I have used the records of Böhm and Halder and the unsigned memorandum in two parts submitted at Nuremberg as evidence." He adds that the fourth account may have been embellished a little by persons who were not present at the meeting at Obersalzberg.[21]

In a second letter of 6 July 1985 on Hitler quotation again to the editor of *The New York Times*, the Armenian historian John stated emphatically: "The document which contains Hitler's alleged statement would not satisfy the United States Provost Marshal at Nuremberg as acceptable in court, and it has not been substantiated since."[22] Indeed, United States Trial Counsel Sidney Alderman did not offer it as evidence because of its flimsy authenticity. He said that this document was given to him through an American journalist and that this journalist had claimed it to be the original protocol of the Obersalzberg meeting. The prosecutor further stated that the journalist in question had told him he had obtained this document from another person, and that the prosecutor was not able to determine if that person was really the one who had written these minutes during the meeting. Hitler's purported declaration on the Armenians is therefore based on a piece of paper the validity of which was not accepted by the prosecutor; neither the author, nor the date the notes were taken is known.[23]

Christopher Browning, Professor of History at Pacific Lutheran University and author of several books on the Holocaust, agrees that definitive accounts of Hitler's speech from German officers indicate no reference to the Armenians. Browning believes the fraudulent version was given to the British Embassy at Berlin in an attempt to persuade London that Hitler had murderous intentions. He thinks it unlikely the German dictator would have suggested then—particularly at that date and to a group of officers—that he planned to commit mass murder.[24] Indeed, while Hitler certainly did not have temperate intentions towards the Jews, his plan for a systemic extermination effort did not materialize until just over two years later, at the Conference at the former Wannsee headquarters of Interpol in Berlin on 20 January 1942.[25]

Much recent research has supported this. In the Fall 2006 issue of *Holocaust and Genocide Studies*, the international multidisciplinary scholarly journal published by the United States Holocaust Memorial Museum in association with Oxford University Press, Professor Jonathan Markovitz indicates that "the authenticity of Hitler's oft-quoted reference" that "(W)ho remembers the extermination of the Armenians? has been challenged on the grounds that the statement appears in a document of questionable origin."[26] And in the September 2008 issue of *Central European History* Matthew Fitzpatrick, Professor of History at Flinders University in Adelaide, Australia, calls it a document the veracity of which is still questioned.[27]

Most importantly, on 22 May 1990 Shayke (Jeshajahu) Weinberg, museum director for the United States Holocaust Memorial Council and who had pioneered the development of the Nahum Goldman Museum of the Jewish Diaspora in Israel, in an interoffice memorandum addressed to Michael Berenbaum, project director for the creation of the museum and for almost two decades the Hyman Goldman Professor of Theology at Georgetown University, noted that the Hitler quote was an open controversy and there seemed to be no positive proof that he said it. According to Weinberg, under the circumstances the United States Holocaust Memorial Museum had to reconsider its plan to use the quote in its exhibition.[28]

And lastly, in another interoffice memorandum of the United States Holocaust Memorial Museum dated 26 July 1992, it is mentioned that the veracity of the Hitler quote has always been in serious doubt. At its best, the text was a third-hand version of Hitler's address, and the circumstances of its creation created more doubt on its accuracy, not less. According to this memorandum, one could not say whether the statement was authentic or bogus, but the weight of evidence seemed to favor the latter judgment. No stenographic record of Hitler's speech survived, because Hitler had ordered his assistants not to take one. Therefore, all evidence on the content of the speech was indirect. The evidence consisted mostly of notes, or accounts based on notes, taken furtively during the speech by members of the audience. The museum memorandum suggests that Abwehr officials compiled the Lochner text from Canaris' notes, and passed it on to British diplomats, perhaps hoping to alert them to Hitler's warlike intentions and concludes that this thesis is perhaps the only interpretation on which all historians agree.[29]

Although this reference was never substantiated, it has assumed a life of its own and has been misused for propaganda aims ever since. Politically, "Hitler" is a magic word that conjures up an all-true image of undisputed evil. He is quoted on the Armenian question for polemic and political purpose, to tie the

Ottoman Turks to Hitler's evil. In the modern world nothing defames so well as associating one's enemies with the Führer.

NOTES

1. Paul Leverkuehn (trans. Alasdair Lean), *A German Officer during the Armenian Genocide: A Biography of Max von Scheubner-Richter* (London: Gomidas Institute, 2008).

2. For a discussion of Hitler's statement, and its falsity, see Heath Lowry, "The United States Congress and Adolf Hitler on the Armenians," *Political Communication and Persuasion*, Vol. 3, No .2 (April 1985), pp. 111-140.

3. Louis Lochner, *What About Germany?* (New York: Dodd, Mead and Company, 1942), pp. 1-4.

4. English translations of the two documents US-29/798 PS and US-30/1014 PS are printed in Documents on German Foreign Policy 1918-1945, Series D (1937-1945) (henceforth referred to as DGFP), Vol.7: The Last Days of Peace August 9-September 3, 1939, Nos.192 and 193, eds., Paul Sweet, Howard Smyth, James Beddie, Arthur Kogan, George Kent (Washington, D.C.: United States Government Printing Office, 1956), pp. 200-206.

5. Naimark, *Fires of Hatred*, p. 57.

6. Cherif Bassiouni, "World War I: The War to End All Wars and the Birth of a Handicapped International Criminal Justice System," *Denver Journal of International Law and Policy*, Vol. 30, No.1, p. 290 fn 352.

7. "Historian of Armenian Descent Says Frequently Used Hitler Quote Is Nothing but a Forgery,"*The Armenian Reporter*, Vol.17, No.40 (2 August 1984), p.1. Brigadier General Telford Taylor was one of the principal American prosecutors at the various Nuremberg war crimes trials after the Second World War.

8. Robert John, Letters, "Did Hitler Say It?" *The New York Times*, 8 June 1985, p. 22.

9. Ian Kershaw, *Hitler 1936-45: Nemesis* (New York and London: W.W. Norton and Company, 2000), p. 207.

10. Heinz Höhne (trans. Maxwell Brownjohn), *Canaris* (New York: Doubleday and Company, Inc., 1979), pp.346-348; Karl Heinz Abshagen (trans. Alan Houghton Brodrick), *Canaris* (London: Hutchinson and Company Ltd., 1956), p. 137; Hans Bernd Gisevius (trans. Richard and Clara Winston), *To the Bitter End* (Boston: Houghton Mifflin Company, 1947), p. 361.

11. Höhne, *Canaris*, p. 348; Donald Cameron Watt, *How War Came: The Immediate Origins of the Second World War, 1938-1939* (New York: Pantheon Books, 1989), pp. 444-445; Documents on British Foreign Policy 1919-1939 (henceforth referred to as DBFP), Third Series, Vol.7, No. 314, eds., Llewellyn Woodward and Rohan Butler (London: Her Majesty's Stationery Office, 1954), pp. 258-259; Office of United States Chief of Counsel for Prosecution of Axis Criminality, *Nazi Conspiracy and Aggression*, Vol.7, (Washington, D. C.: United States Government Printing Office, 1946), pp. 752-754; "Zweite Ansprache des Führers am 22. August 1939," *Akten zur deutschen Auswärtigen Politik, 1918-1945*, Vol. 7, (Baden-Baden: Imprimerie Nationale, 1961),

p. 171 fn1.

12. Leonard Mosley, *On Borrowed Time: How World War II Began* (New York: Random House, 1969), p. 372.

13. Höhne, *Canaris*, p. 348; Peter Hoffmann (trans. Richard Barry), *The History of the German Resistance 1933-1945* (Cambridge, Massachusetts: The MIT Press, 1979), p. 214; George Ogilvie-Forbes' letter to the British Foreign Office enclosing record of speech by Hitler made at Obersalzberg on August 22 is printed in DBFP, Third Series, Vol.7, pp. 257-260. The original copy handed to the British Embassy by Lochner was kept by Ambassador Nevile Henderson and is now among his papers in the National Archives of the United Kingdom.

14. William Byford-Jones, *Berlin Twilight* (London: Hutchinson and Company Limited, 1946), pp. 177-178.

15. Michael Mueller (trans. Geoffrey Brooks), *Canaris: The Life and Death of Hitler's Spymaster* (Annapolis, Maryland: Naval Institute Press, 2007), pp.143-145; Heinz Höhne (trans. Richard Barry), *The Order of the Death's Head: The Story of Hitler's SS* (London: Penguin Books, 2000), pp. 262-263; Richard Breitman, *The Architect of Genocide: Himmler and the Final Solution* (Hanover, New Haven and London: University Press of New England, 1991), p.258 fn 47; Anthony Cave Brown, *Bodyguard of Lies* (Toronto, New York and London: Bantam Books, 1975), p.176. Gerhard Weinberg, a leading authority on the diplomacy of the Third Reich and the Second World War, in *Hitler's Foreign Policy: The Road to World War II 1933-1939* (New York: Enigma Books, 2005), p.911 fn 345 believes that the ribbon copy of the text handed by Lochner to the British Embassy in Berlin was almost certainly prepared in the Abwehr.

16. *Trial of the Major War Criminals Before the International Military Tribunal Nuremberg 14 November 1945-1 October 1946* (henceforth referred to as TMWC), Vol.14, (Nuremberg: International Military Tribunal, 1947; reprint, Buffalo, New York: William Hein, 1995), p.46. The original text in German of Böhm's account is published in "Rede des Fuehrers auf dem Obersalzberg am 22. VIII. 1939," TMWC, Vol. 16, pp.16-25. See also Hermann Böhm, "Zur Ansprache Hitlers vor den Führern der Wehrmacht am 22. August 1939," *Vierteljahreshaft für Zeitgeschichte*, Vol.19 (1971), pp. 294-300.

17. Erich Raeder (trans. Henry Drexel), *My Life* (Annapolis, Maryland: United States Naval Institute, 1960), p. 277.

18. Charles Burdick and Hans-Adolf Jacobsen, eds., *The Halder War Diary 1939-1942* (Novato, California: Presidio Press, 1988), pp. vii and 1-10.

19. See the entry in Halder's notebook for 22 August 1939 in Franz Halder, ed., Hans-Adolf Jacobsen, *Kriegstagebuch: Tägliche Aufzeichnungen des Chefs des Generalstabes des Heeres, 1939-1942*, Vol.1: *Vom Polenfeldzug bis zum Ende der Westoffensive (14.8.1939-30.6.1940)*, (Stuttgart: W. Kohlhammer Verlag, 1962), pp. 22-26 and DGFP, Vol.7, pp. 557-559.

20. Telford Taylor, *Sword and Swastika: Generals and Nazis in the Third Reich* (New York: Simon and Schuster, 1952), pp. 291 and 295.

21. William Shirer, *The Rise and Fall of the Third Reich: A History of Nazi Germany* (New York: Simon and Schuster, 1960), p. 529 fn.

22. Robert John, Letters, "Hitler's Armenian-Extermination Remark, True or False?" *The New York Times*, 6 July 1985, p. 20.

23. William Schabas, *Genocide in International Law: The Crimes of Crimes* (Cambridge: Cambridge University Press, 2000), p. 1 fn 2; David Myer, Review of Kevork

Bardakjian's *Hitler and the Armenian Genocide, Holocaust and Genocide Studies*, Vol. 2, No.1 (January 1987), p. 176. See the explanation provided by Sidney Alderman in TMWC, Vol.2, pp. 285-286.

24. Judith Colp, "Controversy Rages On in Mall Museum," *The Washington Times*, 20 April 1990, p. E2.

25. Bruce Fein, "Genocide Gyrations," *The Washington Times*, 13 October 2000, p. E2.

26. Jonathan Markovitz, "Ararat and Collective Memories of the Armenian Genocide," *Holocaust and Genocide Studies*, Vol. 20, No.2 (Fall 2006), pp. 244 and 253 n.29.

27. Matthew Fitzpatrick, "The Pre-History of the Holocaust? The *Sonderweg* and *Historikerstreit* Debates and the Abject Colonial Past," *Central European History*, Vol. 41, No. 3 (September 2008), p. 495 fn 90.

28. United States Holocaust Memorial Museum Archives (henceforth referred to as USHMMA), Director of the Museum: Subject Files of Shayke (Jeshajahu) Weinberg, 1979-1995, Box 7.

29. USHMMA, Research Institute: Subject Files of the Director Michael Berenbaum, 1987-1997, Box 3, Interoffice Memorandum from David Luebke to Shayke Weinberg, director of the United States Holocaust Memorial Museum and to Michael Berenbaum, project director of the museum, 26 July 1992.

Chapter Five
Legislating History: The Armenian Tragedy and the United States Holocaust Memorial Museum

As mentioned at the outset of the study, the Armenians see the Holocaust and its commemoration ceremonies as the best opportunity to equate their experience with the immense tragedies suffered by the Jews at the hands of the Nazis. This equalization of suffering broadens support for the argument for declaring the Armenian tragedy a genocide.

Within this context Armenians have concentrated their efforts on commemorating their suffering at the United States Holocaust Memorial Museum, which was privately built in Washington D.C. on land donated by the Federal government.[1] To this end American-Armenians successfully campaigned for the appointment of an Armenian-American businessman, Set Momjian, to the thirty-four-member Holocaust Commission by President Jimmy Carter. Momjian had been an active fund-raiser for Carter's election campaign in 1976. For his efforts on behalf of Carter he had earlier been appointed as United States Representative to the United Nations General Assembly (1978-1979) and White House Representative to the Human Rights Commission in Geneva (1979). He was also chairman of the Armenian Assembly of America's Committee on the Armenian Genocide and a member of the Advisory Board for Armenian Studies at Columbia and Stanford Universities.[2]

DEBATES IN THE PRESIDENT'S COMMISSION

Heated debates arose regarding the inclusion of the Armenian case within the parameters of the President's Commission on the Holocaust, later renamed the

United States Holocaust Memorial Council. The council was charged with creating a museum program documenting Jewish suffering and making that history powerful to a general American audience. Preliminary discussions in the late 1970s began to probe the boundaries of the definition of the Holocaust experience by exploring representation of non-Jewish victims, such as homosexuals, Roma, the mentally disabled, and other targeted groups. This would be one of the most vexing issues the United States Holocaust Memorial Museum would face, and the unresolved, perhaps unresolvable, tensions would persist beyond its opening. In his comments at the Commission's meeting in February 1979, for example, historian Raul Hilberg, who characterized the Holocaust as unique, also pointed out that it was not "without its precedents and not without its implications...It would not be a fulfillment of the overall task to ignore the fates of other people, be they Armenians, or be they, during the events, the Soviet prisoners of war that died during captivity, or...other victims." Hilberg wanted to stretch the boundaries of the Holocaust narrative back in time to include the Armenians and he wanted to stretch the boundaries outward to include others murdered by the Nazis. Others cautioned that the unique situation of the Jews in the Holocaust—"never before had one people denied another people the fundamental right to live," argued Lucy Davidowicz—made it crucial to maintain and protect the unique narrative of Jewish suffering during the Holocaust. No other issue—particularly with regard to Armenians and Roma and Sinti—would so engage the attention of those responsible for the creation of the permanent exhibition.[3]

In a subsequent meeting, Kitty Dukakis, president of the Center for Genocide Studies in Brookline, Massachusetts, reporting on the work of the subcommittee on education and curricula, noted: "We discussed the Armenian experience and the sense...was to support a curriculum that included the other dramatic examples of genocide in the twentieth century, including the Armenians." Leo Sarkasian of the Armenian National Committee pleaded that, if the Commission could not recognize that "somewhere, somehow, the Armenian genocide, at least as a backdrop, has a role in {your} work...then we are indeed in trouble...Who will listen if not you?"[4]

In the President's Commission on the Holocaust, *Report to the President* (Washington, D.C., 1979), Elie Wiesel—who served as chairman of the Commission and chairman of the Council until December 1986—sought to solve the problem aphoristically by declaring that while

> Not all victims were Jews, all Jews were victims, destined for annihilation solely because they were born Jewish. They were doomed not because of something they had done or proclaimed or acquired but because of who they were: sons and daughters of the Jewish people. As such they were sentenced to death collectively and individually as part of an official and 'legal' plan unprecedented in the annals of history.

In his concluding remarks at the Commission's meeting on 24 April 1979, Wiesel argued that

> The universality of the Holocaust lies in its uniqueness. If I speak as a Jew about Jews, of course, I speak about others as well. If I were to stop speaking about Jews, I would betray both the others and my own people. I simply do not believe in denials...I understand the motivations. They are good; they are honest. There is so much pain. I was terribly moved by our Armenian friends [who had spoken at the meeting about the importance of their being included in this narrative]. I cannot tell you how much. I understand therefore, the initial impulse to extend and to elaborate and to enlarge...What I am afraid of is if you go too far, we will do neither you...nor ourselves any good.[5]

Inclusion of memory of the Armenian tragedy in the first American national civic commemoration of the Holocaust, held in the Capitol Rotunda on 24 April 1979, involved the President's Commission in a struggle with the Turkish government, which has strongly rejected the claim that the Armenian events of 1915 amounted to genocide. Ankara began an intensive campaign to keep any reference to the Armenian events from entering the boundaries of Holocaust memory—either in commemorative events or in the United States Holocaust Memorial Museum's permanent exhibition. April 24 was, coincidentally, the annual occasion for commemorative ceremonies in the Armenian community, including one scheduled just outside the Capitol. Michael Berenbaum noted:

> The Commission faced the choice of including the Armenians within the Holocaust ceremony and thus running the risk of 'universalizing' the Holocaust, or of having the Armenians stand outside, opposite the ceremony, while Jewish dead were recalled.[6]

Reverend Vartan Hartunian of the First Armenian Church of Belmont, Massachusetts, was invited to recite both in English and in Armenian the traditional prayer for the memory of the dead at the end of the ceremony, and Alex Manoogian, Honorary President of the Armenian General Benevolent Union of America, to light a seventh candle – in addition to the six memorializing the 6 million Jewish dead in the Holocaust – to memorialize victims of genocide around the world. It is said that those who were sensitive to the implications of the Capitol Rotunda Ceremony later spoke with Hartunian about the prayer and he withdrew it. However, in many of the news releases covering the Rotunda ceremony, the participation of Armenians was featured.[7]

Rabbi Irving "Yitz" Greenberg, the Commission's director, wrote:

> To the commission staff, the seventh candle was an appropriately distinguished analogy, particularly since the end result was a seven-branched fully lit menorah. Lessons were drawn from the Holocaust as to the need for human

solidarity and the indivisibility of responsibility, lest the bystander be guilty of complicity. Thus the Holocaust, a uniquely Jewish tragedy, shed a penetrating if baleful light on the moral condition of humanity and, hopefully, moved people to responsibility. Thus the Holocaust was at once particularly Jewish and universal in its implications. However, the inclusion and associations were sharply criticized by a number of figures important in the Holocaust commemoration in the State of Israel. Ultimately, Greenberg supported the inclusion of representation of the Armenian case in the museum. On 8 March 1979, he wrote Dikran Berberian, the executive director of the Armenian Assembly of America, I know that Jews and Armenians unfortunately share in common the experience of being the victims of genocide.[8]

ARMENIAN EXPECTATIONS AND HOPES

There was a great deal of expectation among various Armenian groups that their experiences would be an integral part of the overall exhibit of the museum.

In the first meeting of the Council held on 28 May 1980 in Washington D.C., Momjian was given the following assignments: 1) Committee on Museum/Memorial, 2) Committee on Education and, 3) Committee on the Arts. In addition to these committees he was appointed to the Council's fifteen member Executive Committee. During the meeting, each Council member was invited to make opening remarks. Momjian stated:

> I look forward to the next eight months and to the completed work of this Council when all peoples who have been victims of genocide can look to a museum and educational program that will tell the whole story of man's inhumanity to man. In memory of Henry Morgenthau, who was Ambassador to the Ottoman Empire during the Armenian genocide, the first genocide of the 20th century, where one and one-half million Armenians were slaughtered, and, in the memory of that great rabbi, Steven Wise, who raised tens of thousands of dollars for Armenians during that troubled period, and to show the seriousness the Armenian community places on the work of this Council, I would like to pledge an initial commitment of one million dollars on behalf of the Armenian community for the various projects of the United States Holocaust Memorial Council.[9]

Armenians hoped that the Holocaust Memorial Council would enlarge its scope to that of a United States Genocide Council in order to develop a memorial museum and educational foundation devoted to all victims of 20th century genocide—Armenians, Jews, and many others who had suffered "the unspeakable atrocity of deliberate and systematic destruction of their race." With this aim, Congressman Frank Annunzio wrote on 23 April 1980 to Wiesel, urging that positive action be taken to enlarge the scope of the Council to include all other victims of genocide in the 20th century. The summary text of Annunzio's letter follows:

> Numerous Armenian Americans of my constituency have contacted me in order to express their strong objection to the 27 September 1979 report issued by the President's Commission on the Holocaust. Specifically, my constituents have objected to statements in this report which: (1) Claim the "unique and unprecedented" nature of the Nazi Holocaust, which ignored the historical precedent of the Armenian genocide. (2) The failure of the Commission to voluntarily broaden its scope in order to include the Armenian genocide in some form. Armenian Americans throughout the United States have joined in expressing their bitter disappointment with the Commission's report and have urged that the officials on the United States Holocaust Memorial Council take positive action to include in their program and projects recognition of the Armenian genocide. They suggest enlarging the scope of the United States Holocaust Memorial Council to that of a Genocide Council which, in turn, would develop a memorial museum and educational foundation devoted to all victims of 20th century genocide—not just Jews, but the Armenian (who were the first victims of genocide in this century) and many, many others who came after them.[10]

Armenian scholars such as, Kevork Bardakjian, Vahakn Dadrian, Richard Hovannisian and Gerard Libaridian underlined their continued commitment to working individually and collectively with the United States Holocaust Memorial Museum staff as the situation might require. They inquired whether a more effective means of cooperation could not be worked out through the museum's allocation of a staff person or funds for the development of the concepts concerning the Armenian case. According to them, a formalized medium, like an advisory committee, might also provide for a more effective mechanism for scholarly collaboration. They also wished to bring their contribution to other aspects of the museum development effort, be it the library, the research facilities, its archival section, and educational programs. The Museum Development Committee, however, found the suggestion regarding the allocation of specialized staff and resources as unwarranted.[11]

University of Wisconsin religion professor Edward Linenthal, allowed behind the scenes to write a book on the creation of the museum, stresses that Armenians struggled throughout the 1980s for what they considered "just representation" in the museum's permanent exhibition. According to Linenthal, the Armenian community was willing to accept almost any representation deemed acceptable to the President's Commission. This, in their view, would serve as an important response to Turkish statements that the Armenian deaths in 1915 were not premeditated in intent or effect. They asked the commission to stretch the boundaries of the Holocaust, arguing that a group dedicated to the preservation of truth in the face of "historical denial and the cultivation of redeeming memory" had to lend a sympathetic ear to their claim.[12]

OPPOSITION TO ARMENIAN ENDEAVORS

Linenthal adds that the potential inclusion of the Armenians troubled Yaffa Eliach, a professor of history and literature at Brooklyn College of the City University of New York and director of the Center for Holocaust Studies there. She was willing to include the millions of non-Jewish victims of the Nazis, but not events that took place in 1915. She worried about the slippery slope of inclusion of non-Holocaust-related tragedies.

> Once you include the Armenians as part of Holocaust, I don't see why the American Indians should be excluded, and I don't see why Cambodia should be excluded, and I don't see why other African tribes which are being annihilated at this very moment should not be included. I think we are opening a Pandora's box by not being historically accurate, and this Commission was appointed to deal with the Holocaust.

And, echoing Eliach's concerns expressed years earlier, Miles Lerman, Vice Chairman of the National State of Israel Bonds, spoke for the concerns of many when he worried about extending Holocaust memory too far backward. "If you are introducing the Armenian tragedy to the Holocaust, why not the tragedy of the Cambodians? Why not the tragedy of the American Indians?"[13]

Gerson Cohen, Professor of History and Chancellor of the Jewish Theological Seminary of America, felt that any Holocaust memorial should be devoted exclusively to the victims of the Nazi policy of decimation of the Jews. By including the sufferings of other minorities such as Armenians, the Jews would only dilute the results of any project emerging from the Presidential mandate. Cohen did not want to appear insensitive to the tragedies of other people, but he believed that the treatment of other tragedies would mitigate the public appreciation for the suffering of the Jews of Europe. Accordingly, the distinguished scholar and rabbi thought the Holocaust Commission should recommend to the President of the United States and to Congress that the memorial be dedicated exclusively to the memory of the Jews of Europe.[14]

On the same subject the veteran journalist J.J. Goldberg writes that early in the deliberations, an Armenian-American entrepreneur offered to donate a substantial sum to the museum on the condition that it commemorate the Armenian events of 1915. However, opposition to this plan emerged quickly. Goldberg recounts that lawyer-lobbyist Paul Berger, a top lay figure in the United Jewish Appeal, insisted that the Holocaust should not be compared to other events:

> Once you open the door to things that are not related to the Holocaust, where

do you draw the line? People wanted to involve the Cambodians, the American Indians, even the Palestinians in the Holocaust museum exhibit. I say, where do you draw the line? I think the special historic experience of Jews as Jews is a different story, and reflects how the world has looked at the Jews in a special way. That is not to say there haven't been other kinds of sufferings. But to involve other kinds of suffering distracts from the experience of Jews as Jews.[15]

Yet Momjian insisted that the Armenian events of 1915 should be included in the museum. And he hoped the one million dollars to the fledgling project pledged on behalf of the Armenian community ensured that it would be. To comprehend the importance of Momjian's offer, one must realize that the legislation establishing the United States Holocaust Memorial Council specified that the planned memorial must be paid for by funds raised from the private sector. Therefore, when Momjian made his offer the Council had negligible funds raised, and his one million dollars was seen as the beginning of the fundraising campaign for the actual memorial. The fact of the matter was that the Council members did vote unanimously to accept Armenian money in return for inclusion of the Armenian tragedy, defined as a genocide, in the scope of their planned memorial.

"There was an implicit, if not explicit, understanding that the gift would result in the inclusion of the Armenian massacres in the museum's permanent exhibit," said Stuart Eizenstat, an attorney and the Domestic Policy Advisor to President Carter. And when the Turkish Ambassador to the United States learned of this, he visited Eizenstat at the White House. "I had many blunt and difficult meetings during those years, but this was the most difficult," Eizenstat recalled. The Ambassador reminded that Turkey had been hospitable to Jews over the centuries. Though neutral during the Second World War, Turkey had given refuge to many Jews fleeing Hitler. In modern times, it was the home of a large and thriving Jewish population, and it was one of the few countries with a Muslim majority that had established and maintained diplomatic relations with Israel. The Ambassador added Turkey was adamantly opposed to the inclusion of the Armenian tragedy in the museum, as currently planned.[16]

On 28 August 1980 Leon Picon, a retired United States Foreign Service Officer who served inter alia in Turkey and Japan, wrote to Monroe Freedman, director of the United States Holocaust Memorial Council, expressing his concern over some of the latent and predictable problems that could emerge from the proposed expanded role of the Council. Most students of history would, he believed, recognize that the Holocaust as a genocidal policy adopted by a government was unique, at least during the past half-millenium. Not even the Russian pogroms nor the Spanish Inquisition, dreadful though they were, could be lumped into this category. It seemed to Picon important to distinguish between contemplated genocide, meticulously executed as public policy, on the one hand, and war atrocities, on the other. To include the latter would dilute the impact of the Holocaust as a historical event with a lasting legacy.[17]

Picon said it would open up a "Pandora's Box," especially in the United States, where minorities from all over the world now resident here would delight in the opportunity to brand as genocide the actions of their former political, religious or even economic oppressors. The central question became: "Where does one draw the line, and who draws it?" While serving in Japan, Picon often heard the argument that the atomic bombs dropped on Hiroshima and Nagasaki were the first step "of a Caucasian plot to annihilate the yellow race" and that the bomb never would have been dropped on other Caucasians. It was crucial to recognize that those who made such statements truly believed them, and by that token could legitimately seek inclusion in a broadened Holocaust Memorial, posing thereby some rather difficult choices for the Council. Of course, there were also the more obvious claims to genocide: the Sioux and other American Indians, the Afro-Americans, the Cambodians and the Algerians.

It is instructive to point out that a favorite source of those who advocate and defend the Armenian case is British historian Arnold Toynbee's *Armenian Atrocities: The Murder of a Nation*. It was written at the behest of Lord James Bryce, a long-time friend and sympathist of the Armenians, before the author began his Turkish studies. In his *Western Question in Greece and Turkey: A Study in the Contact of Civilizations*, he states that he had been "employed by His Majesty's Government to compile all available documents on the recent treatment of the Armenians by the Turkish Government in a Blue Book, which was duly published and distributed as war-propaganda." In his *Study of History*, Toynbee continues to call the tragedy massacres. In his sections on genocide, he discusses the Holocaust, but not the Armenian tragedy.[18]

According to James Morgan Read, Professor of History at the University of Louisville, the causes, kinds, and consequences of atrocity propaganda are worthy of careful studies. Atrocious acts are deplorable enough by themselves; but when they are deliberately blown out of proportion by war propagandists, the consequences are significant. He examined the value of the various allegations disseminated during the years of 1914-1919. After reading pages of harrowing atrocity stories, as gathered together in the Blue Book, he concluded most of them were based on hearsay. How many of these events actually occurred was impossible to say. Almost every page of the report contained phrases such as "some said," "I was told," etc., despite Bryce's claim that "by far the larger part" of the information came from eyewitnesses.[19]

Monroe Freedman stated on 30 September 1980 that the President's Commission on the Holocaust also referred to the tragic events of 1915 as "that earlier 20th century attempt at genocide." Accordingly, when he became director of the United States Holocaust Memorial Council in January 1980, he assumed that the museum would include reference to the tragic events under the Ottoman Empire, and he had made public statements reflecting that assumption. In fact, however, the United States Holocaust Memorial Council had not made a policy decision on that issue, because no questions regarding the contents of the museum had as yet been presented to the Council.[20]

On 19 March 1981 Rabbi Rav Soloff of Beth Sholom Congregation at Johnstown, Pennsylvania wrote to Freedman, suggesting he rethink the inclusion of Armenian references in the museum. He said scholars could cite examples of Heinrich Himmler—leader of the SS, head of the German police and Waffen-SS, and Minister of the Interior—justifying the murder of Jews on the basis of the elimination and the near extermination of the Indians by the Americans, who themselves carved out *lebensraum* for themselves in the American continent. Scholars could also demonstrate that Hitler and Himmler justified their anti-Jewish policies with quotations from the New Testament. Soloff said that given that Nazi "justifications" of their genocidal policies included references to countless real or imagined precedents for Jew-hatred, slaughter of innocents, atrocities against civilians, it might be difficult to prevent any such references from appearing in the museum. The Council, Rabbi Soloff said, would have to pass judgment as to which rationalizations were most influential in Nazi decision-making and which were spoken purely for propaganda purposes.[21]

On 12 April 1981 the Assembly of Turkish American Associations, at its annual meeting in New York adopted a resolution, stating that it endorsed and supported the creation of the United States Holocaust Memorial Museum, planned for erection in Washington D.C.; that the Assembly recognized the term Holocaust as referring specifically to the Nazi effort to destroy the Jewish people. It cited as well the historical, traditional, and continuous support to the Jews by the Turkish people and noted in particular that tens of thousands of Jews fled Nazi Germany and Nazi-occupied countries during the Second World War and became full citizens of Turkey.[22]

The United States Holocaust Memorial Council, however, adopted at its meeting of 30 April 1981 the recommendation by the Museum Committee to include the Armenian episode in its program. Momjian brought the Armenian "genocide" into the forefront of discussion and said:

> Since January 1979, when the President's Commission on the Holocaust requested that the Armenian-American community lend its voice to a universal understanding of genocide, suffering, and evil, a surge of renewed hope was born. For sixty-four years, the Armenian people had fervently and solemnly sought to remind all civilized societies of the Armenian genocide and to point out the frightening consequences of indifference. He spoke of the vital importance of remembering, understanding, and remaining vigilant against a repetition of the past. He said that through the process of remembering those of our own people who have suffered and perished, we bond ourselves not only to them, but to each other and to all mankind.[23]

Momjian released the portion of the Council's report referring to the Armenians, which read: "There was unanimous approval of the fact that the Armenian Genocide should be included in the Holocaust Museum Memorial. It was deeply felt that this was part of the entire process that led ultimately to the Holocaust and, therefore, deserved a significant place in the final project." In addition to the Museum Committee resolutions, the Holocaust Council approved broader museum themes. Within the theme, "Death Does Not Have Limited Targets," the following language was unanimously adopted: "The Armenian Genocide is certainly involved in the process. The indifference of the world to that experience was definitely a prelude to the Final Solution." Momjian then stated: "I am overjoyed with these historic decisions. I have always believed that the Holocaust Council would respond as it did. If the Jewish people, who had experienced and survived such brutality, could not understand our suffering, who could?"[24]

In the meeting of the United States Holocaust Memorial Council held on 24 September 1981, Momjian informed that in August, the Armenian-American community sent the final $10,000 of a $100,000 pledge to Hillel Hall at Harvard University. He presented the first payment, of $100,000, of the $1 million pledge to the museum. Momjian said the Armenian community looked forward to the completion of the museum and the educational components.[25]

In August 1981, headlines in the Turkish press announced that a planned Washington memorial to the Jewish Holocaust of the Second World War would also refer to Turkey's "genocide" of Armenians during the First World War. The most widely read İstanbul dailies did not understand the involvement of the United States Holocaust Memorial Council into a conflict unrelated to the Jewish catastrophe. Considering the museum would not give similar attention to other human tragedies of comparable or even greater magnitude, such as the French massacre of the Huguenots, various tribal wars in Africa, Joseph Stalin's deliberate starvation of millions of Ukrainians, and Pol Pot's murder of millions of Cambodians, the museum's decision struck Turks as unfair.[26]

"There was a real uproar," recalled Hyman Bookbinder, a longtime lobbyist for the American Jewish Committee and an original member of the President's Commission and the United States Holocaust Memorial Council that succeeded it. The Turks protested that the two events were not remotely comparable. "I am confidant that the right words can be found to refer to the Armenian tragedy as an example among many of the kind that must not be permitted in the world without pinning any 'genocide' label on it," he said in an interview to the Turkish reporters.[27]

The United States Holocaust Memorial Council solicited Assistant Professor Justin McCarthy's opinion on this matter in December 1981. The main elements of his reply ran as follows: There is no similarity between the Holocaust and the deaths of Armenians in the First World War period. The Holocaust was the deliberate extermination of a people, using all the resources of an organized and powerful state. Although it took place during wartime, in fact the Holocaust had little relation to the war itself. If anything, German resources used for the extermination of Jews and others would have assisted the German war effort, had they been used strategically. The Jews were caught up in Hitler's madness; they were not the victims of war. The Armenians, on the other hand, were victims of wartime murder, starvation, and disease that affected all the inhabitants of Anatolia, not only Armenians. During the First World War eastern Anatolia was the site of both civil war and war between the Russians and the Ottomans. Innocent Armenians and innocent Muslims were forced to take sides in the conflicts. Turks were killed by the Russian army and by Armenians, while Armenians were killed by the Ottoman army and by Turks. In fact, more Muslims died than Armenians. It was a horrible period, a period of anti-human, not simply anti-Armenian excesses. The actions of the Ottoman government toward the Armenians cannot be compared to the actions of the Germans toward the Jews. The Ottomans had an ineffective government that could neither protect its own territory from foreign invasion, nor keep its citizens from killing each other. The German government, on the other hand, was all too effective. The issue of whether or not the Ottoman government ordered the killing of Armenians was never settled, but, even had they wished to, the Ottomans would have been incapable of carrying out such a plan. If a memorial to the dead in Anatolia in the First World War is to be made, it should be a memorial to the innocent dead on both sides—the innocent Muslim and Armenian villagers who were slaughtered. Obviously, no meaningful comparison can be made between the deaths of those in eastern Anatolia and the Holocaust. A more fitting comparison to the deaths in Anatolia would be the recent war between Ethiopia and Somalia, in which villagers on both sides suffered.[28]

The perspective of McCarthy was influential, and zeal to support inclusion of the Armenian tragedy in the museum began to wane. Ross Vartian, director of the Armenian Assembly of America, wrote that his organization was extremely concerned with the following statement attributed to Robert Agus, the newly-appointed director of the United States Holocaust Memorial Council, that appeared in the 8-14 April 1982 issue of *Jewish Week*: "Whether or not the Armenian massacre would be included in this area—another point of controversy—has not been determined." Based on his community's "positive" participation with the Council and a number of Council decisions affirming and reaffirming that the Armenian "genocide" was included, Vartian considered Agus' quotations disturbing. According to the Armenian administrator, the Assembly's activity in support of the Council within his community might be adversely affected if Agus' statements were widely circulated.[29]

In subsequent months, the public debate over the matter intensified. During early 1983, Armenian newsletters declared that the United States Holocaust

Memorial Council had decided to include in the museum a reference to the "genocide" of the Armenians by the Turks as a prelude to the Nazi Holocaust. The Assembly of Turkish American Associations countered that it was ready to assist the Council in authenticating any historical facts bearing on the Turkish-Armenian conflict.[30]

A full-page advertisement was placed by a Turkish American group in the weekly magazine *The Baltimore Jewish Times* on 3 June 1983 under the headline "The Holocaust and Politics." The advertisement said the uniqueness of the Holocaust—as the only documented genocide in history—would be diluted if the Armenian issue was accepted as an event of equal magnitude. Readers were urged to oppose the inclusion of Armenians in any United States memorial commemorating victims of the Holocaust. The statement referred to Armenians as "the most daring" of non-Jewish groups to press claims of persecution "because their claim of genocide is a documented myth made to seem real through the relentless propaganda at the end of the First World War by the victorious Western empires as justification for carving up the Ottoman Empire." "The truth is," it continued, "Armenians and Turks killed each other in a civil war within a global war." The advertisement went further, offering quotations and factual information which indicated Armenians backed Hitler and supported the Holocaust.

During the Second World War, it said, "Armenians set up a provisional government in Berlin, declared themselves Aryans, subscribed to Hitler's racial superiority thesis, thereby supporting the Holocaust, and contributed 20,000 troops to Hitler's army." It was signed by Jewish Members of the Assembly of Turkish American Associations. The same advertisement also appeared in Philadelphia's *Jewish Exponent*, the international edition of the *Jerusalem Post*, and three papers in the *Jewish Floridian* chain.[31]

Stephen Kimatian, a spokesman for the Armenian Association of Greater Baltimore, said in a letter to *The Baltimore Jewish Times* his group wanted a "full-page apology for allowing such a vile and despicable statement to be included in an ostensibly legitimate publication."

"The tragedy which befell the Armenian population residing in Turkey from 1895 through 1915 is absolutely documented history," Kimatian claimed. "The United States Department of State archives are replete with the accounts of the Turkish massacres of Armenians. During that time 1.5 million Armenians were systematically exterminated by the Turks." Gary Rosenblatt, editor of the weekly, acknowledged that the advertisement raised two distinct issues: whether the Holocaust and its memorials should be exclusively Jewish, and whether the Armenian events of 1915 can be labeled as genocide. The editor stated that he does not think "we have been insensitive to the problem." He noted that the paper has done stories in the past about the Armenian killings. But not to have published the advertisement "gets into whether some people are allowed to advertise."[32]

In the meantime, the United States Holocaust Memorial Council had to account for the resolution agreeing to the presentation of the Armenian version of the events of 1915 in the museum. This resolution, which was accepted under strong pressure from the Armenian lobby, actually contradicted the thematic definition outlined in the President's Commission report. The recommendations of the commission delineated the thematic scope of the museum and served as the planning team's guideline for composing the exhibition's story line and structure. Yet the thematic definition, focusing on the Holocaust, did not permit inclusion of a chapter on the Armenians. In 1983, the United States Holocaust Memorial Council accepted a compromise offered by Bookbinder. The museum would include an "appropriate reference" to the Armenians, but its planners had reserved judgment on the use of the word "genocide." "We have to acknowledge some merit to the Turkish claim and be careful about our language," Bookbinder said. "There is some ambiguity here." Armenians vehemently disagreed. Armenian reaction garnered wide coverage in their own press.[33]

On 23 June 1983 Richard Chambers, Associate Professor at the University of Chicago, wrote to Bookbinder reiterating his firm conviction that the Holocaust Memorial should be devoted entirely and exclusively to the European Jewish Holocaust of the Nazi era; that it would be a serious mistake to dilute the impact of the Memorial by including other instances of "Man's Inhumanity to Man"; and that to single out the Armenians from among all the many other people who have at one time or another in history suffered a major communal tragedy would be particularly inappropriate. Chambers contended that since the historical record of exactly what transpired in the eastern provinces of the Ottoman Empire during the First World War was far from complete, whatever might be said at this point would inevitably fall short of the historical truth. According to the Chicago professor, it would be a grave injustice to the Turkish people to brand them with guilt for crimes against humanity when these had yet to be proven.[34]

Throughout the United States Holocaust Memorial Council's anguished attempts to assert the uniqueness of the Holocaust and also to represent the experiences of various victim groups, commitment to telling the story of the Armenian case waxed and waned. In the meeting of the Council held on 4 August 1983, Miles Lerman asked the members that if they chose to include the Armenian tragedy in the narrative of the Holocaust, why not introduce the tragedy of the Cambodians. He continued: "Why not introduce the tragedy of the American Indians. Why not introduce the tragedy of people that were annihilated and wiped off the surface of the earth?" Lerman added:

> There are people that feel that if we step away from the basic concept that this museum is dedicated to the memorialization of the victims of the Holocaust and the other victims of Nazi brutality, we are exposing ourselves to a very dangerous open field, which may distress the main objective.[35]

Momjian was troubled by the now-regular discussion of the Armenian matter:

> Three years ago, The Museum Committee came to this Council with the unanimous decision that the Armenians would be included in a significant way. That was relayed to the Armenian community. The following June this Council voted unanimously again that the Armenians would be included. A month ago under Mark Talisman's chairmanship, the Museum Committee met and there was a consensus of opinion that not only the Armenians but others would be included. It is three years now since that Museum Committee came in with that decision, and I find now that there is a discussion whether there was [an] Armenian genocide or not. The Jewish community I believe has been brought up long before the Holocaust on the stories of the Armenian genocide. The Turkish records have been closed for seventy years. When Monroe Freedman asked them why they don't make them available, they said at that time they did not want to embarrass the Armenians. I understand now they say they're going to make them available. I find it insulting at this stage of the game to have a discussion or dispute as to whether or not there was an Armenian genocide.[36]

In a letter to Wiesel, who did not attend the meeting, Bookbinder noted that "the Armenian tragedy was the principal episode discussed. In light of major events outside the Council to close the door to any kind of reference to the Armenian events, the Council reaffirmed its earlier decisions for an appropriate inclusion of this historic event," the nature of which had not yet been determined.[37]

President Ronald Reagan appointed on 12 July 1985 California Governor George Deukmejian to be a member of the United States Holocaust Memorial Council. The Governor pledged to help make California a leader in the one hundred million dollar fund-raising campaign to build the Holocaust museum. Deukmejian, the second Council member of Armenian descent, emphasized the ties between his Armenian heritage and the Jewish people in a speech on 10 November 1985 in Los Angeles to a star-studded benefit for the Simon Wiesenthal Center. The Governor claimed that Hitler hatched his slaughter of millions of Jews by studying the earlier Turkish massacre of "1,5 million Armenians." "Many of you have grown up hearing the truly tragic stories of friends, families and loved ones who died at the hands of the Nazis during the Holocaust in the 1940s," Deukmejian added.

> Gloria and I grew up hearing those stories too—stories about our relatives who were brutally driven from their homes and massacred during the Armenian genocide in the early 1900s. The civilized world barely noticed, but Hitler did. In formulating his own evil and murderous plans, he surmised that he could get away with it because, as he put it, 'Who nowadays talks about the Armenians.'[38]

On 14 February 1988 the Representatives of the Federation of all Turkish Associations in Israel wrote to Yitzhak David, Advisor to the Israeli Prime Minister, that they had learned of the United States Holocaust Memorial Council's plans to include the Armenian issue in the Holocaust Memorial Museum. They said this was inappropriate and added they were convinced that such a move would not benefit the Jewish people and would undermine the significance of the Holocaust. The Turkish Jews said they had no objection to any people erecting their own memorial to commemorate their own victims wherever they wanted. There was no basis, however, for linking any other people to this tragedy of the Jewish people.[39]

The Turkish Jews maintained that if the United States Holocaust Memorial Council decided to go ahead with this move, Israel should not remain indifferent. They said it would be ungrateful to make the charge of genocide against the Turks, who saved Jews from the Nazis. Turkish Jews therefore called on the Israeli government to work to get the museum's decision revoked.

In response on behalf of the members of the United States Holocaust Memorial Council to various letters criticizing the decision to include a reference to the Armenian tragedy, Sara Bloomfield, Acting Executive Director of the Museum, asserted the primacy of the Holocaust at the museum, in accordance with its Congressional mandate. According to Bloomfield, there would be a "single focus" for the museum on the Holocaust.[40]

Yet shortly afterwards, Berenbaum introduced a plan to have the Armenian issue mentioned in four different occasions at the museum: (1) A nine-minute film on "Hitler's ascent to power (including precedents)" would be shown to the visitors at the beginning of their one and a half hour museum tour. The two or three minutes that would deal with "precedents for mass murder" would make reference in some way to the Armenians, along with references to the Americans and the Indians, the Australians and the Aborigines, and others. (2) There would be a wall dealing with the Nazi invasion of Poland and the Nazi terror in that country. Here, Hitler's purported remark referencing world indifference to the Armenians would be displayed. (3) There would be an exhibition dealing with Henry Morgenthau, Jr.'s efforts within the United States government during the Second World War to save Jews. Morgenthau, Jr.'s diary might be quoted to the effect that his conscience was spurred by memories of the effort made during the First World War on behalf of the Armenians by his father, Henry Morgenthau, who served at the time as United States Ambassador to the Ottoman Empire. (4) On the wall dealing with resistance to the Nazis, there might be a quotation from a Jewish resistance fighter in Bialystock/Poland who likened his fight to Musa Dagh, the scene of Armenian-Turkish conflict made famous in Franz Werfel's novel, *The Forty Days of Musa Dagh* (1933).[41]

These four references remained problematic. As previously mentioned, the quote of Hitler was almost certainly a fabrication, and the quote cannot be confirmed to have ever been spoken.

The notion that the Nazis were following a tradition of mass murder established by others ignores the unique purpose with which they went about the destruction of the Jewish people in Europe. Moreover, the Nazis relied on nineteenth century racial theories and ancient Christian anti-Semitic traditions for their inspiration, not Ottoman Armenian history. Neither the Nazis' motivation, rationale, nor program with respect to the annihilation of Jews emerged from or related to Ottoman history. Only by describing the Holocaust merely as an example of human suffering and the cruelty of war, can the term "precedent" be applied to the Ottoman-Armenian conflict.

The quotation referencing Musa Dagh was also problematic. If a Jewish resistance fighter against the Nazis in fact had made the quoted remark, it demonstrated nothing except that he probably had read the 1933 Franz Werfel novel, *The Forty Days of Musa Dagh*, a fictional account of Armenian conflict against Turks. It is not a historical record of Ottoman-Armenian history.

Mark Epstein, a veteran Jewish leader and former head of the Union of Councils for Soviet Jews, in a letter to the editor of *Washington Jewish Week* of 7 December 1989 commented:

> Today in Germany and elsewhere many contend that the Holocaust was simply a terrible event, neither unique nor particular. To compare the activities of Ottoman Armenians to the situation of Europe's Jews in 1933 or 1939 is a dangerous invitation to revisionism about the Holocaust...If Jews say every terrible event or failed revolution is genocide, why should the world believe the Holocaust is distinctive?[42]

Epstein appropriately gives prominence to some additional points and goes on as follows:

> The Ottoman Empire and Turkish people who stand accused today have an exemplary record in their treatment of the Jews: the Turks offered refuge to Jews fleeing the inquisition in 1492 and blood libels were unknown there, except when instigated by Christians, who were severely punished by the Sultans. In 1912, when Northern Greece became independent of the Ottomans, many Jews fled to Istanbul to remain under Turkish rule. In 1917-1921, as the allies conquered and occupied Syria, at the time of the events in question, many Syrian Jews fled to Istanbul to remain under Turkish rule. During the Holocaust, those European Jews who managed to reach Turkey found ways to stay and survive, even without papers and visas.

And at the end of the letter he directs the pertinent question to the editor:

> Are you so sure of the historical facts, and so confident in those who are asking your support, as to endanger the special significance of the Holocaust as

an historical event and slander a people who offered us refuge and safe haven over the centuries?

In June 1990 the United States Holocaust Memorial Museum Director Shayke Weinberg declared that it was a mistake on Elie Wiesel's part to have promised to deal with the Armenian issue in the museum. Weinberg said he would prefer no reference at all to this issue in the museum, which should deal only with the Holocaust from 1933 to 1945. He knew, however, that the Council was in a bind because it had made a commitment to the Armenians and there was no practical way to get out of it altogether. He therefore set out to fulfill this commitment in as minimal a way as possible.

"We were charged to tell the story of 1933-1945—not to make a museum of world politics," said William Lowenberg, the Council Vice Chairman and member of Board of Governors of the Jewish Agency for Israel. Referencing the Armenian tragedy "would dilute the meaning and wouldn't do anybody any good."[43]

Facing stiff resistance from some members of the Content Committee, Michael Berenbaum was forced to scale back his plans, informing the Museum's executive committee on 15 August 1990 that at least the reference to Armenians in the film and Hitler's quotation should be in the exhibition. The committee stated, however, that

> the only mention of the Armenian genocide would be the quotation from Hitler, and that the Content Committee should decide if and how the 'Rise of Hitler' film...should include a reference to the Armenian genocide or in fact any reference to precedents...Albert Abrahamson asked that the minutes reflect that it is the 'sense' of the Committee that a comparison should not be made in the film or any other place in the Museum to any other mass murder, because the Holocaust is unique.[44]

Berenbaum, who strongly dissented from the committee's decision, continued to press the losing battle for inclusion of the Armenians in the film, the title of which no longer included "genocidal precedents." At a Content Committee meeting on 13 February 1991, a prominent survivor and Council representative lost control and screamed at Berenbaum, "ordering" him not to mention Armenians in his presence again. Only Franklin Littell and Raul Hilberg spoke in Berenbaum's behalf. At the cost of significant political support within the institution—several people mentioned that Berenbaum lost any chance to eventually become museum director because of this issue—he succeeded in salvaging the Hitler quotation for inclusion in the permanent exhibition, for even that had been in jeopardy.[45]

Though the matter was largely settled by this point, Turkish groups both in the United States and Israel continued to press for a complete removal of any reference to the Armenian tragedy. In point of fact, they pressed as well for mentions of Turkey's positive role in saving Jews during the Second World War.

Bülent Başol, president of the Assembly of Turkish American Associations, in a letter of 16 February 1993 to Weinberg, said the museum should feature the stories of Turkish diplomats who rescued numerous Jewish scholars and others from the Holocaust and Turkey's overall efforts to provide safe haven throughout the Second World War. The president of the Assembly of Turkish American Associations was convinced that any attempt to link the Holocaust with the Armenian tragedy would only serve to enhance the claims of extremist and fringe groups who, despite incontrovertible proof, continue to deny the historical reality of the Holocaust.[46]

Even after the decision of the museum, Turkish groups have continued to press the museum on its exhibits and research policies, largely in reaction to less noteworthy decisions and policies of the museum staff.

The Assembly of Turkish American Associations on 27 October 2000 addressed a letter to the museum requesting clarification on fifteen points related to the latter's policies and research methods concerning tragedies other than the Holocaust.[47] Turkish Americans found the apparent position of the museum on the Armenian allegations of genocide deeply unsettling.

The group suggested that going forward, the museum should state from which authority the museum had the right to proclaim on tragedies other than the Holocaust, make clear its policy for selecting tragedies for inclusion among its archives, research materials, and exhibits, make clear its position on whether the Armenian tragedy was a genocide or not, and explain how they reached that conclusion and whether that view is an expression of the United States government position, and finally, make clear that utterances of individual staffers of the museum do not represent the official policy or view of the museum.

In response to a sense that the museum did not have an adequate appreciation of historical events related to the Armenian genocide, it suggested that the museum's research arm objectively examine the complex series of events which characterized the final century of the Ottoman Empire, roughly 1820-1923, the latter part of which period saw the deaths of hundreds of thousands of Armenians and several million Ottoman Muslims. And finally, the group suggested the museum revisit its decision to post a dubious quote from Adolf Hitler.

Notwithstanding these suggestions, the museum has yet to provide a substantive response and the disputed quote by Hitler remains.

NOTES

1. İlhan Selçuk, "Daha Anlayamadık mı?" (Could Not We Understand Yet?), *Cumhuriyet*, 5 December 1985, p.2; Ufuk Güldemir, "Ermeni Soykırımı Müzede" (Armenian

Genocide in the Museum), *Cumhuriyet*, 7 October 1988, p. 12.

2. USHMMA, United States Holocaust Memorial Council: Minutes and Records Relating to Council Meetings, May 1980-June 1994, Box 24, Council Member Biographies/Curriculum Vitaes.

3. Edward Linenthal, "The Boundaries of Memory: The United States Holocaust Memorial Musem," *American Quarterly*, Vol. 46, No.3 (September 1994), p. 430 fn 9.

4. Edward Linenthal, *Preserving Memory: The Struggle to Create America's Holocaust Museum* (New York: Viking Penguin, 1995), p. 229.

5. Linenthal, "The Boundaries of Memory," p. 430 fn 9.

6. Linenthal, *Preserving Memory*, p. 230; Michael Berenbaum, *After Tragedy and Triumph: Essays in Modern Jewish Thought and the American Experience* (Cambridge: Cambridge University Press, 1990), p. 37.

7. USHMMA, President's Commission on the Holocaust: Correspondence and Reading Files, 1978-1979, Box: 5, Letter from Michael Berenbaum, Deputy Director, to Vigen Babayan, Vice President, Science and Technology, Stokely-Van Camp, Inc., Indianapolis/Indiana, 11 May 1979; ibid., Letter from Michael Berenbaum, Deputy Director, to Herbert Rumerman, Belmont/Massachusetts, 15 June 1979.

8. Linenthal, *Preserving Memory*, pp. 230 and 311; Irvin Greenberg, *Living As a Jew: Observing Jewish Holidays* (New York: Summit Books, 1988), p. 343.

9. USHMMA, United States Holocaust Memorial Council: Minutes and Records Relating to Council Meetings, May 1980-June 1994, Box: 1, Transcripts of the Proceedings of the United States Holocaust Memorial Council, 28 May 1980; "Momjian Pledges One Million Dollars on Behalf of the Community to Holocaust Council," *The Armenian Observer*, 25 June 1980, p. 10.

10. Congressional Record, House of Representatives, p. H 2969, 24 April 1980.

11. USHMMA, Research Institute: Subject Files of the Director Michael Berenbaum, 1987-1997, Box 3, Letters Exchanged Between Rouben Adalian, Director of Academic Affairs of the Armenian Assembly of America, Washington, D.C. and Michael Berenbaum, Project Director of the United States Holocaust Memorial Museum, 28 December 1989 and 17 January 1990.

12. Linenthal, *Preserving Memory*, pp. 228-229.

13. USHMMA, President's Commission on the Holocaust: Subject Files Relating to the Commission's Work and Research, 1978-1984, Box: 3, Transcript of Proceedings of the President's Commission on the Holocaust Commission Meeting, Washington, D.C., 24 April 1979, pp. 108-109; Linenthal, *Preserving Memory*, pp. 229 and 232.

14. USHMMA, President's Commission on the Holocaust: Subject Files Relating to the Commission's Work and Research, 1978-1984, Box: 3, Letter from Gerson Cohen, Chancellor of the Jewish Theological Seminary of America, New York to Elie Wiesel, Chairman of the President's Commission on the Holocaust, New York, 5 June 1979.

15. J.J. Goldberg, *Jewish Power: Inside the American Jewish Establishment* (Reading, Massachusetts: Addison-Wesley Publishing Company, 1996), pp. 194-195. Arnold and Porter attorney Paul Berger, who used to be president of the Jewish Federation of Washington, D.C., was also a member of the Board of Governors of the Jewish Agency.

16. Stuart Eizenstat, *Imperfect Justice: Looted Assets, Slave Labor, and the Unfinished Business of World War II* (New York: Public Affairs, 2003), p.18; Judith Miller, *One, by One, by One: Facing the Holocaust* (New York: Simon and Schuster, 1990), pp. 259 and 302 fn 46. See also Israel Charny, "The Conference Crisis: The Turks, Ar-

menians, and the Jews," in Israel Charny and Shamai Davidson, eds., *The Book of the International Conference on the Holocaust and Genocide. Book One: The Conference Program and Crisis* (Tel Aviv: Institute on the Holocaust and Genocide, 1983), pp. 294-295 and 317-321.

17. This and the following paragraph are based on the letter from Leon Picon to Monroe Freedman, director of the United States Holocaust Memorial Council, Bethesda/ Maryland, 28 August 1980.

18. See Arnold Toynbee, *Armenian Atrocities: The Murder of a Nation* (London, New York and Toronto: Hodder and Stoughton, 1915); idem, *Western Question in Greece and Turkey: A Study in the Contact of Civilizations* (London: Constable and Company Ltd., 1922), p. 50 and idem, *A Study of History*, Vol. 7, (London and New York: Oxford University Press, 1946), pp. 290, 304 and 307.

19. James Morgan Read, *Atrocity Propaganda 1914-1919* (New York: Arno Press, reprinted, 1972), p. 221. British propaganda activities during the First World War are described at length in Michael Sanders and Philip Taylor, *British Propaganda during the First World War, 1914-1918* (London and Basingstoke: The Macmillan Press Limited, 1982); Gary Messinger, *British Propaganda and the State in the First World War* (Manchester and New York: Manchester University Press, 1992) and Servet Avşar, *Birinci Dünya Savaşında İngiliz Propagandası* (British Propaganda in the First World War), (Ankara: Kim Yayınları, 2004).

20. USHMMA, President's Commission on the Holocaust: Correspondence and Reading Files, 1978-1979, Box: 7, Letter from Monroe Freedman, director of the United States Holocaust Memorial Council, to Kemal Karpat, Professor of History and chairman of the Middle East Studies Program at the University of Wisconsin, Madison/Wisconsin, 30 September 1980.

21. Letter from Rabbi Rav Soloff of Beth Sholom Congregation to Monroe Freedman, director of the United States Holocaust Memorial Council, Johnston/Pennsylvania, 19 March 1981.

22. Letter from Ülkü Ülgür, president of the Assembly of Turkish American Associations, to Monroe Freedman, director of the United States Holocaust Memorial Council, Washinton, D.C., 23 April 1981.

23. USHMMA, United States Holocaust Memorial Council: Minutes and Records Relating to Council Meetings, May 1980-June 1994, Box: 2, Minutes of the Meetings of the United States Holocaust Memorial Council, 30 April 1981.

24. "Armenian Genocide Included in U.S. Holocaust Council's Program," *Armenian Reporter*, Vol. 14, No. 30, 14 May 1981, p. 1; "U.S. Holocaust Museum to Include 1915 Massacres," *The California Courier*, Vol. 23, No. 43, 14 May 1981, p. 1; "Armenian Genocide Included in Holocaust Council Programs," *Armenian Weekly*, 23 May 1981, p.1.

25. USHMMA, United States Holocaust Memorial Council: Minutes and Records Relating to Council Meetings, May 1980-June 1994, Box: 2, Minutes of the Meetings of the United States Holocaust Memorial Council, 24 September 1981.

26. See, among others, Necdet Berkand, "Amerika'daki Ermeniler Türklere Karşı Yeni Tertipler Peşinde"(Armenians in America Are in Quest of New Plots Against the Turks), *Tercüman*, 19 August 1981, pp. 1 and 13; "Katil Ermeniler Şimdi de Amerikan Yahudileri İle İşbirliği Yapmaya Başladı"(Murderer Armenians Now Began to Co-operate With American Jews), *Günaydın*, 19 August 1981, p. 4; Rauf Tamer, "Ateşle

Oynamak(2)"{ To Play With Fire(2)}, *Tercüman*, 20 August 1981, p. 2; "Türkiye'deki Musevilerin Dini Lideri Hahambaşı Ermeni Girişimine Karşı Çıktı" (The Religious Leader of the Jews in Turkey Chief Rabbi Has Opposed the Armenian Attempt), *Günaydın*, 22 August 1981, pp. 8 and 4; Rauf Tamer, "Bu Haftadan Kalan"(That Remains From This Week), *Tercüman*, 23 August 1981, p. 2; Bedii Faik, "Mişonyan Anıtı"(Mişonyan Monument), *Hürriyet*, 23 August 1981, p. 6; Saynur Gören, "Soykırım Müzesinde Ermenilere Yer Verilmeyecek"(No Place Will Be Allotted to Armenians in the Holocaust Museum), *Milliyet*, 28 August 1981, p. 8.

27. See, for example, "ABD'deki Türklerin Adalet Mücadelesi" (The Struggle for Justice of the Turks in the United States of America), *Yeni Asır*, 6 September 1981, p.6; Tuna Köprülü, "Yahudi Soykırım Müzesi Amerika'da Mesele Oluyor" (Jewish Genocide Museum Is Becoming a Problem in America), *Hürriyet*, 16 September 1981, p. 21; Oktay Ekşi, "Bilelim de..." (Let Us Know Any Way), Editorial, *Hürriyet*, 16 September 1981, p. 3; Sezai Orkunt, "Yahudi Katliamının Anısına Yapılacak Anıt-Müzede Ermeniler Yer Kapmaya Uğraşıyor" (Armenians Are Endeavoring to Seize a Place in the Museum to Be Constructed in Memory of the Jewish Genocide), *Milliyet*, 1 October 1981, p. 7.

28. Letter from Justin McCarthy, Assistant Professor at the University of Louisville/Kentucky, to Hillel Levine, Deputy Director of the United States Holocaust Memorial Council, Louisville/Kentucky, 15 December 1981.

29. USHMMA, United States Holocaust Memorial Council: Records of the Chairperson—Elie Wiesel, 1978-1986, Box: 7, Letter from Ross Vartian, Director of the Armenian Assembly of America, to Elie Wiesel, Chairman of the United States Holocaust Memorial Council, Washington, D.C., 12 April 1982.

30.USHMMA, United States Holocaust Memorial Council: Records of the Chairperson—Elie Wiesel, 1978-1986, Box: 7, Letter from Ali Sevin, Secretary General of the Assembly of Turkish American Associations, to Elie Wiesel, Chairman of the United States Holocaust Memorial Council, Washington, D.C., 4 March 1983.

31. "The Holocaust and Politics," *The Baltimore Jewish Times*, 3 June 1983, p. 55. Full text of the advertisement will be found in Appendix. See also Frank Somerville, "Pro-Turkish Ad in Jewish Times Enrages Armenian Community," *The Sun*, 6 July 1983, p. F14 and "Ad in United States Sparks Armenian Protest," *Turkish Daily News*, 8 July 1983, p. 1. Christopher Walker, basing himself on British archival documents, concurs in his *Armenia: The Survival of a Nation* (London: Routledge, 1980), p. 357 on the Armenian collaboration with the Nazis during the Second World War. He notes that on 30 December 1941 an Armenian battalion commanded by Andranik was created by the Wehrmacht. The battalion, which totaled 20,000 was operational in the Crimea and the North Caucasus. On 15 December 1942, an Armenian National Council headed by Ardashes Abeghian was founded in Berlin. It was proved to the Nazis that the Armenians were Aryans. For the most detailed published description of Armenian-German relations in the period of the Second World War see Enno Meyer and A.J. Berkian, *Zwischen Rhein und Arax, 900 Jahre Deutsch-Armenische beziehungen* (Oldenburg: Heinz Holzberg Verlag, 1988), pp. 101-157.

32. Stephen Kimatian, "Armenian Genocide," Letters, *The Baltimore Jewish Times*, 5 August 1983, p. 7; Lila Terzian Chorbajian, "Turkish Ad," Letters, *The Baltimore Jewish Times*, 8 July 1983, pp. 6 and 17; Aram Kondayan, "Armenian Genocide," Letters, *The Baltimore Jewish Times*, 15 July 1983, pp. 7 and 39; "Armenians Protest Against

Turkish Ad in Jewish Weekly," *The Jerusalem Post*, 8 July 1983, p. 4; Mimsi Milton, "Caught in the Crossfire: The Jewish Community Finds Itself in the Middle of a Bitter Conflict Between the Armenians and the Turks," *The Baltimore Jewish Times*, 12 August 1983, pp. 65-67 and 75; Sheldon Laskin, "Well Handled," Letters, *The Baltimore Jewish Times*, 9 September 1983, p. 7.

33. Jeshajahu Weinberg and Rina Elieli, *The Holocaust Museum in Washington* (New York: Rizzoli International Publications, 1995), p. 164; Mary Leonard, "War of Words; Armenians, Turks Revive Persecutions of 1915," *Detroit News*, 30 April 1984, p. 3.

34. Letter from Richard Chambers, Associate Professor in the Department of Near Eastern Languages and Civilizations at the University of Chicago, to Hyman Bookbinder, Washington Representative of the American Jewish Committee and Member of the United States Holocaust Memorial Council, Chicago, 23 June 1983.

35. USHMMA, United States Holocaust Memorial Council: Minutes and Records Relating to Council Meetings, May 1980-June 1994, Box: 4, Minutes of the Meeting of the United States Holocaust Memorial Council, 4 August 1983; Linenthal, *Preserving Memory*, p. 231.

36. Ibid.

37. Linenthal, *Preserving Memory*, p. 312.

38. Leo Wolinsky, "Deukmejian Woos Jewish Voters, Cites Links to Armenians," *Los Angeles Times*, 11 November 1985, p. 3.

39. This and the following paragraph are based on the letter from the Representatives of the Federation of all Turkish Associations in Israel to Yitzhak David, Advisor to the Israeli Prime Minister, Jerusalem, 14 February 1988.

40. Letter from Sara Bloomfield, Acting Executive Director of the United States Holocaust Memorial Museum, to Rabbi Rav Soloff of Beth Sholom Congregation, Washington, D.C., 10 July 1989.

41. Weinberg and Elieli, *The Holocaust Museum in Washington*, p. 164.

42. This and the following paragraph are based on Mark Epstein, "Armenia, Turks," Letters, *Washington Jewish Week*, 7 December 1989, p. 13.

43. Judith Weinraub, "How Passion, Politics, Money and Will Created the U.S. Holocaust Museum," *The Washington Post*, 18 April 1993, p. A29.

44. Linenthal, *Preserving Memory*, p. 234.

45. Ibid.

46. Letter from Bülent Başol, president of the Assembly of Turkish American Associations, to Shayke Weinberg, director of the United States Holocaust Memorial Museum, Washington, D.C., 16 February 1993.

47. Letter from Güler Köknar, executive director of the Assembly of Turkish American Associations, to Wesley Fisher, director of external affairs of the United States Holocaust Memorial Museum, Washington, D.C., 27 October 2000. The following description of the views of the Assembly of Turkish American Associations' is based on this source.

Conclusion

In view of the trail of compelling evidence presented above one can safely arrive at the conclusion that the Armenian relocations are not comparable with the Holocaust and they are different fundamentally in nature, purpose, scope and kind. The Holocaust was proven and established as a genocide before the International Military Tribunal at Nuremberg with those accused afforded all due process. Unlike in the case of Jewish calamity, there had so far been no verdict by an international court labeling the events of 1915 as genocide. Armenians have forgone bringing their genocide allegation before the International Court of Justice at The Hague. Following the First World War, when the British had access to all documents of the defeated Ottoman Empire and had the alleged perpetrators of atrocities under British control on the island of Malta, they failed to indict or try any of them for the very atrocities claimed in British wartime propaganda. Had there been a moment to establish genocide and related crimes as a historical fact that would have been it. And yet, Britain decided against it.

At its core, the Holocaust was motivated purely by a quasi-racist ideology. Pursuing the extermination of the Jews either failed to contribute to, or detracted from, the German war effort. Jews did not revolt against German rule until their demise was imminent; they posed no threat to German rule over its conquered territories.

Moreover, the nature of the Nazi genocide – a mechanized and massive destruction of an entire people in a short period of time – had never before been attempted. The German government planned and directed the slaughter of the Jews of Germany and Europe.

By comparison, the deaths of Armenians at the hands of the Ottomans occurred often following Armenian separatist actions and resistance to Ottoman rule. Neither those deaths, nor the planning of them, reflected the kind of strategy, forethought, or consideration so common to the Nazi Holocaust. In notable cases, Armenian deaths occurred in direct contravention of Ottoman policies – and Ottoman authorities were the ones who punished those responsible. The records demonstrate the Ottomans intended to return the relocatees to their homes. No discussions of any plan to wipe the Armenians off the face of the earth, as the Nazis later sought to do the Jews appear in the minutes of the Ottoman Council of Ministers at the time. In fact, Armenians in many parts of the empire, including Armenians of high authority in the Sublime Porte, were unharmed throughout the historical period in question. By comparison, Nazi Germany was ruthlessly efficient in discovering and removing any Jews from within its borders.

Given the basic qualitative differences in intent, motive, scale and methodology behind them, the Holocaust was not a repetition of the forced Armenian displacements and subsequent deaths; while both are tragedies, they were radically different.

Genocide is a legal term in international criminal law and its definition is given by the United Nations Convention on the Prevention and Punishment of the Crime of Genocide of 1948. Turkey and Armenia are among the parties to this convention. Neither Turkey nor Armenia entered any reservations or deposited additional instruments with their signatures to or ratifications of the convention. The instrument remained in effect for a period of ten years from the date of its coming into force, after which its validity was extended for successive periods of five years for such contracting parties.

The 1948 convention declared that the core of the crime of genocide was a specific intent to destroy a national, ethnical, religious or racial group, as such. There could be no genocide without intent. Two ad-hoc tribunals established by the United Nations to try violations of international humanitarian law committed in the former Yugoslavia and Rwanda, respectively, have addressed the central role of intent in the crime of genocide. The intent requirement of the 1948 convention is also reaffirmed in Article 30 of the Rome Statute of the International Criminal Court adopted in 1998. Using this authoritative definition, the forced Armenian population movement was not an example of genocide. Ottoman archival records clearly show that there was no intention on the part of the Sublime Porte to exterminate the Armenians. The Ottoman government never at any time planned, wanted, organized or carried out anything approaching genocide. Rather the Armenian losses were the result of other actions, such as brigandage, disease and famine or a combination of circumstances.

One cannot say the same for the Holocaust, which was hardly incidental, but planned and intentional. The Holocaust is an instance of genocide in which the intentions and plans of the perpetrators are fully known. The record of the Nazi slaughter is unambiguous. Hitler and his Nazi party in Germany used genocide against all those who opposed them. They made and carried out a plan to kill every Jew they could find. Equating that genocide with the events of 1915 dilutes the moral force that recollection of the Holocaust should generate for all. Application of the term genocide to the tragedies of 1915 deprives it of its real meaning.

The term genocide should therefore apply to those situations which merit it, and not those which do not. Those Armenian victims of tragedy are similar to the millions of others who have suffered terribly as a result of war, whether the Boer, the Vietnamese, the Chinese, or the Russians. These people, touched by tragedy, are all treated by historians as victims, and correctly so. But they were not victims of genocide – that distinction must be held apart, and not be appropriated without caution and care.

Appendix:
Advertisement that ran in
The Baltimore Jewish Times,
3 June 1983, p. 55

HOLOCAUST AND POLITICS

Anyone who has read, or seen on the stage or TV, Elie Wiesel's inspired play, "The Madness of God," carries with him, possibly forever, the imprint of the hero's determination to preserve his heritage in the face of political pressures, political intrigues and bargaining, political encirclement, and political pay-offs. Throughout post-Biblical history, Jews of Diaspora have uncompromisingly clung to their traditions, through the Babylonian Captivity, the Spanish and Portuguese Inquisitions, the Russian pogroms, and the Nazi Holocaust.

Of these and of all the human tragedy that have beset this planet, undoubtedly nothing can match the madness of Adolph Hitler's Holocaust. The Holocaust, even in the context of Jewish history, was unique. Unique, because it was, and remains, the only documentable genocide. Unique, because it was deliberately Jewish. Unique, because it was undertaken as a national policy, energetically and meticulously carried out. Unique, because it was unprovoked and total carnage.

Now, the United States Government is determined to build a living monument, not only to preserve a record of the Holocaust, but to declare to all mankind the commitment of this nation to the banishment from the earth of anything parallel to Holocaust. But nothing, nothing parallels the Holocaust. It is unique.

We support the move to establish a Jewish Holocaust Memorial, because it has been in the Turkish tradition to rise in defense of the Jewish people. Turks did this by providing a safe haven to the Jews who fled the Iberian Inquisitions, and after their settlement in the Ottoman Empire, placed many in high governmental positions. In the XVIth century, one of the Ottoman Sultans offered the Jews a homeland—in Palestine—which, because of their comfort and freedoms under Ottoman rule, they did not accept. After the Turkish Republic was established, Turkey risked her declared neutrality by providing Turkish ships to smuggle some 40.000 Jews destined for the Holocaust out of Eastern Europe. Turks were among the first to recognize the State of Israel, and until the time of Camp David the only Moslem people to do so.

But now, for political reasons, the central purpose of the Holocaust Memorial is being diluted. Other groups are knocking at the door seeking admission in order to further their nationalistic goals.

Of these, the most daring are the Armenians. Daring, because their claim of genocide is a documented myth made to seem real through the relentless propaganda at the end of World War I by the victorious Western empires as justification for carving up the Ottoman Empire. The truth is Armenians and Turks killed each other in a civil war within a global war. The Armenian attempt to infiltrate the Holocaust Memorial as innocent victims of a genocide is also curious, because, during the rise of Hitler, their publication *Hairenik* in 1936 carried statements like this: "Sometimes it is difficult to eradicate these poisonous elements (the Jews) when they have struck deep root like a chronic disease. And when it becomes necessary for a people (the Nazis) to eradicate them in an uncommon method, these attempts are regarded revolutionary. During a surgical operation the flow of blood is a natural thing. Under such conditions dictatorship seems to have the role of a saviour."

Curious also, because during World War II, Armenians set up a provisional government in Berlin, declared themselves Aryans, subscribed to Hitler's racial superiority thesis, thereby supporting the Holocaust and contributed 20.000 troops to Hitler's army.

Most Jews in this country are unaware that this intrusion is happening. Most who learn of it are shocked.

This much is clear. To dejudaicize the Jewish Holocaust Memorial is to water down its meaning. Who gets in and who doesn't now becomes a political issue, settled too frequently by political intrigue and pay-offs—call it votes.

This must not happen. Keep the Memorial Jewish. Write. Let the Council know that the broadening its scope will lose them your support.

Jewish Members of the Assembly of Turkish American Associations

Bibliography

I. UNPUBLISHED PRIMARY SOURCES

Official

Department of State Papers (USNA), National Archives and Records Administration, College Park, Maryland
Foreign Office Papers (FO), National Archives, Kew, London
Prime Minister's Office Ottoman Archives (BOA), İstanbul
Turkish General Staff Military History and Strategic Studies Directorate Archives (ATESE), Ankara
War Office Papers (WO), National Archives, Kew, London

Private

American Board of Commissioners for Foreign Missions Papers, Houghton Library, Harvard University
Breckinridge Long Papers, Library of Congress, Manuscript Division, Washington, D.C.
John Aram Shishmanian Papers, Hoover Institution Library and Archives, Stanford University, California
Laurence Steinhardt Papers, Library of Congress, Manuscript Division, Washington, D.C.
United States Holocaust Memorial Museum Archives, Washington, D.C.

II. PUBLISHED PRIMARY SOURCES

Official

Britain

British Documents on the Origins of the War 1898-1914, G.P. Gooch and Harold Temperley, (eds.), Vols. 5 and 10, London: His Majesty's Stationery Office, 1938.

Documents on British Foreign Policy 1919-1939, Llewellyn Woodward and Rohan Butler, (eds.), Third Series, Vol. 7, London: Her Majesty's Stationery Office, 1954.

Great Britain, Parliamentary Papers, 1878, Vol. 83.

Great Britain, Parliamentary Papers, Accounts and Papers (1909), CV, (Cd.4529).

The Treatment of Armenians in the Ottoman Empire 1915-1916, Parliamentary Papers Miscellaneous No.31, London: Joseph Causton, 1916.

League of Nations

Treaty Series.

Turkey

Akbay, Cemal, *Birinci Dünya Harbinde Türk Harbi* (Turkish War in the First World War), Vol.1: *Osmanlı İmparatorluğunun Siyasi ve Askeri Hazırlıkları ve Harbe Girişi* (Political and Military Preparations of the Ottoman Empire and Its Entry Into the War), Ankara: Genelkurmay Basımevi, 1991.

Armenians in Ottoman Documents 1915-1920, Ankara: Başbakanlık Basımevi, 1995.

Arşiv Belgeleriyle Ermeni Faaliyetleri 1914-1918 (Armenian Activities Through Archival Documents), 8 Vols., Ankara: Genelkurmay Basımevi, 2005-2008.

Aspirations et agissements révolutionnaires des Comités Arméniens avant et après la proclamation de la Constitution Ottomane, İstanbul: Matbaai Orhaniye, 1917.

Belen, Fahri, *Birinci Cihan Harbinde Türk Harbi 1914-1918 Yılı Hareketleri* (Turkish War in the First World War: Movements of the Years 1914-1918), 5 Vols., Ankara: Genelkurmay Basımevi, 1965-1967.

Birinci Dünya Harbinde Türk Harbi Kafkas Cephesi Üçüncü Ordu Harekatı (Turkish War in the First World War: Caucasian Front Operations of the Third Army), 2 Vols., Ankara: Genelkurmay Basımevi, 1993.

Genç et al., Yusuf İhsan, *Başbakanlık Osmanlı Arşivi Rehberi* (Guide to the Prime Minister's Office Ottoman Archives), Ankara: Başbakanlık Basımevi, 1992.

Küçük et al., Mustafa, *Başbakanlık Osmanlı Arşivi Katalogları Rehberi* (Guide to the Prime Minister's Office Ottoman Archives Catalogs), Ankara: Başbakanlık Basımevi, 1995.

La Verité sur le mouvement révolutionnaire arménien et les mesures gouvernementales, İstanbul: Imprimerie Tanine, 1916.

Sertoğlu, Murat, *Muhteva Bakımından Başvekalet Arşivi* (Contents of the Prime Minister's Office Archives), Ankara: Türk Tarih Kurumu Basımevi, 1955.

Takvimi Vekayi (Official Gazette).

Türk Parlamento Tarihi (History of the Turkish Parliament), Vols.1 and 2, Ankara: Türkiye Büyük Millet Meclisi Basımevi, 1998.

Türkiye Cumhuriyeti Genelkurmay ATESE ve Denetleme Başkanlığı Yayın Kataloğu (Publications Catalog of the Turkish General Staff Directorate of Military History and Strategic Studies and Directorate of Inspection), Ankara: Genelkurmay Basımevi, 2005.

United States

Documents on German Foreign Policy 1918-1945, Series D (1937-1945), Paul Sweet, Howard Smyth, James Beddie, Arthur Kogan, George Kent (eds.), Vol.7, Washington, D.C.: United States Government Printing Office, 1956.

Duncan, Evan (comp.), *Principal Officers of the Department of State and United States Chiefs of Mission 1778-1990*, Washington, D.C.: United States Government Printing Office, 1991.

Foreign Relations of the United States, Diplomatic Papers, Vols.14 and 16, Washington, D.C.: United States Government Printing Office, 1959.

Guide to the National Archives of the United States, Washington, D.C.: National Archives and Records Service, 1974.

Office of United States Chief of Counsel for Prosecution of Axis Criminality, *Nazi Conspiracy and Aggression*, Vol.7, Washington, D.C.: United States Government Printing Office, 1946.

Papers Relating to the Foreign Affairs of the United States, The Lansing Papers 1914-1920, Vol.1, Washington, D.C.: United States Government Printing Office, 1929.

Trial of the Major War Criminals Before the International Military Tribunal Nuremberg 14 November 1945-1 October 1946, 42 Vols., Nuremberg: International Military Tribunal, 1947-1949.

Private (Memoirs, Correspondences, Statements, Contemporary Studies)

Adıvar, Halidé Edib, *House with Wisteria: Memoirs of Halidé Edib*, Charlottesville, Virginia: Leopolis Press, 2nd ed., 2003.

———, *Memoirs of Halidé Edib*, Piscataway, New Jersey: Gorgias Press, reprinted, 2004.

Altay, Fahrettin, *10 Yıl Savaş ve Sonrası 1912-1922* (10 Year War and Its Beyond 1912-1922), İstanbul: İnsel Yayınları, 1970.

Andonian, Aram (comp.), *The Memoirs of Naim Bey: Turkish Official Documents Relating to the Deportations and Massacres of Armenians*, New Square, Pennsylvania: Armenian Historical Research Association, reprinted, 1965.

Atay, Falih Rıfkı, *Ateş ve Güneş* (Fire and Sun), İstanbul: Pozitif Yayınları, 2nd ed., 2008.

———, *Zeytindağı* (Mount of Olives), İstanbul: Bateş Yayınları, reprinted, 1981.

Baer, George (ed.), *A Question of Trust: The Origins of U.S.-Soviet Diplomatic Relations: The Memoirs of Loy Henderson*, Stanford, California: Hoover Institution Press, 1986.

Balakian, Grigoris (Peter Balakian, trans.), *Armenian Golgotha*, New York: Alfred Knopf, 2009.

Barton, James, *Daybreak in Turkey*, Boston: The Pilgrim Press, 2nd ed., 1908.

———, *Story of Near East Relief (1915-1930): An Interpretation*, New York: The Macmillan Company, 1930.

Bayar, Celal, *Ben de Yazdım Milli Mücadeleye Gidiş* (I Also Wrote: Going Into the National Struggle), 8 Vols., İstanbul: Baha Matbaası, 1965-1966.

Baydar, Mustafa, *Hamdullah Suphi Tanrıöver ve Anıları* (Hamdullah Suphi Tanrıöver and His Reminiscences), İstanbul: Menteş Kitabevi, 1968.

Bennett, John, *Witness: The Story of a Search*, London: Hodder and Stoughton, 1962.

Beylerian, Arthur (ed. and comp.), *Les grandes puissances, L'Empire Ottoman et les Arméniens dans les Archives Françaises (1914-1918)*, Paris: Université de Paris I, Panthéon- Sorbonne, 1983.

Birgen, Muhittin (Zeki Arıkan, ed.), *İttihat ve Terakki'de On Sene* (Ten Years in the Committee of Union and Progress), 2 Vols., İstanbul: Kitap Yayınları, 2006.

Blaisdell, Dorothea Chambers, *Missionary Daughter: Witness to the End of the Ottoman Empire*, Bloomington, Indiana: 1st Books Library, 2002.

Bourne, Kenneth and Donald Cameron Watt (eds.), British Documents on Foreign Affairs: Reports and Papers from the Foreign Office Confidential Print, Part I, Series B, The Near and Middle East, 1856-1914, Vol.20, Frederick, Maryland: University Publications of America, 1985.

Breitman, Richard, Barbara McDonald Stewart, and Severin Hochberg (eds.), *Advocate for the Doomed: The Diaries and Papers of James McDonald 1932-1935*, Bloomington, Indiana: Indiana University Press, 2007.

Bryce, James and Arnold Toynbee (eds.), *The Treatment of Armenians in the Ottoman Empire 1915-1916*, Princeton, New Jersey: Gomidas Institute, Uncensored Edition, 2000.

Burdick, Charles and Hans-Adolf Jacobsen (eds.), *The Halder War Diary 1939-1942*, Novato, California: Presidio Press, 1998.

Byford-Jones, William, *Berlin Twilight*, London: Hutchinson and Company Limited, 1946.

Cavit Bey (Osman Selim Kocahanoğlu, ed.), *Felaket Günleri Mütareke Devrinin Feci Tarihi* (Days of Disaster: Tragic History of the Armistice Period), 2 Vols., İstanbul: Temel Yayınları, 2000.

Cemal Paşa (Behçet Cemal, ed.), *Hatıralar* (Memoirs), İstanbul: Selek Yayınları, 1959.

Chambers, Frank, *The War Behind the War 1914-1918: A History of the Political and Civilian Fronts*, London: Faber and Faber Limited, 1939.

Chambers, William Nesbitt, *Yoljuluk: Random Thoughts on a Life in Imperial Turkey*, London: Simpkin Marshall Limited, 1928.

Childs, W. J., *Across Asia Minor on Foot*, Edinburgh and London: William Blackwood and Sons, 1917.

Clark, Alice, *Letters from Cilicia*, Chicago: A.D. Weinthrop and Company, 1924.

Cox, Samuel, *Diversions of a Diplomat in Turkey*, New York: Charles Webster and Company, 1887.

Djemal Pasha, *Memories of a Turkish Statesman 1913-1919*, New York: George Doran Company, 1922.

Erden, Ali Fuad (Alpay Kabacalı, ed.), *Birinci Dünya Harbinde Suriye Hatıraları* (Recollections of Syria in the First World War), İstanbul: Türkiye İş Bankası Kültür Yayınları, reprinted, 2003.

Erden, Ali Fuad, *Dördüncü Ordunun Mücmel Tarihçesi* (A Brief Enumerative History of the Fourth Army), Ankara: Genelkurmay Yayınları, 1948.

————, *Paris'ten Tih Sahrasına* (From Paris to the Tih Desert), Ankara: Ulus Basımevi, reprinted, 1949.

Ertürk, Hüsamettin (Samih Nafiz Tansu, ed.), *İki Devrin Perde Arkası* (Behind the Curtain of Two Eras), İstanbul: Sebil Yayınevi, reprinted, 1996.

Franck, Harry, *The Fringe of the Moslem World*, New York: Grosset and Dunlop Publishers, 1928.

Graves, Philip, *Briton and Turk*, London: Hutchinson and Company, 1941.

Guse, Felix, *Die Kaukasusfront im Weltkrieg: Bis zum Frieden von Brest*, Leipzig: Koehler und Amelang, 1940.

Gust, Wolfgang (ed.), *Der Völkermord an den Armeniern 1915/16 Dokumente aus dem Politischen Archiv des deutschen Auswärtigen Amts*, Springe: Zu Klampen, 2005.

Halder, Franz (Hans-Adolf Jacobsen, ed.), *Kriegtagebuch: Tägliche Aufzeich-nungen des Chefs des Generalstabes des Heeres, 1939-1942*, Vol.1: *Vom Polenfeldzug bis zum Ende der West-offensive (14.8.1939-30.6.1940)*, Stuttgart: W. Kohlhammer Verlag, 1962.

Halid, Halil, *The Diary of a Turk*, London: Adam and Charles Black, 1903.

Hedin, Sven, *Till Jerusalem*, Leipzig: F.A. Brockhaus, 1918.

Hirschmann, Ira, *Caution to the Winds*, New York: David McKay Company, 1952.

————, *The Embers Still Burn*, New York: Simon and Schuster, 1949.

————, *Lifeline to a Promised Land*, New York: The Vanguard Press, 1946.

Hurewitz, J.C. (ed.), *Diplomacy in the Near and Middle East: A Documentary Record*, Vol.1: 1535-1914, Princeton, New Jersey: D. Van Nostrand Com-pany, Inc., 1956.

Jabotinsky, Eri, *The Sakaria Expedition: A Story of Extra Legal Immigration into Palestine*, Johannesburg: Jewish Community of Johannesburg, 1945.

Kadri, Hüseyin Kazım (İsmail Kara, ed.), *Meşrutiyetten Cumhuriyete Anılarım* (My Reminiscences from the Constitutionalism to the Republic), İstanbul: Dergah Yayınları, reprinted, 2001.

Korganoff, Gabriel, *La participation des Arméniens à la guerre mondiale sur le front du Caucase 1914-1918*, Paris: Massis, 1927.

Loti, Pierre, *La Turquie Agonisante*, Paris: Calman-Lévy, 1913.

————, *Les Massacres d'Arménie*, Paris: Calman-Lévy, 1918.

Mehmet Asaf (İsmet Parmaksızoğlu {ed.}), *1909 Adana Ermeni Olayları ve Anılarım* (1909 Armenian Incidents of Adana and My Reminiscences), An-kara: Türk Tarih Kurumu, 1982.

Melbourne, Roy, *Conflict and Crises: A Foreign Service Story*, Lanham, Mary-land and London: University Press of America, 1993.

Menteşe, Halil (İsmail Arar, ed.), *Osmanlı Mebusan Meclisi Reisi Halil Menteşe'nin Anıları* (Memoirs of the President of the Ottoman Chamber of Deputies Halil Menteşe), İstanbul: Hürriyet Vakfı Yayınları, 1986.

Neumark, Fritz, *Zuflucht am Bosporus*, Frankfurt: Verlag Joseph Knecht, 1981.

Odian, Yervant (Ara Stepan Melkonian, trans.), *Accursed Years: My Exile and Return from Der Zor, 1914-1919*, London: Gomidas Institute, 2009.

Oran, Baskın (ed.), *"M.K." Adlı Çocuğun Tehcir Anıları 1915 ve Sonrası* (Re-location Reminiscences of a Child Called "M.K." 1915 and Its Beyond), İstanbul: İletişim Yayınları, 2005.

Paléologue, Maurice, *La Russie Des Tsars Pendant la Grande Guerre*, 3 Vols., Paris: Plon-Nourrit, 1921.

Pasdermadjian, Garegin (Aram Torossian, trans.), *Armenia: A Leading Factor in the Winning of the War*, New York: Council for Armenia, 1919.

Pomiankowski, Joseph, *Der Zusammenbruch des Ottomanischen Reiches: Erinnerungen an die Türkei aus der Zeit des Weltkrieges*, Zürich, Leipzig, Wien: Amalthea Verlag, 1928.

Raeder, Erich (Henry Drexel, trans.), *My Life*, Annapolis, Maryland: United States Naval Institute, 1960.

Rasim, Ahmet (Hikmet Dizdaroğlu, ed.), *Muharrir Bu Ya* (Such Is the Author), İstanbul: Milli Eğitim Bakanlığı Yayınları, 2nd ed., 1989.

Rustem Bey, Ahmed, *La Guerre Mondiale et la Question Turco-Arménienne*, Berne: Imprimerie Staempfli et Cie, 1918.

Ryan, Andrew, *The Last of the Dragomans*, London: Geoffrey Bles, 1951.

Simavi, Lütfi, *Osmanlı Sarayının Son Günleri* (The Last Days of the Ottoman Court), İstanbul: Hürriyet Yayınları, reprinted, 1973.

Söylemezoğlu, Galip Kemali, *Hariciye Hizmetinde Otuz Sene* (Thirty Years in the Service of the Ministry of Foreign Affairs), 2 Vols., İstanbul: Şaka Matbaası, 1949.

Sutherland, James Kay, *The Adventures of an Armenian Boy: An Autobiography and Historical Narrative Encompassing the Last Thirty Years of the Ottoman Empire*, Ann Arbor, Michigan: Ann Arbor Press, 1964.

Talat Paşa, *Hatıralarım ve Müdafaam* (My Reminiscences and Defense), İstanbul: Kaynak Yayınları, reprinted, 2006.

Ülkümen, Selahattin, *Emekli Diplomat Selahattin Ülkümen'in Anıları Bilinmeyen Yönleriyle Bir Dönemin Dışişleri* (The Memoirs of the Retired Diplomat Selahattin Ülkümen: The Ministry of Foreign Affairs of a Period with Its Unknown Aspects), İstanbul: Gözlem Gazetecilik, 1993.

von Kressenstein, Friedrich Freiherr Kress, *Mit den Türken zum Suezkanal*, Berlin: Vorhut-Verlag, 1938.

von Oppenheim, Max, *Die Nachrichtenstelle der Kaiserlich Deutschen Botschaft in Konstantinopel und die deutsche wirtschaftliche Propaganda in der Türkei*, Berlin: Reichsdruckerei, 1916.

von Papen, Franz, *Der Wahrheit eine Gasse*, München: Paul List Verlag, 1952.

Yalçın, Hüseyin Cahit (Osman Selim Kocahanoğlu, ed.), *İttihatçı Liderlerin Gizli Mektupları* (The Secret Letters of the Unionist Leaders), İstanbul: Temel Yayınları, 2002.

Yalçın, Hüseyin Cahit (Rauf Mutluay, ed.), *Siyasal Anılar* (Political Reminiscences), İstanbul: Türkiye İş Bankası Yayınları, reprinted, 2000.

Yalçın, Hüseyin Cahit, *Talat Paşa*, İstanbul: Yedigün Neşriyat, 1943.

Yalçın, Hüseyin Cahit (Cemil Koçak, ed.), *Tanıdıklarım* (My Acquaintances), İstanbul: Yapı Kredi Yayınları, reprinted, 2001.

Yalman, Ahmed Emin (Erol Şadi Erdinç, ed.), *Yakın Tarihte Gördüklerim ve Geçirdiklerim* (Those I Have Seen and Experienced in Recent History), 2 Vols., İstanbul: Pera Turizm ve Ticaret A.Ş., reprinted, 1997.

Zahm, J.A, *From Berlin to Baghdad and Babylon*, New York and London: D. Appleton and Company, 1922.

III. Newspapers

English: *Asbarez* (Fresno), *Daily Chronicle* (London), *Daily News* (London), *Detroit News*, *Ha'aretz* (Jerusalem), *Jewish Exponent* (Philadelphia), *Jewish Floridian*, *Los Angeles Times*, *Manchester Guardian*, *Philadelphia Inquirer Public Ledger*, *San Francisco Examiner*, *The Baltimore Jewish Times*, *The Boston Daily Globe*, *The Boston Globe*, *The Boston Sunday Globe*, *The Chicago Daily Tribune*, *The Christian Science Monitor* (Boston), *The Daily Telegraph* (London), *The Jerusalem Post*, *The Levant Herald* (İstanbul), *The New York Times*, *The Sun* (New York), *The Times* (London), *Turkish Daily News* (Ankara), *The Washington Post*, *Washington Jewish Week*, *Washington Times*.

French: *La République* (İstanbul), *La Turquie* (İstanbul).

German: *Frankfurter Zeitung* (Frankfurt), *Vossische Zeitung* (Berlin).

Turkish: *Cumhuriyet* (İstanbul), *Günaydın* (İstanbul), *Hürriyet* (İstanbul), *İkdam* (İstanbul), *İttihad* (İstanbul), *Milliyet* (İstanbul), *Star* (İstanbul), *Tanin* (İstanbul), *Tercüman* (İstanbul), *Vakit* (İstanbul), *Yeni Asır* (İzmir), *Yeni Gazete* (İzmir).

IV. Secondary Sources

Books

Abbott, G.F., *Turkey in Transition*, London: Edward Arnold, 1909.

Abshagen, Karl Heinz (Alan Houghton Brodrick, trans.), *Canaris*, London: Hutchinson and Company Ltd., 1956.

Adams, Henry and Robin, *Rebel Patriot: A Biography of Franz von Papen*, Santa Barbara, California: McNally and Loftin Publishers, 1987.

Aghjayan, George, *Genocide Denial: The Armenian and Jewish Experiences Compared*, Worcester: Armenian National Committee of Central Massachusetts, 1998.

Ahmad, Feroz, "İkinci Meşrutiyet Döneminde Jön Türk-Ermeni İlişkileri 1908-1914" (Young Turk-Armenian Relations in the Period of Second Constitutionalism 1908-1914), in Metin Hülagü, Şakir Batmaz, Gülbadi Alan, Süleyman Demirci (eds.), *Hoşgörü Toplumunda Ermeniler* (Armenians in the Society of Tolerance), Vol.2, Kayseri: Erciyes Üniversitesi Yayını, 2007.

————, "The Special Relationship: The Committee of Union and Progress and the Ottoman Jewish Political Elite, 1908-1918," in Avigdor Levy (ed.), *Jews, Turks, Ottomans: A Shared History, Fifteenth Through the Twentieth Century*, Syracuse, New York: Syracuse University Press, 2002.

Akbayar, Nuri, Raşit Çavaş, Yücel Demirel, Bahattin Öztuncay, Mete Tunçay (eds.), *İkinci Meşrutiyetin İlk Yılı 23 Temmuz 1908-23 Temmuz 1909* (The First Year of the Second Constitutionalism: 23 July 1908-23 July 1909), İstanbul: Yapı Kredi Yayınları, 2008.

Akçora, Ergünöz, *Van ve Çevresinde Ermeni İsyanları 1896-1916* (Armenian Revolts in Van and Its Vicinity 1896-1916), İstanbul: Türk Dünyası Araştırmaları Vakfı Yayınları, 1984.

Akşin, Sina, *İstanbul Hükümetleri ve Milli Mücadele* (İstanbul Governments and the National Struggle), 2 Vols., Ankara: Türkiye İş Bankası Kültür Yayınları, 1998.

————, *Jön Türkler ve İttihat ve Terakki* (Young Turks and the Committee of Union and Progress), Ankara: İmge Kitabevi, reprinted, 2006.

Aktan, Gündüz, *Açık Kriptolar Ermeni Soykırım İddiaları Avrupa'da Irkçılık ve Türkiye'nin AB Üyeliği* (Open Ciphered Telegrams Armenian Genocide Allegations Racism in Europe and the EU Membership of Turkey), Ankara: Aşina Kitaplar, 2006.

Angel, Marc, *The Jews of Rhodes: The History of a Sephardic Community*, New York: Sepher-Hermon Press, Inc. and The Union of Sephardic Congregations, 1978.

Arendt, Hannah, *Eichmann in Jerusalem: A Report on the Banality of Evil*, New York: The Viking Press, rev. and enlarged ed., 1975.

Arslan, Ali, *Darülfünundan Üniversiteye* (From the Chamber of Sciences to the University), İstanbul: Kitabevi, 1995.

Artuç, Nevzat, *Cemal Paşa*, Ankara: Türk Tarih Kurumu, 2008.

Aslan, Betül, *Erzurum'da Ermeni Olayları* (Armenian Events in Erzurum), Erzurum: Atatürk Üniversitesi Yayınları, 2004.

Ata, Feridun, *İşgal İstanbul'unda Tehcir Yargılamaları* (Trials for Relocations in Occupied İstanbul), Ankara: Türk Tarih Kurumu, 2005.

Atamian, Sarkis, *The Armenian Community: The Historical Development of a Social and Ideological Conflict*, New York: Philosophical Library, 1955.

Atnur, İbrahim Ethem, "Kadınlar ve Çocuklar" (Women and Children), in Hikmet Özdemir (ed.), *Türk-Ermeni İhtilafı   Makaleler* (Turkish-Armenian Conflict: Articles), Ankara: Türkiye Büyük Millet Meclisi Kültür, Sanat ve Yayın Kurulu Yayınları, 2007.

————, *Türkiye'de Ermeni Kadınları ve Çocukları Meselesi* (The Question of Armenian Women and Children in Turkey), Ankara: Babil Yayınları, 2005.

Auron, Yair, *The Banality of Denial: Israel and the Armenian Genocide*, New Brunswick, New Jersey: Transaction Publishers, 2003.

————, *The Banality of Indifference: Zionism and the Armenian Genocide*, New Brunswick, New Jersey: Transaction Publishers, 2003.

Avagyan, Arsen and Gaidz Minasyan (Ludmilla Denisenko and Mutlucan Şahan, trans.), *Ermeniler ve İttihat ve Terakki İşbirliğinden Çatışmaya* (Armenians and the Committee of Union and Progress: From Cooperation to Conflict), İstanbul: Aras Yayıncılık, 2005.

Avşar, Servet, *Birinci Dünya Savaşında İngiliz Propagandası* (British Propaganda in the First World War), Ankara: Kim Yayınları, 2004.

Aydemir, Şevket Süreyya, *Makedonya'dan Ortaasya'ya Enver Paşa* (From Macedonia to Central Asia: Enver Paşa), 3 Vols., İstanbul: Remzi Kitabevi, 2nd ed., 1995.

Babacan, Hasan, *Mehmet Talat Paşa 1874-1921*, Ankara: Türk Tarih Kurumu, 2005.

Bakar, Bülent, *Ermeni Tehciri* (Armenian Relocations), Ankara: Atatürk Araştırma Merkezi, 2009.

Bakar, Bülent, Necdet Öztürk, and Süleyman Beyoğlu (eds.), *Tarihi Gerçekler ve Bilimin Işığında Ermeni Meselesi* (Historical Realities and the Armenian Question in the Light of Science), İstanbul: IQ Kültür Sanat Yayıncılık, 2007.

Bardakjian, Kevork, *Hitler and the Armenian Genocide*, Cambridge, Massachusetts: The Zoryan Institute, Special Report No. 3, 1985.

Baron, Salo, *A Social and Religious History of the Jews*, Vol. 18, New York: 2nd rev. ed., Columbia University Press, 1980.

Başyurt, Erhan, *Ermeni Evlatlıklar Saklı Kalmış Hayatlar* (Armenian Adopted Children: Hidden Lives), İstanbul: Karakutu Yayınları, 2006.

Bayur, Yusuf Hikmet, *Türk İnkılabı Tarihi* (History of the Turkish Revolution), 3 Vols., Ankara: Türk Tarih Kurumu, 1940-1967.

Belasel, Yusuf, *Osmanlı ve Türkiye Yahudileri* (Jews of the Ottoman Empire and Turkey), İstanbul: Gözlem Gazetecilik, 2004.

Benbassa, Esther and Aron Rodrigue, *Türkiye ve Balkan Yahudileri Tarihi* (History of Jews of Turkey and the Balkans), İstanbul: İletişim Yayınları, 2001.

Bengi, Hilmi, *Gazeteci, Siyasetçi ve Fikir Adamı Olarak Hüseyin Cahit Yalçın* (Hüseyin Cahit Yalçın As Journalist, Politician, and Intellectual), Ankara: Atatürk Araştırma Merkezi, 2000.

Berenbaum, Michael, *After Tragedy and Triumph: Essays in Modern Jewish Thought and the American Experience*, Cambridge: Cambridge University Press, 1990.

————, "The Americanization of the Holocaust," in Ilya Levkov (ed.), *Bitburg and Beyond: Encounters in American, German and Jewish History*, New York: Shapolsky Publishers, 1987.

————, *The World Must Know: The History of the Holocaust as Told in the United States Holocaust Memorial Museum*, New York: Little, Brown and

Company, 1993.

Birinci, Ali, *Hürriyet ve İtilaf Fırkası* (Party of Liberty and Entente), İstanbul: Dergah Yayınları, 1990.

Bloxham, Donald, *Genocide, the World Wars and the Unweaving of Europe*, London and Portland, Oregon: Vallentine Mitchell, 2008.

Bloxham, Donald and Tony Kushner, *The Holocaust: Critical Historical Approaches*, Manchester: Manchester University Press, 2005.

Bozkurt, Gülnihal, *Alman-İngiliz Belgelerinde ve Siyasi Gelişmelerin Işığı Altında Gayrımüslim Osmanlı Vatandaşlarının Hukuki Durumu 1839-1914* (The Legal Situation of the Non-Muslim Ottoman Citizens According to German-British Documents and in Light of Political Developments 1839-1914), Ankara: Türk Tarih Kurumu, 1996.

Braude, Benjamin and Bernard Lewis (eds.), *Christians and Jews in the Ottoman Empire: The Functioning of a Plural Society*, 2 Vols., New York: Holmes and Meier, 1982.

Breitman, Richard, *The Architect of Genocide: Himmler and the Final Solution*, Hanover, New Haven and London: University Press of New England, 1991.

Brogan, Patrick, *World Conflicts: Why and Where They Are Happening*, London: Bloomsbury Publishing Limited, 1989.

Brown, Anthony Cave, *Bodyguard of Lies*, Toronto, New York and London: Bantam Books, 1975.

Budak, Mustafa, *İdealden Gerçeğe Misak-i Milli'den Lozan'a Dış Politika* (Foreign Policy: From the Ideal to the Reality, from the National Pact to Lausanne), İstanbul: Küre Yayınları, 2002.

Burg, Avraham (Israel Amrani, trans.), *The Holocaust Is Over: We Must Rise from Its Ashes*, New York: Palgrave Macmillan, 2008.

Byford-Jones, William, *Berlin Twilight*, London: Hutchinson and Company Limited, 1946.

Charny, Israel, "The Conference Crisis: The Turks, Armenians, and the Jews," in Israel Charny and Shamai Davidson (eds.), *The Book of the International Conference on the Holocaust and Genocide. Book One: The Conference Program and Crisis*, Tel Aviv: Institute on the Holocaust and Genocide, 1983.

Chorbajian, Levon and George Shirinian (eds.), *Studies in Comparative Genocide*, London: Macmillan and New York: St. Martin's Press, 1999.

Conquest, Robert, *The Soviet Deportation of Nationalities*, London: Macmillan, 1960.

Crowe, David, *The Holocaust: Roots, History, and Aftermath*, Boulder, Colorado: Westview Press, 2008.

Çakır, Ömer, "Birlikte Yaşamak: Faik Ali Bey ve Kütahya Ermenileri" (Living Together: Faik Ali Bey and the Armenians of Kütahya), in Metin Hülagü, Şakir Batmaz, Gülbadi Alan, Süleyman Demirci (eds.), *Hoşgörü Toplu-*

munda Ermeniler (Armenians in the Society of Tolerance), Vol. 3, Kayseri: Erciyes Üniversitesi Yayını, 2007.

Çarkcıyan, Yervant Gomitas, *Türk Devleti Hizmetinde Ermeniler 1453-1953* (Armenians at the Service of the Turkish State 1453-1953), İstanbul: Kesit Yayınları, reprinted, 2006.

Çavdar, Tevfik, *Talat Paşa: Bir Örgüt Ustasının Yaşam Öyküsü* (Talat Paşa: Life Story of a Master of Organization), Ankara: Dost Kitabevi, 1984.

Çetin, Attila, *Başbakanlık Arşivi Kılavuzu* (Guide to the Prime Minister's Office Archives), İstanbul: Enderun Kitabevi, 1979.

Çetin, Fethiye, *Anneannem* (My Grandmother), İstanbul: Metis Yayınları, 2005.

Çiçek, Kemal, *Ermenilerin Zorunlu Göçü, 1915-1917* (Relocation of Armenians, 1915-1917), Ankara: Türk Tarih Kurumu, 2005.

Dabağyan, Levon Panos, *Emperyalistler Kıskacında Ermeni Tehciri* (In the Pincer of Imperialists: Armenian Relocations), İstanbul: IQ Kültür Sanat Yayıncılık, 2007.

———, *Türkiye Ermenilerinin Tarihi* (History of the Armenians of Turkey), İstanbul: IQ Kültür Sanat Yayıncılık, 2003.

Dadrian, Vahakn, *The History of the Armenian Genocide: Ethnic Conflict from the Balkans to Anatolia to the Caucasus*, New York: Berghahn Books, 6th ed., 2003.

———, *The Key Elements in the Turkish Denial of the Armenian Genocide: A Case Study of Distortion and Falsification*, Toronto: Zoryan Institute, 1999.

———, "The Role of the Special Organization in the Armenian Genocide during the First World War," in Panikos Panayi (ed.), *Minorities in Wartime: National and Racial Groupings in Europe, North America and Australia during the Two World Wars*, Oxford: Berg Publishers, 1993.

Danışman, Basri, *Artçı Diplomat Son Osmanlı Hariciye Nazırlarından Mustafa Reşit Paşa* (The Rearguard Diplomat: From the Last Ottoman Ministers of Foreign Affairs Mustafa Reşit Paşa), İstanbul: Arba Yayınları, 1998.

Dawidowicz, Lucy, *The Holocaust and the Historians*, Cambridge, Massachusetts and London: Harvard University Press, 1981.

———, *The War Against the Jews 1933-1945*, New York: Holt, Rinehart and Winston, 1975.

Demirci, Aliyar, "İkinci Meşrutiyet Birinci ve İkinci Yasama Döneminde (1908-1914) Osmanlı Ayan Meclisinin Ermeni Üyeleri ve Faaliyetleri," (Armenian Members of the Ottoman Chamber of Notables and Their Activities in the First and Second Legislative Terms [1908-1914] of the Second Constitutionalism), in Şenol Kantarcı, Kamer Kasım, İbrahim Kaya, Sedat Laçiner (eds.), *Ermeni Araştırmaları Birinci Türkiye Kongresi Bildirileri* (Communications Presented at the First Turkish Congress on Armenian Studies), Vol.1, Ankara: Avrasya Stratejik Araştırmalar Merkezi Ermeni Araştırmaları Enstitüsü Yayınları, 2003.

Der Matossian, Bedross, Ethnic Politics in Post-Revolutionary Ottoman Empire: Armenians, Arabs, and Jews during the Second Constitutional Period (1908-1909), doctoral dissertation, Columbia University, 2008.

Deringil, Selim, *Turkish Foreign Policy during the Second World War: An Active Neutrality*, Cambridge: Cambridge University Press, 1989.

Dündar, Fuat, *Modern Türkiye'nin Şifresi İttihat ve Terakki'nin Etnisite Mühendisliği (1913-1918)* [Cipher of Modern Turkey: Ethnicity Engineering of the Committee of Union and Progress (1913-1918)], İstanbul: İletişim Yayınları, 2008.

Eckardt, Alice and Roy Eckardt, *Long Night's Journey Into Day: A Revised Retrospective on the Holocaust*, Detroit, Michigan: Wayne State University Press, 1988.

Eizenstat, Stuart, *Imperfect Justice: Looted Assets, Slave Labor, and the Unfinished Business of World War II*, New York: Public Affairs, 2003.

Emgili, Fahriye, "İkinci Dünya Savaşı Sırasında Türkiye'den Filistin'e Transit Geçen Yahudi Mülteci Gemileri"(Jewish Refugee Ships Passing Transit from Turkey to Palestine during the Second World War), in *Onbirinci Askeri Tarih Sempozyumu Bildirileri, 4-5 Nisan 2007 Onsekizinci Yüzyıldan Günümüze Orta Doğu'daki Gelişmelerin Türkiye'nin Güvenliğine Etkileri* (Communications Presented at the Eleventh Military History Symposium, 4-5 April 2007: Effects of the Developments in the Middle East on Turkey's Security from the Eighteenth Century to Our Day), Vol.2, Ankara: Türkiye Cumhuriyeti Genelkurmay Askeri Tarih ve Stratejik Etüt Başkanlığı Yayınları, 2008.

Epstein, Mark, "A Lucky Few: Refugees in Turkey," in Michael Berenbaum and Abraham Peck (eds.), *The Holocaust and History: The Known, the Unknown, the Disputed, and the Reexamined*, Bloomington and Indianapolis: Indiana University Press, 1998.

Erickson, Edward, *Ordered to Die: A History of the Ottoman Army in the First World War*, Westport, Connecticut and London: Greenwood Press, 2001.

———, *Ottoman Army Effectiveness in World War I: A Comparative Study*, New York and London: Routledge, 2007.

Esatlı, Mustafa Ragıb (İsmail Dervişoğlu, ed.), *İttihat ve Terakki'nin Son Günleri Suikastler ve Entrikalar* (The Last Days of the Committee of Union and Progress: Assassinations and Intrigues), İstanbul: Bengi Yayınları, 2007.

Feingold, Henry, *Bearing Witness: How America and Its Jews Responded to the Holocaust*, Syracuse, New York: Syracuse University Press, 1995.

———, *The Politics of Rescue: The Roosevelt Administration and the Holocaust, 1938-1945*, New Brunswick, New Jersey: Rutgers University Press, 1970.

Ferriman, Duckett, *Turkey and the Turks*, London: Mills and Boon Limited, 1911.

Findley, Carter Vaughn, *Bureaucratic Reform in the Ottoman Empire: The Sublime Porte, 1789-1922*, Princeton, New Jersey: Princeton University Press, 1980.

———, *Ottoman Civil Officialdom: A Social History*, Princeton, New Jersey: Princeton University Press, 1989.

Finkelstein, Norman, *The Holocaust Industry: Reflections on the Exploitation of Jewish Suffering*, New York: Verso Books, 2000.

Fleming, Katherine Elisabeth, *Greece: A Jewish History*, Princeton and Oxford: Princeton University Press, 2008.

Fremantle, Anne, *Loyal Enemy*, London: Hutchinson and Co., 1938.

Friedman, Isaiah, *Germany, Turkey, and Zionism 1897-1918*, Oxford: Oxford University Press, 1977.

———, *The Question of Palestine British-Jewish-Arab Relations: 1914-1918*, New Brunswick, New Jersey and London: Transaction Publishers, 2nd expanded ed., 1992.

Gaillard, Gaston, *The Turks and Europe*, London: Thomas Murby and Company, 1921.

Galanté, Abraham, *Histoire des Juifs de Turquie*, 9 Vols., İstanbul: İSİS, 1987.

Gatrell, Peter, *A Whole Empire Walking: Refugees in Russia During World War I*, Bloomington and Indianapolis: Indiana University Press, 1999.

George, David Lloyd, *Armenia's Charter: An Appreciation of the Services of Armenians to the Allied Cause*, London: Spottiswoode, 1918.

Gidney, James, *A Mandate for Armenia*, Oberlin, Ohio: The Kent University Press, 1967.

Gilbert, Martin, *Winston S. Churchill*, Vol.3: *1914-1916 The Challenge of War*, Boston: Houghton Mifflin Company, 1971.

Gisevius, Hans Bernd (Richard and Clara Winston, trans.), *To the Bitter End*, Boston: Houghton Mifflin Company, 1947.

Goldberg, J.J., *Jewish Power: Inside the American Jewish Establishment*, Reading, Massachusetts: Addison-Wesley Publishing Company, 1996.

Göyünç, Nejat, *Osmanlı İdaresinde Ermeniler* (Armenians Under Ottoman Rule), İstanbul: Gültepe Yayınları, 1983.

Grabill, Joseph, *Protestant Diplomacy and the Near East: Missionary Influence on American Policy, 1810-1927*, Minneapolis: University of Minnesota Press, 1971.

Greenberg, Irvin, *Living As a Jew: Observing Jewish Holidays*, New York: Summit Books, 1988.

Grenke, Arthur, *God, Greed, and Genocide: The Holocaust through the Centuries*, Washington, D.C.: New Academia Publishing, 2005.

Gruen, George, "Turkey," in Reeva Spector Simon, Michael Menachem Laskier and Sara Reguer (eds.), *The Jews of the Middle East and North Africa in Modern Times*, New York: Columbia University Press, 2003.

Gunter, Michael, *"Pursuing the Just Cause of Their People": A Study of Contemporary Armenian Terrorism*, Westport, Connecticut: Greenwood Press, 1986.

Gutman, Israel (ed.), *The Encyclopedia of the Righteous Among the Nations: Rescuers of Jews during the Holocaust, Europe (Part I) and Other Countries*, Jerusalem: Yad Vashem The Holocaust Martyrs' and Heroes' Remembrance Authority, 2007.

Güçlü, Yücel, *Eminence Grise of the Turkish Foreign Service: Numan Menemencioğlu*, Ankara: Grafiker Basımevi, 2002.

———, *The Life and Career of a Turkish Diplomat: Cevat Açıkalın*, Ankara: Grafiker Basımevi, 2002.

———, *The Question of the Sanjak of Alexandretta: A Study in Turkish-French-Syrian Relations*, Ankara: Turkish Historical Society Printing House, 2001.

Halaçoğlu, Yusuf, *Ermeni Tehciri* (Armenian Relocations), İstanbul: Babıali Kültür Yayıncılığı, 2005.

———, *Sürgünden Soykırıma: Ermeni İddiaları* (From Exile to Genocide: Armenian Claims), İstanbul: Babıali Kültür Yayıncılığı, 2006.

Hamerow, Theodore, *Why We Watched: Europe, America, and the Holocaust*, New York: W.W. Norton and Company, Inc., 2008.

Hamilton, Richard and Holger Herwig, *Decisions for War, 1914-1917*, Cambridge: Cambridge University Press, 2004.

Hanioğlu, Şükrü, *A Brief History of the Late Ottoman Empire*, Princeton, New Jersey: Princeton University Press, 2008.

Haskan, Nermi and Çelik Gülersoy, *Hükümet Kapısı Bab-ı Ali Kuruluşundan Cumhuriyete Kadar* (Government Gate The Sublime Porte: From Its Founding Up to the Republic), (İstanbul: Çelik Gülersoy Vakfı Yayını, 2000).

Hayes, Peter (ed.), *Lessons and Legacies: The Meaning of the Holocaust in a Changing World*, Evanston, Illinois: Northwestern University Press, 1991.

Herf, Jeffrey, *The Jewish Enemy: Nazi Propaganda During World War II and the Holocaust*, Cambridge, Massachusetts and London: The Belknap Press of Harvard University Press, 2006.

Hoffmann, Peter (Richard Barry, trans.), *The History of the German Resistance 1933-1945*, Cambridge, Massachusetts: The MIT Press, 1979.

Hovannisian, Richard, *The Armenian Holocaust: A Bibliography Relating to the Deportations, Massacres, and Dispersion of the Armenian People 1915-1923*, Cambridge, Massachusetts: Armenian Heritage Press, 1980.

———, "The Question of Altruism During the Armenian Genocide of 1915," in Pearl Oliner, Samuel Oliner, Lawrence Baron, Lawrence Blum, Dennis Krebs, and Zuzanna Smolenska (eds.), *Embracing the Other: Philosophical, Psychological, and Historical Perspectives on Altruism*, New York and London: New York University Press, 1992.

Höhne, Heinz (Maxwell Brownjohn, trans.), *Canaris*, New York: Doubleday and Company, Inc., 1979.

Höhne, Heinz (Richard Barry, trans.), *The Order of the Death's Head: The Story of Hitler's SS*, London: Penguin Books, 2000.

Hull, Isabel, *Absolute Destruction: Military Culture and the Practices of War in Imperial Germany*, Ithaca, New York and London: Cornell University Press, 2005.

İnalcık, Halil, *Osmanlı İmparatorluğunun Ekonomik ve Sosyal Tarihi (1300-1600)* [Economic and Social History of the Ottoman Empire (1300-1600)], 2 Vols., İstanbul: Eren Yayınları, 2000.

İrtem, Süleyman Kani (Osman Selim Kocahanoğlu, ed.), *Ermeni Meselesinin İçyüzü Ermeni İsyanları Tarihi, Bomba Hadisesi, Adana Vakası, Meclisi Mebusan Zabıtları* (The True Nature of the Armenian Question: History of Armenian Revolts, Bomb Incident, Adana Event, Proceedings of the Chamber of Deputies), İstanbul: Temel Yayınları, 2004.

İstepenyan, Torkom, *Atatürk'ün Doğumunun 100. Yılında Türk-Ermeni İlişkileri* (Turkish-Armenian Relations at the 100th Birthday Anniversary of Atatürk), İstanbul: Murat Ofset, 1984.

Kaligian, Dikran Mesrob, *Armenian Organization and Ideology under Ottoman Rule 1908-1914*, New Brunswick, New Jersey and London: Transaction Publishers, 2009.

Kansu, Aykut, *Politics in Post-Revolutionary Turkey 1908-1913*, Leiden: E.J. Brill, 2000.

―――, *The Revolution of 1908 in Turkey: Social, Economic and Political Studies of the Middle East and Asia*, Leiden: E.J. Brill, 1997.

Karal, Enver Ziya, *Osmanlı Tarihi İslahat Fermanı Devri (1856-1861)* {Ottoman History: Era of Reform Rescript (1856-1861)}, Vol.6, Ankara: Türk Tarih Kurumu, reprinted, 1988.

―――, *Osmanlı Tarihi Nizam-ı Cedit ve Tanzimat Devirleri (1789-1856)* {Ottoman History: Eras of New Order and Reorganization (1789-1856)}, Vol.5, Ankara: Türk Tarih Kurumu, reprinted, 1988.

Katz, Steven, *Historicism, the Holocaust and Zionism: Critical Studies in Modern Jewish Thought and History*, New York and London: New York University Press, 1992.

―――, *The Holocaust in Historical Context*, Vol.1: *The Holocaust and Mass Death before the Modern Age*, New York and Oxford: Oxford University Press, 1994.

―――, *Post-Holocaust Dialogues: Critical Studies in Modern Jewish Thought*, New York and London: New York University Press, 1983.

―――, "The Uniqueness of the Holocaust: The Historical Dimension," in Alan Rosenbaum (ed.), *Is the Holocaust Unique? Perspectives on Comparative Genocide*, Boulder, Colorado: Westview Press, 1966.

Kedourie, Elie, "Minorities," in *The Chatham House Version and other Middle-Eastern Studies*, London: Weidenfeld and Nicolson, 1970.

Keller, Werner (Richard and Clara Winston, trans.), *Diaspora: The Post-Biblical History of the Jews*, New York: Harcourt, Brace and World, Inc., 1969.

Kershaw, Ian, *Fateful Choices: Ten Decisions That Changed the World 1940-1941*, New York: The Penguin Press, 2007.

————, *Hitler 1936-45: Nemesis*, New York and London: W.W. Norton and Company, 2000.

Keser, Ulvi, "İkinci Dünya Savaşı Sürecinde Orta Doğu'ya Yahudi Göçü, Göçmen Yahudilere Türkiye'nin Yardım Faaliyeti ve İngiltere'nin Kıbrıs'ta Açtığı Mülteci Kampları"(Jewish Immigration to the Middle East during the Second World War, Turkey's Assistance to the Immigrant Jews and the Refugee Camps Opened by the British in Cyprus), in *Onbirinci Askeri Tarih Sempozyumu Bildirileri, 4-5 Nisan 2007 Onsekizinci Yüzyıldan Günümüze Orta Doğu'daki Gelişmelerin Türkiye'nin Güvenliğine Etkileri* (Communications Presented at the Eleventh Military History Symposium, 4-5 April 2007: Effects of the Developments in the Middle East on Turkey's Security from the Eighteenth Century to Our Day), Vol. 2, Ankara: Türkiye Cumhuriyeti Genelkurmay Askeri Tarih ve Stratejik Etüt Başkanlığı Yayınları, 2008.

Kévorkian, Raymond, "The Cilician Massacres, 1909," in Richard Hovannisian and Simon Payaslian (eds.), *Armenian Cilicia*, Costa Mesa, California: Mazda Publishers, Inc., 2008.

Kieser, Hans-Lukas and Dominik Schaller (eds.), *Der Völkermord an Den Armeniern Und Die Shoah*, Zürich: Kronos Verlag, 2002.

Knight, E.F., *The Awakening of Turkey: A History of the Turkish Revolution*, London: John Milne, 1909.

Kodaman, Bayram and Mehmet Ali Ünal (eds.), *Son Vakanüvis Abdurrahman Şeref Efendi Tarihi İkinci Meşrutiyet Olayları (1908-1909)*{History of the Last Chronicler Abdurrahman Şeref Efendi: Events of Second Constitutionalism (1908-1909)}, Ankara: Türk Tarih Kurumu, 1996.

Krikorian, Mesrob, *Armenians in the Service of the Ottoman Empire 1860-1908*, London: Routledge and Kegan Paul, 1977.

Kuneralp, Sinan, *Son Dönem Osmanlı Erkan ve Ricali 1839-1922 Prosopografik Rehber* (The Late Period Ottoman Statesmen and Officialdom 1839-1922: Prosopographical Guide), İstanbul: İSİS, 1999.

Kurat, Akdes Nimet, *Birinci Dünya Savaşı Sırasında Türkiye'de Bulunan Alman Generallerinin Raporları* (Reports of the German Generals Who Have Been in Turkey during the First World War), Ankara: Türk Kültürünü Araştırma Enstitüsü Yayınları, 1966.

Langer, William, *Diplomacy of Imperialism: 1890-1902*, Vol.1, New York: Alfred A. Knopf, 1935.

Laqueur, Walter, *Generation Exodus: The Fate of Young Jewish Refugees from Nazi Germany*, Hanover and London: Brandeis University Press, 2001.

Larcher, Maurice, *La Guerre turque dans la guerre mondiale*, Paris: Chiron et Berger-Levrault, 1926.

Lemkin, Raphael, *Axis Rule in Occupied Europe: Laws of Occupation, Analysis of Government, Proposals for Redress*, Washington, D.C.: Carnegie Endowment for International Peace Division of International Law, 1944.

Lengyel, Emil, *Turkey*, New York: H. Wolff, 1941.

Leverkuehn, Paul (Alasdair Lean, trans.), *A German Officer during the Armenian Genocide: A Biography of Max von Scheubner-Richter*, London: Gomidas Institute, 2008.

Levi, Avner, *Türkiye Cumhuriyetinde Yahudiler* (Jews in the Republic of Turkey), İstanbul: İletişim Yayınları, 1992.

Levi, Neil and Michael Rothberg (eds.), *The Holocaust: Theoretical Readings*, New Brunswick, New Jersey: Rutgers University Press, 2003.

Levin, Nora, *The Holocaust Years: The Nazi Destruction of European Jewry, 1933-1945*, Malabar, Florida: Krieger Publishing Company, 1992.

Levy, Avigdor (ed.), *The Jews of the Ottoman Empire*, Princeton: The Darwin Press, 1994.

——— (ed.), *Jews, Turks, Ottomans: A Shared History, Fifteenth Through the Twentieth Century*, Syracuse, New York: Syracuse University Press, 2002.

Lewis, Bernard, *The Emergence of Modern Turkey*, London: Oxford University Press, 2nd ed., 1968.

———, *From Babel to Dragomans: Interpreting the Middle East*, Oxford and New York: Oxford University Press, 2004.

———, *The Middle East: A Brief History of the Last 2,000 Years*, New York: Scribner, 1995.

———, *Notes and Documents from the Turkish Archives: A Contribution to the History of the Jews in the Ottoman Empire* (Oriental Notes and Studies, No.3), Jerusalem: The Israel Oriental Society, 1953.

———, *The Political Language of Islam*, Chicago and London: The University of Chicago Press, 1988.

———, *Semites and Anti-Semites: An Inquiry into Conflict and Prejudice*, New York and London: W.W. Norton and Company, 1986.

Lewkowicz, Bea, *The Jewish Community of Salonika: History, Memory, Identity*, London and Portland, Oregon: Vallentine Mitchell, 2006.

Lewy, Guenter, *The Armenian Massacres in Ottoman Turkey: A Disputed Genocide*, Salt Lake City: The University of Utah Press, 2005.

Lieberman, Benjamin, *Terrible Fate: Ethnic Cleansing in the Making of Modern Europe*, Chicago: Ivan Dee Publishers, 2006.

Lieven, Dominic, *The Russian Empire and Its Rivals*, London: John Murray Publishers Ltd., 2000.

Linenthal, Edward, *Preserving Memory: The Struggle to Create America's Ho-locaust Museum*, New York: Viking Penguin, 1995.

Lochner, Louis, *What About Germany?* New York: Dodd, Mead and Company, 1942.

Lohr, Eric, *Nationalizing the Russian Empire: The Campaign Against Enemy Aliens During World War I*, Cambridge, Massachusetts: Harvard University Press, 2003.

Maier, Charles, *The Unmasterable Past: History, Holocaust, and German National Identity*, Cambridge, Massachusetts: Harvard University Press, 1988.

Mann, Michael, *The Dark Side of Democracy: Explaining Ethnic Cleansing*, New York: Cambridge University Press, 2005.

Marrus, Michael (ed.), *The Nazi Holocaust: Historical Articles on the Destruction of European Jews*, Vol. 2: *The Origins of the Holocaust*, Westport, Connecticut and London: Meckler Corporation, 1989.

Mazian, Florence, *Why Genocide? The Armenian and Jewish Experiences in Perspective*, Ames, Iowa: Iowa State University Press, 1990.

Mazower, Mark, *Salonica, City of Ghosts: Christians, Muslims, and Jews, 1430-1950*, London: HarpersCollins, 2004.

McCarthy, Justin, *Death and Exile: The Ethnic Cleansing of Ottoman Muslims, 1821-1922*, Princeton, New Jersey: The Darwin Press, Inc., 1995.

———, *Muslims and Minorities: The Population of Ottoman Anatolia at the End of the Empire*, New York and London: New York University Press, 1983.

McCarthy, Justin and Carolyn McCarthy, *Turks and Armenians: A Manual on the Armenian Question*, Washington, D.C.: Assembly of Turkish American Associations, 1989.

McCarthy, Justin, Esat Arslan, Cemalettin Taşkıran and Ömer Turan, *The Armenian Rebellion at Van*, Salt Lake City: The University of Utah Press, 2006.

McMeekin, Sean, *The Berlin-Baghdad Express: The Ottoman Empire and Germany's Bid for World Power, 1898-1918*, London: Allen Lane, 2010.

Melson, Robert, *Revolution and Genocide: On the Origins of the Armenian Genocide and the Holocaust*, Chicago: University of Chicago Press, 1992.

Messinger, Gary, *British Propaganda and the State in the First World War*, Manchester and New York: Manchester University Press, 1992.

Meyer, Enno and A.J. Berkian, *Zwischen Rhein und Arax, 900 Jahre Deutsch-Armenische beziehungen*, Oldenburg: Heinz Holzberg Verlag, 1988.

Michman, Don, *Holocaust Historiography: A Jewish Perspective*, London and Portland, Oregon: Vallentine Mitchell, 2003.

Miller, Judith, *One, by One, by One: Facing the Holocaust*, New York: Simon and Schuster, 1990.

Morse, Arthur, *While Six Million Died: A Chronicle of American Apathy*, New York: Random House, 1967.

Mosley, Leonard, *On Borrowed Time: How World War II Began*, New York: Random House, 1969.

Mosse, George, *The Crisis of German Ideology: Intellectual Origins of the Third Reich*, New York: Grosset and Dunlap, 1964.

Mueller, Michael (Geoffrey Brooks, trans.), *Canaris: The Life and Death of Hitler's Spymaster*, Annapolis, Maryland: Naval Institute Press, 2007.

Naimark, Norman, *Fires of Hatred: Ethnic Cleansing in Twentieth-Century Europe*, Cambridge, Massachusetts: Harvard University Press, 2001.

Nicolle, David, *The Ottoman Army 1914-1918*, London: Reed International Books, 1996.

Novick, Peter, *The Holocaust in American Life*, Boston and New York: Houghton Mifflin Company, 2000.

Ofer, Dalia, *Escaping the Holocaust: Illegal Immigration to the Land of Israel 1939-1944*, New York: Oxford University Press, 1990.

Orel, Şinasi and Süreyya Yuca, *The Talat Pasha Telegrams: Historical Fact or Armenian Fiction?* Nicosia: Rustem, 1986.

Ortaylı, İlber, "Jenosit Kavramı" (Genocide Concept), in Aysel Ekşi (ed.), *Belgeler ve Tanıklarla Türk-Ermeni İlişkilerinde Tarihi Gerçekler* (Historical Realities in Turkish-Armenian Relations with Documents and Witnesses), İstanbul: Alfa Basım Yayım Dağıtım Ltd. Şti., 2006.

————, *Osmanlı Barışı* (Pax Ottomana), İstanbul: Timaş Yayınları, 2007.

————, "Osmanlı İmparatorluğunda Millet Sistemi" (*Millet* System in the Ottoman Empire), in Hasan Celal Güzel, Kemal Çiçek, Salim Koca (eds.), *Türkler* (Turks), Vol. 10, Ankara: Yeni Türkiye Yayınları, 2002.

Öke, Mim Kemal, *The Armenian Question*, Ankara: Türk Tarih Kurumu, 2001.

Özdemir, Hikmet, *Cemal Paşa ve Ermeni Göçmenler (4. Ordu'nun İnsani Yardımları)* [Cemal Paşa and Armenian Emigrants (Humanitarian Assistance of the 4th Army)], İstanbul: Remzi Kitabevi, 2009.

————, *Ermeni İddiaları Karşısında Türkiye'nin Birikimi* (The Accumulation of Turkey Regarding the Armenian Claims), Ankara: Türkiye Büyük Millet Meclisi Kültür, Sanat ve Yayın Kurulu Yayınları, 2008.

Özdemir, Hikmet (Şaban Kardaş, trans.), *The Ottoman Army 1914-1918: Disease and Death on the Battlefield*, Salt Lake City: The University of Utah Press, 2008.

Özdemir, Hikmet, Kemal Çiçek, Ömer Turan, Ramazan Çalık, and Yusuf Halaçoğlu, *Sürgün ve Göç* (Exile and Emigration), Ankara: Türk Tarih Kurumu, 2004.

Palalı, İrfan, *Tehcir Çocukları Nenem Bir Ermeniymiş* (Children of the Relocations: My Grandmother Had Been An Armenian), İstanbul: Su Yayınları, 2005.

Paldiel, Mordecai, *Diplomat Heroes of the Holocaust*, Jersey City, New Jersey: KTAV Publishing House, Inc., 2007.

————, *The Righteous Among the Nations*, Jerusalem: The Jerusalem Publishing House, 2007.

Palut, Joshua Eli, *Greek Jewry in the Twentieth Century, 1913-1983: Patterns of Jewish Survival in the Greek Provinces before and after the Holocaust*, Cranbury, New Jersey: Associated University Presses, 1996.

Pamukciyan, Kevork, *Ermeni Kaynaklarından Tarihe Katkılar* (Contributions to the History from the Armenian Sources), Vol. 3: *Zamanlar, Mekanlar, İnsanlar* (Times, Places, Men) and Vol. 4: *Biyografileriyle Ermeniler* (Armenians With Their Biographies), İstanbul: Aras Yayıncılık, 2003.

————, *İstanbul Yazıları* (İstanbul Writings), Vol. 1: *İstanbul'da Ermeniler* (Armenians in İstanbul), İstanbul: Aras Yayıncılık, 2002.

Pears, Edwin, *Turkey and Its People*, London: Methuen and Company Limited, 1911.

Pedersen, Susan, *Eleanor Rathbone and the Politics of Conscience*, New Haven and London: Yale University Press, 2004.

Peterson, Merrill, *"Starving Armenians" America and the Armenian Genocide, 1915-1930 and After*, Charlottesville and London: University of Virginia Press, 2004.

Poliakov, Leon, *The Aryan Myth: A History of Racist and Nationalistic Ideas in Europe*, New York: New American Library, 1974.

Powel, Alexander, *The Struggle for Power in Moslem Asia*, New York and London: The Century Company, 1923.

Price, Philips, *A History of Turkey: From Empire to Republic*, London: George Allen and Unwin, 1956.

Quataert, Donald, "Ottoman History Writing at a Crossroads," in Donald Quataert and Sabri Sayarı (eds.), *Turkish Studies in the United States*, Bloomington, Indiana: Indiana University Ottoman and Modern Turkish Studies Publications, 2003.

Read, James Morgan, *Atrocity Propaganda 1914-1919*, New York: Arno Press, reprinted, 1972.

Reisman, Arnold, *Turkey's Modernization: Refugees from Nazism and Atatürk's Vision*, Washington, D.C.: New Academia Publishing, 2006.

Robinson, Nehemiah, *The Genocide Convention: A Commentary*, New York: Institute of Jewish Affairs, 1960.

Rodrigue, Aron, "From *Millet* to Minority: Turkish Jewry," in Pierre Birnbaum and Ira Katznelson (eds.), *Paths of Emancipation: Jews, States, and Citizenship*, Princeton, New Jersey: Princeton University Press, 1995.

————, *Jews and Muslims: Images of Sephardi and Eastern Jewries in Modern Times*, Seattle: University of Washington Press, 2003.

————, "The Sephardim in the Ottoman Empire," in Elie Kedourie (ed.), *Spain and the Jews: The Sephardi Experience 1492 and After*, London: Thames and Hudson, 1992.

Rogger, Hans, *Jewish Policies and Right-Wing Politics in Imperial Russia*, Berkeley and Los Angeles, California: University of California Press, 1986.

Rosen, Robert, *Saving the Jews: Franklin Delano Roosevelt and the Holocaust*, New York: Thunder's Mouth Press, 2006.

Roth, Cecil, *A History of Jews: From Earliest Times Through the Six Day War*, New York: Schocken Books, 1971.

Rozen, Minna (Karen Gold, trans.), *The Last Ottoman Century and Beyond: The Jews in Turkey and the Balkans 1808-1945*, 2 Vols., Jerusalem: Graphit Press Limited, 2002.

Rubin, Barry, *Istanbul Intrigues*, New York: McGraw-Hill Publishing Company, 1989.

Rubinstein, William, *Genocide: A History*, Harlow: Pearson Education Ltd., 2004.

Rummel, R.J., *Death by Government*, New Brunswick, New Jersey: Transaction Publishers, 1994.

Rutherford, Philip, *Prelude to the Final Solution: The Nazi Program for Deporting Ethnic Poles, 1939-1941*, Lawrence, Kansas: University Press of Kansas, 2007.

Sanders, Michael and Philip Taylor, *British Propaganda during the First World War, 1914-1918*, London and Basingstoke: The Macmillan Press Limited, 1982.

Sanjian, Avedis, *The Armenian Communities in Syria under Ottoman Dominion*, Cambridge, Massachusetts: Harvard University Press, 1965.

Saray, Mehmet, *Ermeniler ve Türk-Ermeni İlişkileri* (Armenians and Turkish-Armenian Relations), Ankara: Atatürk Araştırma Merkezi Yayınları, 2005.

Schabas, William, *Genocide in International Law: The Crimes of Crimes*, Cambridge: Cambridge University Press, 2000.

Schilcher, Linda Schatkowski, "The Famine of 1915-1918 in Greater Syria," in John Spagnolo (ed.), *Problems of the Modern Middle East in Historical Perspective*, Reading: Ithaca Press, 1992.

Schmuhl, Hans-Walter, "Der Völkermord an den Armeniern 1915-1917 in vergleichender Perspektive," in Fikret Adanır and Bernd Bonwetsch (eds.), *Osmanismus, Nationalismus, und der Kaukasus: Muslime und Christen, Türken und Armenier im 19. und 20. Jahrhundert*, Wiesbaden: Reichert Verlag, 2005.

Sevilla-Sharon, Moshe, *Türkiye Yahudileri* (Jews of Turkey), İstanbul: İletişimYayınları, 1992.

Shaw, Stanford, *The Jews of the Ottoman Empire and the Turkish Republic*, New York: New York University Press, 1991.

———, *The Ottoman Empire in World War I*, 2 Vols., Ankara: Türk Tarih Kurumu, 2008.

———, "Ottoman Jewry During World War I," in *Onbirinci Türk Tarih Kon-*

gresi, 5-9 Eylül 1990 Kongreye Sunulan Bildiriler (Communications Presented at the Eleventh Turkish History Congress, 5-9 September 1990), Vol. 5, Ankara: Türk Tarih Kurumu, 1994.

———, "Roads East: Turkey and the Jews of Europe during World War II," in Avigdor Levy (ed.), *Jews, Turks, Ottomans: A Shared History, Fifteenth Through the Twentieth Century*, Syracuse, New York: Syracuse University Press, 2002.

———, *Turkey and the Holocaust: Turkey's Role in Rescuing Turkish and European Jewry from Nazi Persecution, 1933-1945*, New York: New York University Press, 1993.

Shirer, William, *The Rise and Fall of the Third Reich: A History of Nazi Germany*, New York: Simon and Schuster, 1960.

Shmuelevitz, Aryeh, "Relations Between Jews and Christians in the Ottoman Empire: The Armenian Case," in *Onbirinci Türk Tarih Kongresi, 5-9 Eylül 1990 Kongreye Sunulan Bildiriler* (Communications Presented at the Eleventh Turkish History Congress, 5-9 September 1990), Vol. 5, Ankara: Türk Tarih Kurumu, 1994.

Smith, Daniel, *Robert Lansing and American Neutrality, 1914-1917*, Berkeley, California: University of California Press, 1958.

Stern, Fritz, *The Politics of Cultural Despair: A Study in the Rise of German Ideology*, Berkeley, California: University of California Press, 1961.

Stone, Frank Andrews, *Academies for Anatolia: A Study of the Rationale, Program and Impact of the Educational Institutions Sponsored by the American Board in Turkey: 1830-1980*, Lanham, Maryland: University Press of America, 1984.

Stone, Norman, *World War One: A Short History*, London: Allen Lane, 2007.

Şahin, Seyit, "Birinci Dünya Harbinde Dördüncü Ordunun Faaliyetleri' (Activities of the Fourth Army in the First World War), doctoral dissertation, Selçuk University, 1997.

Taylor, Telford, *Sword and Swastika: Generals and Nazis in the Third Reich*, New York: Simon and Schuster, 1952.

Ter Minassian, Anahide, "The Role of the Armenian Community in the Foundation and Development of the Socialist Movement in the Ottoman Empire and Turkey: 1876-1923," in Mete Tunçay and Erich Zürcher (eds.), *Socialism and Nationalism in the Ottoman Empire 1876-1923*, London: British Academy Press, 1994.

Ternon, Yves, *La cause arménienne*, Paris: Editions du Seuil, 1983.

Toprak, Zafer, *İttihad-Terakki ve Cihan Harbi* (Committee of Union and Progress and the Great War), İstanbul: Homer Kitabevi, 2003.

Toynbee, Arnold, *Armenian Atrocities: The Murder of a Nation*, London, New York and Toronto: Hodder and Stoughton, 1915.

————, *A Study of History*, Vol. 7, London and New York: Oxford University Press, 1946.

————, *Western Question in Greece and Turkey: A Study in the Contact of Civilizations*, London: Constable and Company Ltd., 1922.

Tuğlacı, Pars, *Tarih Boyunca Batı Ermenileri* (Western Armenians throughout History), Vol. 3: *1891-1922*, İstanbul: Pars Yayın ve Ticaret Limited Şirketi, 2004.

Tunaya, Tarık Zafer, *Türkiye'de Siyasi Partiler* (Political Parties in Turkey), Vol.3: *İttihat ve Terakki, Bir Çağın, Bir Kuşağın, Bir Partinin Tarihi* (Committee of Union and Progress, the History of an Age, a Generation, a Party), İstanbul: İletişim Yayınları, 3rd ed., 2000.

Turfan, Naim, *Rise of the Young Turks: Politics, the Military, and Ottoman Collapse*, London and New York: I.B. Tauris Publishers, 2000.

Uras, Esat, *Tarihte Ermeniler ve Ermeni Meselesi* (Armenians in History and the Armenian Question), İstanbul: Belge Yayınları, 2nd rev. and expanded ed., 1987.

Valentino, Benjamin, *Final Solutions: Mass Killing and Genocide in the 20th Century*, Ithaca and London: Cornell University Press, 2004.

Valyi, Felix, *Spiritual and Political Revolutions in Islam*, London: Kegan Paul, Trench, Trubner and Company Ltd., 1925.

Vassillian, Hamo (ed.), *The Armenians: A Colossal Bibliographic Guide to Books Published in the English Language*, Glendale, California: Armenian Reference Books, 1993.

Veinstein, Gilles (ed.), *Salonique 1850-1918: La "ville des Juifs" et le réveil des Balkans*, Paris: Editions Autrement, 1993.

Walker, Christopher, *Armenia: The Survival of a Nation*, London: Routledge, 1980.

Watt, Donald Cameron, *How War Came: The Immediate Origins of the Second World War, 1938-1939*, New York: Pantheon Books, 1989.

Weber, Frank, *The Evasive Neutral, Germany, Britain and the Quest for a Turkish Alliance in the Second World War*, Columbia and London: University of Missouri Press, 1979.

Weems, Samuel, *Armenia: Secrets of a "Christian" Terrorist State*, Dallas, Texas: St. John Press, 2002.

Weiker, Walter, *Ottomans, Turks, and the Jewish Polity: A History of the Jews of Turkey*, Lanham, Maryland and London: University Press of America, 1992.

————, *The Unseen Israelis: The Jews from Turkey*, Lanham, Maryland and London: University Press of America, 1988.

Weinberg, Gerhard, *Hitler's Foreign Policy: The Road to World War II 1933-1939*, New York: Enigma Books, 2005.

Weinberg, Jeshajahu and Rina Elieli, *The Holocaust Museum in Washington*, New York: Rizzoli International Publications, 1995.

Weiner, Amir (ed.), *Landscaping the Human Garden: Twentieth-Century Population Management in a Comparative Framework*, Stanford, California: Stanford University Press, 2003.

Wistrich, Robert, *Hitler and the Holocaust*, New York: Modern Library, 2001.

Woods, Charles, *The Danger Zone of Europe: Changes and Problems in the Near East*, London: T. Fisher Unwin, 1911.

Wyman, David, *The Abandonment of the Jews: America and the Holocaust, 1941-1945*, New York: Pantheon Books, 1984.

———, *Paper Walls: America and the Refugee Crisis, 1938-1941*, Amherst, Massachusetts: University of Massachusetts Press, 1968.

Yavuz, Celalettin, "Göçmenler ve Cemal Paşa"(Emigrants and Cemal Paşa), in Hikmet Özdemir (ed.), *Türk-Ermeni İhtilafı Makaleler* (Turkish-Armenian Conflict: Articles), Ankara: Türkiye Büyük Millet Meclisi Kültür, Sanat ve Yayın Kurulu Yayınları, 2007.

Yetkin, Çetin, *Türkiye Devlet Yaşamında Yahudiler* (Jews in Turkish Public Life), İstanbul: Gözlem Gazetecilik Basın ve Yayın A.Ş., 1996.

Zmarzlik, Hans-Günter, "Social Darwinism in Germany, Seen as a Historical Problem," in Hajo Holborn (ed.), (Ralph Manheim, trans.), *Republic to Reich: The Making of the Nazi Revolution*, New York: Random House, 1972.

Zürcher, Erik Jan, *Turkey: A Modern History*, London and New York: I.B. Tauris, 3rd ed., 2004.

Articles

Ahmad, Feroz and Dankwart Rustow, "İkinci Meşrutiyet Döneminde Meclisler 1908-1918" (Chambers in the Period of Second Constitutionalism 1908-1918), *Güney-Doğu Avrupa Araştırmaları Dergisi*, Nos. 4-5 (1976).

Ahmad, Mahrad, "İkinci Dünya Savaşında Alman İşgal Bölgelerinde Yaşayan Türk Yahudilerinin Akibeti" (Fate of the Turkish Jews Living in the German Occupation Zones in the Second World War), *Tarih ve Toplum*, Vol. 18, No. 108 (December 1992).

Akçam, Taner, "Deportation and Massacres in the Cipher Telegrams of the Interior Ministry in the Prime Ministerial Archive (Başbakanlık Arşivi)," *Genocide Studies and Prevention*, Vol. 1, No. 3 (December 2006).

Amado, Selim, "İsrail'de Türkiye Kökenli Yahudiler Kopmayan Bağ" (Jews from Turkey in Israel: Unruptured Links), *Görüş*, Special Supplement on Jews from Turkey (September 2003).

"The Armenian Question Before the Peace Conference: A Memorandum Presented Officially by the Representatives of Armenia to the Peace Conference at Versailles on 26 February 1919,"*The Armenian Review*, Vol. 27, No. 3-107 (Autumn 1974).

Astourian, Stephan, "Why Genocide? The Armenian and Jewish Experiences in Perspective," *Slavic Review*, Vol. 50, No. 4 (Winter 1991).

Auchterlonie, Paul, "Review of Arnold Reisman's *Turkey's Modernization: Refugees from Nazism and Atatürk's Vision*," *British Journal of Middle Eastern Studies*, Vol. 35, No. 1 (April 2008).

Aydın, Suavi, "Yahudiler ve Türk Milliyetçiliği" (Jews and Turkish Nationalism), *Tarih ve Toplum*, Vol. 15, No. 89 (May 1991).

Baer, Marc David, "Turkish Jews Rethink 500 Years of Brotherhood and Friendship," *The Turkish Studies Association Bulletin*, Vol. 24, No. 2 (Fall 2000).

Bali, Rifat, "Savaş Yıllarında Türkiye Yahudileri" (Jews of Turkey During the War Years), *Toplumsal Tarih*, Vol. 13, No. 121 (January 2004).

Bassiouni, Cherif, "World War I: The War to End All Wars and the Birth of a Handicapped International Criminal Justice System," *Denver Journal of International Law and Policy*, Vol. 30, No. 1.

Beyoğlu, Süleyman, "1915 Ermeni Tehciri Hakkında Bazı Değerlendirmeler" (Some Assessments on the Armenian Relocations of 1915), *Türk Dünyası Araştırmaları*, No. 131 (April 2001).

Birnbaum, Eleazar, "Jews in the Ottoman Empire: Some Recent Historiography," *Middle East Studies Association Bulletin*, Vol. 28, No. 1 (July 1994).

Bliss, Frederick, "Djemal Pasha: A Portrait," *The Nineteenth Century and After*, Vol. 136, No. DX14 (December 1919).

Böhm, Hermann, "Zur Ansprache Hitlers vor den Führern der Wehrmacht am 22. August 1939," *Vierteljahreshaft für Zeitgeschichte*, Vol. 19 (1971).

"Capture of the Sublime Porte," *The Near East*, Vol. 4, No. 9 (31 January 1913).

"Carnegie Report on the Balkan Atrocities," *The Literary Digest*, Vol. 158, No. 22 (30 May 1914).

Cavendish, Lucy, "The Peril of Armenia," *The Contemporary Review*, Vol. CIII, No. 1 (January 1913).

Charlton, Zeeneb, "Six Ottoman Patriots," *The Nineteenth Century and After*, Vol. 124, No. CCCCXLII (December 1913).

"Constantinople Letter," *The Near East*, Vol. 3, No. 76 (18 October 1912).

Çalık, Ramazan, "Alman Kaynaklarına Göre Cemal Paşa" (Cemal Paşa: According to German Sources), *Osmanlı Araştırmaları*, No. 19 (1999).

Dadrian, Vahakn, "The Documentation of the World War I Armenian Massacres in the Proceedings of the Turkish Military Tribunal," *International Journal of Middle East Studies*, Vol. 23, No. 4 (November 1991).

———, "The Naim-Andonian Documents on the World War I Destruction of Ottoman Armenians: The Anatomy of a Genocide," *International Journal of Middle East Studies*, Vol. 18, No. 3 (August 1986).

————, "A Textual Analysis of the Key Indictment of the Turkish Military Tribunal Investigating the Armenian Genocide," *Journal of Political and Military Sociology*, Vol. 22, No. 1 (1994).

————, "The Turkish Military Tribunal's Prosecution of the Authors of the Armenian Genocide: Four Major Court Martial Series," *Holocaust and Genocide Studies*, Vol. 11, No. 1 (Spring 1997).

Dawidowicz, Lucy, "The Holocaust Was Unique in Intent, Scope, and Effect," *Center Magazine*, Vol. 14, No. 4 (July-August 1981).

Des Pres, Terrance, "On Governing Narratives: the Turkish-Armenian Case," *Yale Review*, Vol. 75, No. 75, No. 4 (1986).

Dinkel, Christoph, "German Officers and the Armenian Genocide," *The Armenian Review*, Vol. 44, No. 1 (1991).

Eckardt, Roy, "Is the Holocaust Unique?" *Worldview*, Vol. 17, No. 9 (September 1974).

Eckardt, Roy and Alice Eckardt, "The Holocaust and the Enigma of Uniqueness: A Philosophical Effort at Practical Clarification," *The Annals of the American Academy of Political and Social Science*, Vol. 450 (July 1980).

Enginün, İnci, "Cemal Paşa'nın Hatıraları," (Memoirs of Cemal Paşa), *Hisar*, Vol. 17, No. 171 (1978).

Erickson, Edward, "Armenian Massacres: New Records Undercut Old Blame," *Middle East Quarterly*, Vol. 13, No. 3 (Summer 2006).

————, "The Armenians and Ottoman Military Policy, 1915," *War in History*, Vol. 15, No. 2 (April 2008).

————, "The Turkish Official Military Histories of the First World War: A Bibliographic Essay," *Middle Eastern Studies*, Vol. 38, No. 3 (July 2003).

Fein, Helen, "A Formula for Genocide: Comparison of the Turkish Genocide (1915) and the German Holocaust (1939-1945)," *Comparative Studies in Sociology*, Vol. 1, No. 1 (1978).

Fitzpatrick, Matthew, "The Pre-History of the Holocaust? The *Sonderweg* and *Historikerstreit* Debates and the Abject Colonial Past," *Central European History*, Vol. 41, No. 3 (September 2008).

Gatrell, Peter, "Refugees and Forced Migrants during the First World War," *Immigrants and Minorities*, Vol. 26, Nos. 1-2 (March-July 2008).

Geber, M.N., "An Attempt to Internationalize Salonika: 1912-1913," *Jewish Social Studies*, Vol. 17, No. 4 (October 1955).

Geft, Liebe and Harold Brackman, "Gilberto Bosques and Jewish Rescue during World War II," *Midstream*, Vol. 53, No. 2 (March/April 2007).

Goekjian, Gregory, "Genocide and Historical Desire," *Semiotica*, Vol. 83, No.3/4 (1991).

Goffmann, Daniel, "The Quincentennial of 1492 and Ottoman-Jewish Studies: A Review Essay," *Shofar*, Vol. 11, No. 4 (Summer 1993).

Gulbekian, Edward, "The Poles and Armenians in Hitler's Political Thinking," *The Armenian Review*, Vol. 41, No. 3-163 (Autumn 1988).

Gunter, Michael, "Notes and Comments," *International Journal of Middle East Studies*, Vol. 19, No. 4 (November 1987).

———, "Notes and Comments," *International Journal of Middle East Studies*, Vol. 40, No. 4 (November 2008).

Güçlü, Yücel, "The Basic Principles and Practices of the Turkish Foreign Policy under Atatürk," *Belleten*, Vol. 64, No. 241 (December 2000).

———, "Will Untapped Ottoman Archives Reshape the Armenian Debate?" *Middle East Quarterly*, Vol. 16, No. 2 (Spring 2009).

Hamlin, Cyrus, "The Genesis and Evolution of the Turkish Massacre of Armenian Subjects," *Proceedings of the American Antiquarian Society*, April 1898.

Harbord, James, "Investigating Turkey and Trans-Caucasia," *The World's Work*, Vol. 15 (May 1920-October 1920).

———, "Mustapha Kemal Pasha and His Party," *The World's Work*, Vol. 15 (May 1920-October 1920).

Heller, Joseph, "Sir Louis Mallet and the Ottoman Empire: The Road to War," *Middle Eastern Studies*, Vol. 12, No. 1 (January 1976).

Ignatieff, Michael, "Lemkin's Word," *New Republic*, No.4493 (26 February 2001).

Jacobson, Abigail, "A City Living through Crisis: Jerusalem during World War I," *British Journal of Middle Eastern Studies*, Vol. 36, No. 1 (April 2009).

Karacakaya, Recep, "Meclisi-i Mebusan Seçimleri ve Ermeniler 1908-1914" (Chamber of Deputies Elections and the Armenians 1908-1914), *Yakın Dönem Türkiye Araştırmaları*, No. 3 (2003).

Katz, Steven, "The Unique Intentionality of the Holocaust," *Modern Judaism*, Vol. 1, No. 2 (September 1981).

Laufer, Max, "A Tale of Two Genocides," *Journal of Armenian Studies*, Vol. 2, No. 2 (Fall-Winter 1985-1986).

Lemkin, Raphael, "Genocide as a Crime in International Law," *American Journal of International Law*, Vol. 41, No. 1 (January 1947).

Levene, Mark, "Is the Holocaust Simply Another Example of Genocide?" *Patterns of Prejudice*, Vol. 28, No. 2 (April 1994).

Levi, Avner, "İkinci Dünya Savaşı ve Öncesinde Türk Yahudileri" (Turkish Jews During and Before the Second World War), *Tarih ve Toplum*, Vol. 26, No. 154 (October 1996).

Lewis, Bernard, "The Ottoman Archives as a Source for the History of the Arab Lands," *Journal of the Royal Asiatic Society*, Nos. 3-4 (October 1951).

———, "Studies in the Ottoman Archives, I," *Bulletin of the School of Oriental and African Studies*, Vol. 16 (1954).

Lewy, Guenter, "The First Genocide of the 20th Century?" *Commentary*, Vol. 120, No. 5 (December 2005).

———, "Reply to Tony Barta, Norbert Finzsch and Davis Stannard," *Journal of Genocide Research*, Vol. 10, No. 2 (June 2008).

———, "Revisiting the Armenian Genocide," *Middle East Quarterly*, Vol. 12, No. 4 (Fall 2005).

Lieven, Dominic, "Dilemmas of Empire 1850-1918: Power, Territory, Identity," *Journal of Contemporary History*, Vol. 34, No. 2 (April 1999).

Linenthal, Edward, "The Boundaries of Memory: The United States Holocaust Memorial Museum," *American Quarterly*, Vol. 46, No. 3 (September 1994).

Lohr, Eric, "The Russian Army and the Jews: Mass Deportation, Hostages, and Violence during World War I," *Russian Review*, Vol. 60, No. 3 (July 2001).

Lowry, Heath, "The United States Congress and Adolf Hitler on the Armenians," *Political Communication and Persuasion*, Vol. 3, No. 2 (April 1985).

Mango, Andrew, "Turks and Kurds," *Middle Eastern Studies*, Vol.30, No.4 (October 1994).

Markovitz, Jonathan, "Ararat and Collective Memories of the Armenian Genocide," *Holocaust and Genocide Studies*, Vol. 20, No. 2 (Fall 2006).

Matas, David, "Prosecuting Crimes Against Humanity: The Lessons of World War I," *Fordham International Law Journal*, Vol. 13, No. 1 (1989-1990).

Myer, David, "Review of Kevork Bardakjian's *Hitler and the Armenian Genocide*," *Holocaust and Genocide Studies*, Vol. 2, No. 1 (January 1987).

Naar, Devin, "From the "Jerusalem of the Balkans" to the *Goldene Medina*: Jewish Immigration from Salonika to the United States," *American Jewish History*, Vol. 93, No. 4 (December 2007).

Olson, Robert, "The Young Turks and the Jews," *Turcica*, No. 18 (1986).

Pamukciyan, Kevork, "Divrikli Noradunkyan Ailesi ve Kapriel Noradunkyan Efendi (Noradounghian Family of Divrik and Gabriel Noradounghian Efendi), *Tarih ve Toplum*, Vol. 9, No. 49 (January 1988).

———, "Kumkapı Patrikhane Kilisesi Ne Zamandan Beri Ermenilerin Elindedir?" (Since When the Armenians Own the Patriarchate Church at Kumkapı?), *Tarih ve Toplum*, Vol. 14, No. 1 (September 1990).

Papazian, Pierre, "A 'Unique Uniqueness'?" and "Was the Holocaust Unique? Responses to Pierre Papazian," *Midstream*, Vol. 30, No. 4 (April 1984).

Pears, Edwin, "The Baghdad Railway," *The Contemporary Review*, Vol. 154, No. 5 (November 1908).

———, "Developments in Turkey," *The Contemporary Review*, Vol. 157, No. 6 (June 1910).

———, "Turkey and the War," *The Contemporary Review*, Vol.CVI, No.5 (November 1914).

———, "Turkey: Developments and Forecasts," *The Contemporary Review*, Vol. 155, No. 6 (June 1909).

————, "Turkey, Present and Future," *The Contemporary Review*, Vol. CIII, No. 6 (June 1913).

————, "The Turkish Revolution," *The Contemporary Review*, Vol. 154, No. 3 (September 1908).

Petrie, Jon, "The Secular Word Holocaust: Scholarly Myths, History, and 20th Century Meanings," *Journal of Genocide Research*, Vol. 2, No. 1 (March 2000).

Poidebard, Antoine, "Rôle militaire des Arméniens sur le front du Caucase après la défection de l'armée russe (décembre 1917-novembre 1918)," *Revue des études arméniennes*, Vol. 1, No. 2 (1920).

Price, Philips, "The Problem of Asiatic Turkey," *The Contemporary Review*, Vol. CV, No. 2 (February 1914).

Quataert, Donald, "Recent Writings in Late Ottoman History," *International Journal of Middle East Studies*, Vol. 35, No. 1 (February 2003).

"The Rebirth of a Nation," *The Literary Digest*, Vol. 50, No. 13 (27 March 1915).

Reynolds, Nancy, "Difference and Tolerance in the Ottoman Empire: Interview of Aron Rodrigue," *Stanford Humanities Review*, Vol. 5, No. 1 (1995).

Salt, Jeremy, "The Narrative Gap in Ottoman Armenian History," *Middle Eastern Studies*, Vol. 39, No. 1 (January 2003).

Sarınay, Yusuf, "Türk Arşivleri ve Ermeni Meselesi" (Turkish Archives and the Armenian Question), *Belleten*, Vol. 70, No. 257 (April 2006).

————, "What Happened on April 24, 1915?: The Circular of April 25, 1915, and the Arrest of Armenian Committee Members in İstanbul," *International Journal of Turkish Studies*, Vol. 14, Nos. 1-2 (Fall 2008).

Sarkiss, Harry Jewell, "The Armenian Renaissance, 1500-1863," *Journal of Modern History*, Vol. 9, No. 4 (December 1937).

Schorsch, Ismar, "Historical Reflections on the Holocaust," *Conservative Judaism*, Vol. 31, Nos. 1-2 (Fall-Winter 1976-1977).

Seropyan, Sarkis, "Vicdanlı Türk Valisi Faik Ali Ozansoy" (Conscientous Turkish Governor Faik Ali Ozansoy), *Toplumsal Tarih*, Vol. 4, No. 23 (November 1995).

Sezer, Ayten, "Ermeni Meselesinde Misyonerlerin Rolü" (Role of the Missionaries in the Armenian Question), *Türk Kültürü*, No. 467 (March 2002).

"Situation in Cilicia," *The Orient*, Vol .2, No. 28 (25 October 1911).

Spector, Robert, "Review of Arthur Grenke's *God, Greed, and Genocide: The Holocaust through the Centuries*," *European History Quarterly*, Vol. 39, No. 1 (January 2009).

Ter Minassian, Anahide, "A Family of Armenian Amiras: The Dadians," *The Armenian Review*, Vol. 45, No. 3/179 (Autumn 1992).

Tetik, Ahmet, "4. Ordu Komutanlığının Bölgesinde Salgın Hastalıklarla Mücadele ve İnsani Yardım Çalışmaları" (Struggle against Contagious Diseases and Humanitarian Assistance Activities in the Zone of the Fourth Army Command), *Ermeni Araştırmaları Dergisi*, No. 30 (2008).

Toktaş, Şule, "Turkey's Jews and their Immigration to Israel," *Middle Eastern Studies*, Vol. 42, No. 3 (May 2006).

"Transformation of Turkish Law," *Levant Trade Review*, Vol. 6, No. 1 (June 1916).

Türkgeldi, Emin Ali, "Brest-Litovsk Hatıraları" (Brest-Litovsk Reminiscences), *Belgelerle Türk Tarihi Dergisi*, Vol. 3, No. 13 (March 1986).

"The Voice of Turkey," *The Literay Digest*, Vol. 159, No. 24 (12 December 1914).

von Kressenstein, Friedrich Freiherr Kress, "Zwischen Kaukasus und Sinai," *Jahrbuch des Bundes der Asienkämpfer*, Vols. 1 and 2 (1921-1922).

Vratzian, Simon, "The Armenian Revolution and the Armenian Revolutionary Federation," *The Armenian Review*, Vol. 3, No. 3 (Autumn 1950).

Williams, Aneurin, "Armenia, British Pledges and the Near East," *The Contemporary Review*, Vol. 121, No. 4 (April 1922).

Williams, W.Llew., "Armenians and the Partition of Asia Minor," *The Fortnightly Review*, Vol. 158, No. July-December 1915.

Yegparian, Garen, "Armenian Issues in the Congressional Record, 1965-1983," *The Armenian Review*, Vol. 40, No. 1-157 (Spring 1987).

Index of Subjects

About the Author

Yücel Güçlü is a historian. His previously published works include *The Question of the Sanjak of Alexandretta: A Study in Turkish-French-Syrian Relations*, Ankara: Turkish Historical Society, 2001; *Eminence Grise of the Turkish Foreign Service: Numan Menemencioğlu*, Ankara: Grafiker Yayıncılık, 2002; *The Life and Career of a Turkish Diplomat: Cevat Açıkalın*, Ankara: Grafiker Yayıncılık, 2002; *The Turcomans and Kirkuk*, Philadelphia/Pennsylvania: Xlibris Corporation, 2007; *Armenians and the Allies in Cilicia, 1914-1923*, Salt Lake City: The University of Utah Press, 2010, and numerous articles on Turkish diplomatic history. He is the winner of the Afet İnan Historical Studies Prize in 1996.